In Search *of the* Nonprofit Sector

In Search
of the
Nonprofit
Sector

Peter Frumkin
Jonathan B. Imber
editors

Transaction Publishers
New Brunswick (U.S.A.) and London (U.K.)

Library of Congress Catalog Number: 2003064556
ISBN: 0-7658-0518-9
Printed in the United States of America

Library of Congress Cataloging-in-Publication Data

In search of the nonprofit sector / edited by Peter Frumkin and Jonathan B. Imber.
    p. cm.
    Includes bibliographical references and index.
    ISBN 0-7658-0518-9 (alk. paper)
      1. Nonprofit organizations—Government policy—United States. 2. Nonprofit organizations—United States—Finance. 3. Public-private sector cooperation—United States. 4. Charities—United States. 5. Voluntarism—United States. 6. Church and social problems—United States. I. Frumkin, Peter. II. Imber, Jonathan B., 1952-.

HD2769.2.U615 2003
361.7'63'0973—dc22   2003064556

Contents

Preface   vii
Peter Frumkin and Jonathan B. Imber

Part 1: Nonprofits and Government: Rhetoric and Reality

1. Government and Nonprofits in the Modern Age: 3
   Is Independence Possible?
   Steven Rathgeb Smith

2. Social Welfare Organizations, Politics, and Regulation   19
   Elizabeth Reid

3. What Is the Political Role of Nonprofits in a Democracy?   37
   Mark E. Warren

Part 2: Nonprofits and Business: Blurred Boundaries

4. Sector-Bending: Blurring the Lines Between Nonprofit   51
   and For-Profit
   J. Gregory Dees and Beth Battle Anderson

5. Commercialism and the Mission of Nonprofits   73
   Estelle James

6. How Important Is a Nonprofit's Bottom Line?   85
   The Uses and Abuses of Financial Data
   Mark Hager and Janet Greenlee

Part 3: Philanthropy and Volunteerism: New Practices

7. Inside Venture Philanthropy   99
   Peter Frumkin

8. Charity and Philanthropy After September 11th   115
     Peter Frumkin

9. National Service in Theory and Practice   131
     Peter Frumkin

**Part 4: Nonprofits, Religion, and Government:
          Opportunities and Challenges**

10. Understanding Religious Organizations: 153
     Implications and Concerns for Public Policy and
     Social Welfare Services
     Thomas H. Jeavons

11. Nonprofit and Faith-Based Welfare-to-Work Programs: 171
     Government's Partners or Government's Captives?
     Stephen V. Monsma

12. Faith in Communities: A Solid Investment   185
     Amy L. Sherman

Bibliography   199

Contributors   219

Index   225

Preface

America's nonprofit sector is at once a potent force for change and innovation in society and an unruly collection of contradictions. Its profile has increased in recent decades, in part due to the growing limitations on the amount of new discretionary social spending government can entertain under the weight of large entitlement commitments. In many areas, nonprofit initiatives—not new public programs—have proved to be the most likely venues for new programmatic ideas to be tested, refined, and disseminated. Nonprofits have come to depend on a mix of funding sources, including fees and dues, individual contributions, government contracts, and foundation and corporate grants. These multiple sources have allowed nonprofits to achieve a measure of financial stability, while at the same time they have exposed nonprofits to tough market competition and significant public oversight. Caught between competition from business firms and pressures from government funders and regulators, nonprofit organizations have been forced to adjust and react to an ever changing and sometimes hostile environment.

The ultimate impact of these pressures has been to erode some of the perceived distinctiveness of the nonprofit sector or, put in somewhat harsher terms, to reveal the fact that nonprofits are really not that different from all other organizations. Critics of nonprofits have in fact suggested that the mythology of an independent and distinctive sector should have been abandoned long ago in favor of a more realistic conceptualization and assessment of the contribution made by nonprofits to society. Instead of clinging to the myth that nonprofits are either morally or practically superior to other organizational forms, it might simply be wiser to accept the fact that nonprofits display characteristics that often mimic and replicate those in business and government. In many instances, the boundaries between societal sectors are now hopelessly blurred and confused. Pressures on both from both sides—business and government—have led business firms into direct competition with nonprofits and allowed government contractors to assert greater control over nonprofits in the name of accountability.

Competitive pressures in the nonprofit sector are not new. The most obvious source of competition for nonprofits has long been other nonprofit organizations. Nonprofits have engaged in pitched competitive battles with other nonprofits, fighting for control of neighborhoods, client bases, and donors. In some major metropolitan areas, multiple nonprofits with very similar missions now compete against one another in close geographical proximity. In many cases, this competitive struggle is a function of a lack of coordination and collaboration between nonprofits. In other cases, it is a function of different values and missions competing in a common field for dominance, be it affordable housing, professional theater, community health, or any number of other fields. A new and different source of competition has recently arisen from outside the nonprofit sector: Business firms, including some very large multinational corporations, have moved into many fields that have long been dominated by nonprofits, such as nursing home care, health care, and welfare-to-work services. This growing inter-sector rivalry has at times raised questions about the relative importance of effectiveness versus efficiency in service provision, as business firms have been able to undercut the prices that nonprofits charge for services, leaving nonprofits to argue that corporations are simply cutting corners and delivering inferior quality services. This new competitive challenge has profoundly affected the nonprofit sector as a whole, and it has raised tough questions about the real identity and purpose of the nonprofit world and the boundary between nonprofits and businesses.

One consequence of the permeability of this sectoral boundary has been that nonprofit organizations have had a chance to absorb some of the rhetoric and practices of businesses, no matter how much they might protest the incursion. One of the most pronounced trends in the nonprofit sector has been the rise of commercial activity, whether in the form of charging fees to clients or in the form of business income generated by the operation of all kinds of ventures, some related to the mission, others wholly unrelated. From educational tours of Europe offered by universities to cafes run by museums, earned income is very attractive to nonprofits because it can be used to cover costs that donors and clients are unwilling to subsidize. Unlike project funding or targeted grants that can only be used for narrowly circumscribed purposes, commercial revenue or earned income comes with no strings and can be used for whatever purposes suit the nonprofit. Although nonprofit commercialism risks at some level distorting the mission of nonprofits in that it may make it harder for nonprofits to serve the neediest clients if the focus is on generating revenues, it also has the potential to make nonprofits more market savvy and realistic about the demand for their various services. No matter the programmatic consequences, the growing competition with business firms and the movement of nonprofits toward greater reliance on earned sources of income have contributed to the blurring of the boundaries between sectors.

Like competitive pressures, demands for accountability are not new, but they are growing more intense. For decades, government has been deeply connected to nonprofit service providers through contractual relations that have moved many critical elements of service provision from public agencies to nonprofit organizations. The rise of contractual relations between federal, state, and local governments and nonprofits has imbued parts of the sector with a sense of purpose and delivered, particularly in the health and human services fields, substantial financial resources. At the same time, contracts have also given government the ability to dictate to nonprofits the kinds of services to be delivered and to define the accountability mechanisms that will be required. As a result of decades of close contact with government, nonprofits have gotten progressively more professionalized, more detailed in their accounting and record keeping, and more organized in their operation. While some have bemoaned the de-radicalization and homogenization that public funding has brought to the nonprofit sector, the effects have been fairly subtle. The flow of funds between government and nonprofits has eroded some of the differences between the sectors and moved nonprofits closer to being public organizations than previously was the case.

For most nonprofits, the private values of the founder, staff, and chief supporters coexist more or less comfortably with the public purposes of the organization. After all, by virtue of their tax-exempt status, nonprofits are expected to provide something of value to the public and cannot simply be vehicles for the satisfaction of narrow and mostly private purposes. Still, one of the characteristics of successful nonprofits is often the powerful connection and synergy between deeply held private values and significant community needs. Nonprofits that find this potent intersection are often able to offer services that are different from those of more generic government interventions and that speak directly to local concerns. The rise of government funding has at least the potential of shifting the private-public mix within nonprofits toward a more agnostic and neutral public orientation. Because public funding is critical to many fields of nonprofit activity, a difficult question has arisen about the long-term ability of nonprofits to protect their autonomy. One clear manifestation of the tension between public accountability and nonprofit autonomy has been the heated debate over the role of faith in service provision that has taken place over the past decade. The struggle to find a compromise resulted in the passage of legislation aimed at ensuring that nonprofits with religious grounding are not unduly penalized and constrained in the work they do under government contracts.

As boundaries between sectors have been blurred and as nonprofits have been led to imitate and accommodate business and government, many gaps in our basic understanding of key aspects of nonprofits have been revealed and many difficult conceptual questions have remained unanswered. While there are certain truisms that are recited over and over again about nonprofits, they often mask deeper and more complex issues and problems.

We know that there are over one and a half million nonprofits registered with government. What we do not know, however, is how many of these organizations are functioning and financed. Some researchers have argued that the number of nonprofits with meaningful revenues (around $25,000 a year) is actually very small, perhaps around 100,000. This raises the question of what the vast majority of organizations are doing, if anything. There are many nonprofits on the government books that are simply nonfunctional and unfunded, but that persist as legal fictions. One reason why the organizational population includes so many poor or nonperforming organizations stems from the very low barriers of entry, and the fact that many nonprofits are created before a need is really established for the services to be offered. Nonprofits can be and often are the expressions of personal convictions and beliefs on the part of individuals. Still, at the most basic level of data, the nonprofit sector lags far behind business and government in its ability to count and measure itself.

We know that the largest and most visible nonprofits (including hospitals, universities, and cultural organizations) do provide valuable services that clients and patrons are willing to pay for either in the form of fees or in the form of donations. What we do not know is how to measure the comparative performance of these organizations against one another within fields, or, for that matter, across fields. The quality of performance measurement systems in the nonprofit sector remains low and the ability of evaluators to deliver convincing analyses of value added of nonprofit programs is questionable, no matter the claims made recently about progress in this domain. The nonprofit sector remains far behind the business sector when it comes to performance measurement. While firms can look at a host of issues, such as share value, profit margins, market share, and other common tools for assessing how well in the short run and in the long run the central goal of operating profitably is being achieved, nonprofits are far more limited in what they can truly do to assess their performance. Most of these constraints come down to the fact that nonprofits are first and foremost about fulfilling their missions.

We know that nonprofits have many stakeholders, including trustees, clients, donors, and government regulators, and that none of these stakeholders is truly able to assert a meaningful ownership claim over nonprofits. What we do not know is whether governance issues are significantly exacerbated by the lack of a residual claimant, or whether this feature actually makes nonprofits freer to take chances and govern themselves wisely. Most nonprofits have governing boards that work like corporate boards in that they set overall strategy and direction. However, like government agencies, nonprofits are open to and responsive to the many stakeholders that surround them.

Amidst all this uncertainty and confusion and against the backdrop of shifting boundaries around the nonprofit sector, we present a collection of essays that all chase after this elusive sector, pinpoint in one way or another its many contradictions and challenges, and analyze its attempts to operate somewhere between the state and the market. The essays were for the most part commissioned for publication in *Society*. Most of the chapters were also initially delivered at a conference cosponsored by *Society*, the Institute for the Study of Economic Culture at Boston University, and the Ethics and Public Policy Center, held in Washington, D.C., in April 2002. Funding for the conference was provided by the Lynde and Harry Bradley Foundation. Four of the chapters were commissioned after the conference to complete the volume and cover topics not fully addressed at the conference.

The volume is organized into four main parts. In the first part, contributors explore the boundary issues between nonprofits and government. Steven Rathgeb Smith considers the complex dynamic of interdependence that now characterizes the relationship between government and nonprofits. Rather than accept arguments either for total sectoral autonomy or for more complete interpenetration, Smith suggests that public-nonprofit relations must be grounded in the reality that financial ties between the sectors are here to stay, and that what we need are creative strategies for making this relationship work. Elizabeth Reid focuses on the confused identity and role of advocacy or social welfare organizations, which are treated differently than most other charitable organizations. She finds that the government regulation of advocacy organizations is not always clear and consistent, and that much work needs to be done to refine public policy affecting nonprofits that engage the political process. Mark Warren examines the positive and negative effects nonprofits have on democracies. He argues that policies need to be crafted in light of these differential effects, rather than on the uncritical assumption that all contributions made by nonprofits enhance democratic values.

The second part of the book discusses vexed questions about the boundary between nonprofits and business. Gregory Dees and Beth Battle Anderson look at the phenomenon of "sector-bending," by which they mean organizational forms that defy easy classification because they combine the attributes of business and nonprofit organizations. In these trans-sectored organizations, they find both potential and risks, and they suggest ways to assess the consequences of the blurring of the boundaries between nonprofit organizations and business firms. Estelle James focuses on the issue of commercialization in the nonprofit sector and considers its causes and effects on mission. She argues that nonprofit commercialism may increase the resources available to nonprofits, but that this movement poses a threat to the managerial values of nonprofits, may lead to misallocated tax privileges, and can produce a diversion of public funds into private gain. Mark Hager and Janet Greenlee consider the problems associated with using purely financial measures to assess the worthiness of nonprofits. They highlight the uses and abuses of financial data in the context of mission focused organizations, in which the most important measurement issues often have to do with programmatic effectiveness, not the bottom line.

The third part of the book considers the boundary issues from a different perspective. It looks at important recent developments in the areas of philanthropy and voluntarism and the impact business practices and government policy have had on each. In venture philanthropy, Peter Frumkin finds an interesting if flawed effort to apply the logic and principles of venture capitalism to the world of philanthropy. While there is nothing wrong with an effort to improve the practices of philanthropy, the venture philanthropy movement has a long way to go before its effort to translate business concepts to philanthropy is convincing. In the recent charitable efforts following September 11th, Frumkin looks at the difficulty of coordinating public and private relief efforts and asks whether charity can ever really respond sensibly to major catastrophes such as the ones in New York and Washington. Although private charities raised billions of dollars for the families of victims, their efforts were plagued by criticisms over the efficiency of the dispersal system and the ultimate effectiveness of the grants made. Finally, in the area of national service programs, Frumkin focuses on the many questions that arise when government attempts to foster volunteerism by recruiting and placing young people in stipend-supported positions in nonprofit organizations through programs such as AmeriCorps. He probes what we really know about the value of these programs and sets forward a framework for organizing our thinking about the effects of national service programs.

The final part of the book looks at the role of faith-based organizations and the special challenges these nonprofits face when competing for public support. Amy Sherman argues that faith-based organizations have at least one substantial advantage over government and secular private programs, namely the disproportionate provision of social services that they provide compared to the relative cost and effectiveness of other programs. She insists on viewing these services "from the ground up" rather than through the lens of present debates about "charitable choice." Thomas Jeavons, in a more sobering analysis, raises concerns about being too enthusiastic about defining nonprofits founded on religious convictions as exclusively devoted to the purposes of social service, however those purposes may be understood. Their independence, as religious congregations, is precisely founded on such purposes not being their raison d'être. Jeavons provides an inventory of the diversity of approaches and goals that have shaped religiously inspired organizations. Stephen Monsma's study of welfare-to-work programs asks whether there is any way out of the dilemma of large-scale secular programs losing their independence when receiving government funds, and of much smaller faith-based programs maintaining their independence with nominal government-funding, but at the expense of serving only small numbers of clients. Monsma believes that clearer congressional oversight would help in improving both types of programs in the long run.

Across each of these four parts of this volume, a recurrent theme or story line is that of contested sectoral boundaries leading to changing organizational identities. The nonprofit sector may well have been "invented" less than a century ago, but the consequences of this act of invention are still being felt today and will continue to be felt for a long time. Clear boundaries between public, business, and nonprofit organizations no longer exist today, and probably never existed all that neatly. A more accurate vision of the sectoral terrain is one in which all three sectors struggle for power and resources, interact with each other regularly, and produce alternatively competition, collaboration, and contention. This is the vision that emerges from the chapters contained in this volume.

Fortunately for all, the quantity and quality of research about nonprofit organizations has increased measurably in recent decades. The growth of a research community dedicated to nonprofit organizations has helped clarify many of the management challenges facing nonprofits. However, some of the more complex conceptual issues are still far from resolved. The title of this book is intended to capture the still elusive and complex nature of the nonprofit sector. By looking at the points of conceptual tension and boundary conflicts, this volume's contributors seek to work that part of the nonprofit terrain that remains largely untilled. Future research should continue to focus in greater depth and with a critical eye on the question of what, if anything, really defines nonprofit organizations, and how, when, and why their structure, governance, and activities share many features with business and public sector organizations. Rather than accept the idea that the nonprofit sector is a clearly defined, autonomous, and bounded entity, we should begin to treat the nonprofit sector as a far more complex and contingent construct that is neither organizationally stable nor consistent in its many ideological and institutional manifestations. We hope this volume contributes to the process of developing this kind of new understanding.

Peter Frumkin
John F. Kennedy School of Government,
Harvard University

Jonathan B. Imber
Wellesley College

Part 1

Nonprofits and Government:
Rhetoric and Reality

1

Government and Nonprofits in the Modern Age: Is Independence Possible?

Steven Rathgeb Smith

In recent years, several high profile and important public policy issues have involved a debate on the independence of the nonprofit sector. President Bush's Faith-Based and Community Initiatives are predicated, in part, on the idea that many nonprofit organizations providing health and social services are professionalized agencies with very close ties to government. The President hopes to involve congregations and faith-based service agencies that are more independent of government in service delivery. A few years ago, Representative Ernest Istook (R-OK) introduced legislation barring many types of advocacy by nonprofit organizations if they received any federal funds whatsoever, even if they did not use federal funds for their lobbying. Again, the underlying assumption of the amendment was that many nonprofit organizations have close ties to government and thus they had a great incentive to lobby for the continuance of social programs. While the amendment did not become law, the appropriate level of advocacy activity by nonprofit, charitable organizations remains a hotly contested issue. More generally, the push for the devolution of federal policy is motivated, in part, by a desire to shift federal responsibilities back to local communities who do not have the close connections to the federal government of the existing network of nonprofit advocacy organizations based in Washington, D.C.

Nonprofit organizations, in short, are central to the ongoing debate in American politics on the proper role of the state. For policymakers interested in shrinking the state and its role in society, nonprofit organizations offer the possibility of local citizens assuming federal responsibilities without the distorting influence of government. It is a vision of a nonprofit sector that is distinctly separate and different from government, one that is independent from government (and the market). Other people value the role of nonprofit organizations and their contributions to representation and the provision of services, but believe that direct and indirect assistance from government is essential. Given these differing perspectives, it is often argued that government should provide assistance, but allow nonprofits to remain independent and autonomous.

This chapter examines this idea and vision of distinctiveness and independence of the nonprofit sector in view of contemporary developments in American public policy and politics. My basic argument is that the government and nonprofit organizations have become increasingly intertwined in the last twenty-five years due to direct government funding and new government regulations, as well as the increase in overall government policy activity. Government also influences nonprofit behavior in many different ways so that the term "independent sector" (or the related term "nonprofit autonomy") does not convey the diverse interconnections between government and nonprofit organizations, including the way in which nonprofit staff and volunteers choose their own priorities based, in part, on the actions of government. To be sure, nonprofit organizations can also influence government policy and play a critical role in promoting citizen participation in public affairs, broadly defined. But the capacity of nonprofit organizations to promote citizen engagement and influence policy is also dependent upon the capacity of political institutions to respond to the goals and expectations of nonprofit organizations.

The Intellectual Roots of Independence

The vision of nonprofit organizations as a distinctively different and independent sector has deep roots in American political culture. Alexis de Tocqueville (1956) forcefully argued that America's democracy rested on its extensive network of voluntary associations. In his view, voluntary associations were vital to democracy because they served as an intermediate entity between the individual and the state. Thus, voluntary associations helped foster individual freedom by serving as vehicles for the representation of citizen views and offering a bulwark against state infringements on individual liberties. Through voluntary associations, citizens could also come together to influence government policy. To de Tocqueville, voluntary associations were inherently positive for democracy, and the more voluntary associations, the better.

In the twentieth century, this Tocquevillian perspective has been articulated by many different scholars and policymakers. Robert Nisbet, a political theorist, argued in his influential book, *The Quest for Community*, that, "Most of the tendencies in contemporary society toward the erosion of cultural differences and the standardization of cultural tastes, beliefs and activities, which are so often charged, mistakenly, against technology and science, are the product of a centralization of authority and function and a desiccation of local and cultural associations" (Nisbet 1953, 267). The implications of his views were quite far-reaching: Government and voluntary associations had opposing agendas and values, and further, the growth of government would directly lead to undermining community. Whether it was the arts or social services, the growth of government would undermine voluntarism and other local forms of service. Government was a direct threat to creativity, innovation, and pluralism. Similarly, Ernest van den Haag (1979) argued against government subsidies of the arts because it would inevitably reduce the quality of art and actually compromise the integrity of local arts organizations and individual artists.

This Tocquevillian perspective was advanced by Peter Berger and Richard John Neuhaus in their widely read book, *To Empower People*, published in 1977. Therein, they argued that voluntary organizations are crucial mediating institutions between the individual and government, protecting individual freedom, and enhancing community responsibility for social problems. Other scholars including Robert Woodson (1981), Jack Meyer (1982), and Nathan Glazer (1989) followed with books of similar perspectives. Glazer, for example, suggested that we, as a society, should move toward a "self-service society" with voluntary associations, community groups, and individuals addressing social problems rather than government. The image of the government-nonprofit relationship was one of inherent tension with government as a coercive force undermining local and community responsibility and reducing the effectiveness of social programs.

The independence and distinctiveness of the nonprofit sector is also raised by the widely publicized work of Robert Putnam. In his book on Italy, *Making Democracy Work*, Putnam (1993) argued that voluntary associations were critical to building "social capital," or the networks of cooperation and collaboration that exist in a community or region. His research suggested that areas with higher levels of social capital also had more satisfied citizenry, more effective government programs, and higher levels of economic development. Participation in voluntary associations helped build social capital by bringing people together, including people who previously may not have known each other. The mechanism by which social capital translates into improved government is presumed to be an indirect one whereupon social capital makes collective action for the common good more likely, so eventually citizens come to demand and expect more from their government officials.

Putnam (1993, 1995, 1999) is especially concerned with voluntary organizations that rely primarily on volunteers and bring diverse people together. In the United States, the local PTA chapter, choral society, or soccer club are good examples. Thus, he is concerned about the potential of the many contemporary nonprofit service agencies and advocacy organizations to build social capital. As he and others, including Theda Skocpol (1999), have noted, many service and advocacy organizations do not have a large number of volunteers or members and they rely heavily on a paid, professionalized staff. Without an extensive membership that meets regularly, these agencies are arguably not well-positioned to build social capital. Putnam (1993) also argues that government can have both positive and negative effects on nonprofit organizations and their ability to create social capital. Inappropriate regulations or unstable funding can undermine the health of local community organizations, especially smaller agencies and associations. Government can also help nurture the nonprofit infrastructure through favorable regulations and incentives for people and agencies to collaborate and volunteer at the local level.

Implicit in Putnam's work on social capital is an important issue that connects to de Tocqueville and others: that the process of social capital building, and more generally the formation of nonprofit organizations, is a "bottoms-up" process in which individuals come together at the local level to participate in voluntary associations, and as a by-product, produce social capital, facilitated by friendly government policies and leadership.

Citizen engagement in voluntary associations as a valued goal is also reflected in many other works. Harry Boyte lamented "the eclipse of the citizen" and suggested several strategies to promote the importance of "public life, community, and active citizenship" (Boyte 1989, 5), including increased participation in local community organizations. Carmen Sirianni and Lewis Friedland (2001) argue that grassroots community organizing and development can be a very effective means of citizen empowerment and achieving positive change in government policy. And, Lappe and Du Bois (1994) suggest that participation in voluntary groups and organizations can transform individuals from "clients to citizens."

In these works, the imagery is of separate distinct organizations that act as vehicles for independent citizen action. This perspective also relates to the social movement literature which calls attention to the key role of social movement organizations in changing public policy and government in recent years. The political scientist, Sidney Tarrow (1994) defines social movements as "collective challenges by people with common purposes and solidarity in sustained interaction with elites, opponents and authorities" (as quoted by Hasenfeld and Gidron 2001, 3). Many social movements such as the civil rights movement or the women's movement begin as loosely, structured informal associations and groups without any formal legal status. Eventually, many of these associations formally incorporate as legal entities in order to raise money and enhance their effectiveness and sustainability.

This social movement perspective contains two key ideas with direct relevance to the government-nonprofit relationship. First, nonprofit organizations representing social movements may have a deliberately conflictual relationship with government. Indeed, the entire raison d'être of many social movements is to change government policy. Many of the social movements have also been supported by private, nonprofit foundations (Clemens 1999; Jenkins and Halcli 1999; Raynor 1999). Second, the successful transformation of government policy by social movements is a major contributing factor to the growth of nonprofit organizations in the last thirty years. For instance, the women's movement successfully pressed for the establishment of domestic violence shelters, rape crisis centers, and women's health clinics. Many political advocacy groups have emerged to press for action by government on women's issues. The civil rights movement worked, in part, through nonprofit advocacy organizations and locally based nonprofit, community action agencies (Marris and Rein 1982; Morone 1990; A. O'Connor 1999, 2001). The same basic pattern has been repeated with social movements focused on AIDS, developmental disabilities, the mentally ill, the environment, and civil rights. These social movements provided the organizational and political mechanism for translating previous private concerns into public issues. Social movement organizations, then, can act as an independent source of citizen action to change and reform government policy.

Rethinking the Independence Model

In public discourse, the argument for independence of the nonprofit sector has often been put forth at a normative level. Scholars from de Tocqueville to Berger and Neuhaus to Boyte argue that nonprofit organizations should be independent of government (and the market) because of the value of nonprofit organizations to pluralism, diversity, service effectiveness, and freedom. This perspective has then been reinforced by policymakers and groups representing nonprofit organizations. (The proposed restrictions on nonprofit advocacy embodied in the Istook amendment are just one example.) While these arguments are valuable and important, they do not necessarily capture the complex relationship between government and the nonprofit sector, and can actually inadvertently undermine the representative and service role of nonprofit organizations. To better clarify the issues, it is useful to highlight the key issues of resources, regulations, and political institutions as they pertain to the role of nonprofit organizations in contemporary American society.

Many studies demonstrate the importance of government funding to nonprofit organizations, although the extent of government funding varies substantially depending upon the service category (Gronbjerg 1993; Smith and Lipsky 1993; Boris and Steuerle 1999; Gronbjerg and Smith 1999, forthcoming; Salamon 1999; Smith 2002). In the United States, government funding of nonprofit agencies has a long tradition. But widespread government funding of nonprofits did not develop until the 1960s with growth of the federal government's support for new social policies. Indeed, many of the key federal social programs of the 1960s, including community mental health centers, neighborhood health clinics, community action agencies, and new child welfare programs, were predominantly new services provided by non-profit organizations with public funds. Since the 1960s, the extent of government contracting with nonprofit and for-profit service agencies has continued to grow substantially despite periodic funding cutbacks. For instance, the number of nonprofit social service agencies is at an all-time high and government support of nonprofit social and health agencies is more extensive than ever (Smith 2002).

Public financial support of nonprofit organizations has also grown through the diversification of "policy tools." Increasingly, government has many different policy tools by which to address public problems (Salamon 2002). Direct funding through grants and contracts is one major approach. But nonprofits greatly benefit by many more indirect policy tools, including tax credits, vouchers, and tax-exempt bonds. For instance, in the United States, the federal government now spends billions of dollars through tax credits (Howard 1997). A good example is the federal Low Income Housing Tax Credit (LIHTC) program which allows private investors to reduce their tax liability by purchasing tax credits to build low-income housing. Investors get a tax break and their investment money is directed to community development and housing organizations to build low-income and affordable housing. Tax credits also exist for child care and hiring low-income and disadvantaged workers.

Many nonprofit organizations are also eligible for tax-exempt bond financing and loans to help with their capital needs. This has been particularly true for larger nonprofit institutions such as universities, hospitals, and museums. But more recently, many smaller nonprofits including human service agencies and community development corporations have also obtained access to tax-exempt bond financing.

Vouchers are a subsidy tied to the individual recipient as opposed to the organization. They are perhaps most prominent in low-income housing and child care in which vouchers or allowances are used to subsidize housing or child care for low-income and disadvantaged citizens. But their use is likely to grow in education and social services such as drug and alcohol treatment.

The significance of direct and indirect public funding of nonprofit organizations goes well beyond the actual transfer of resources. The opportunity for funding means that many nonprofit agencies "adjust" their behavior, including their organizational goals and mission, depending upon the priorities of government funding agencies. For instance, many child welfare agencies in recent years have shifted their mission and focus in order to qualify for federal Medicaid funds. Many other nonprofit agencies have de-emphasized services with declining funding opportunities (such as general counseling) and added new programs such as home care. Also, the decision to create a nonprofit can be influenced, in part, on the funding opportunities available (Smith and Lipsky 1993). Indeed, the big increase in the actual number of nonprofits in the last thirty years reflects the wide array of funding opportunities available to eligible nonprofits.

The availability of government funding is also relevant to nonprofit advocacy. Many nonprofit organizations emerge from community grassroots organizing or social movements. Their missions and methods can sometimes be deliberately confrontational, seeking dramatic change to existing public policies. Often, these organizations begin as informal groups, associations, and networks of colleagues without any formal legal status. A good example is a neighborhood association that wants to rid its neighborhood of drug abuse. Eventually, this association may obtain formal 501(c)(3) status as a nonprofit and obtain grants to fund their activities. Initially, these grants may be from foundations or private donors. But eventually these initial start-up grants will end and then the organization needs to find new sources of support. Often these organizations are tempted or forced to seek public funding of their activities.

Public support may alter the advocacy efforts of these nonprofit organizations in two ways. First, public funding is usually reserved for direct service such as counseling or job training rather than advocacy. Consequently, an agency may be forced to shift its mission and focus from advocacy to direct services if it wants public funds. This can be particularly problematic in many developing countries in which the initial grant to support advocacy organizations comes from foreign donors in the United States and Europe. Once these grants end, these advocacy organizations have few options to support themselves other than public grants since few countries have the tradition of private donations and giving (or the wealth) characteristic of industrialized countries.

An agency may feel it necessary to change their advocacy with the receipt of public funds. For instance, a community-based poverty agency may have initially focused on advocating broadly for the health and income needs of the local disadvantaged population. But then the agency accepts sizable government contracts for job training. Especially if the agency does not have other significant revenue sources, the agency may feel very constrained in its ability to directly criticize government policy regarding the disadvantaged and public job training programs in particular.

This advocacy role of many nonprofit service agencies is further complicated by the relatively small staffs of many nonprofit service agencies. Often, these agencies do not have the capacity to engage in significant advocacy. One strategy to overcome the small size of many nonprofit staffs is for an agency to contribute to the creation of an umbrella coalition or association that represents many nonprofit organizations. A typical example would be a state or national association of home care providers or child welfare agencies.

These umbrella coalitions tend to concentrate their advocacy on issues of most direct relevance to their member agencies—that is, rates, funding, and contract regulations. Much less incentive exists to engage in broad-based advocacy work on behalf of the clients of member agencies (Smith and Lipsky 1993).

Despite the growth of political activity by nonprofit organizations and the keen interest of many nonprofit organizations in public policy, many nonprofit service organizations with a 501(c)(3) designation as a charitable institution remain very reluctant to engage government directly, lest they anger or alienate government officials and hence jeopardize their contracts or their tax-exempt status (Berry 2003). For instance, social service agencies representing low-income people rarely engage in direct advocacy to change government policies related to the poor. This is not to imply that nonprofit agencies are absent completely from other policy issues. Many nonprofit agencies, for example, opposed welfare reform. But welfare reform was decided at the national level and local nonprofit agencies only took part in the debate indirectly.

The muting of political advocacy is a product, in part, of the regulatory policies of the Internal Revenue Service. It is a more general example of the powerful role of government regulations in shaping the place of nonprofit organizations within American society. Conceptually, one can consider regulation as a distinctly different "tool" of government from other tools such as contracting and tax credits (Salamon 2002). However, many of these tools such as contracting and tax credits are accompanied by regulations. One important reason for the growth of regulation is the big increase in government spending which then creates a dynamic that pushes government to "rationalize" their spending (Brown 1983). Regulations are one important strategy in this rationalization process.

Another important manifestation of this rationalization process—evident in the United States as well as in many other countries—has been a restructuring of the relationship between government and private nonprofit service agencies. In the United States and elsewhere, many nonprofit agencies often received grants or subsidies for services for children or adults who were government's responsibility. But these subsidies rarely were accompanied by extensive regulations or accountability standards. Private agencies were expected to do their own monitoring and the government simply reimbursed them for their costs (although many subsidy arrangements failed to fully cover private agency costs). With a big increase in government funds, administrators had to monitor a far-flung service system. In response, government officials shifted from subsidy or grant arrangements to formal contracts with much more detailed expectations in the area of performance evaluation. And more recently, contracts in social and health services have been progressively tightened and restructured, giving government more control over the allocation of funds (Gutch 1993; Smith and Lipsky 1993;). Contract agencies also have less discretion in terms of billing. More and more government jurisdictions impose performance measures on their contract agencies (Osborne and Gaebler 1991; Behn 2001).

This emphasis on performance evaluation is also related to the devolution of government policy, which has placed new demands on state and local governments in the funding and administration of nonprofit organizations. Faced with new management pressures, states and localities have instituted new performance assessment strategies to enhance their ability to hold nonprofits accountable for the expenditure of public funds. In unexpected ways, the changing regulatory role of government also altered the behavior of private philanthropy in the United States, creating further blurring between the public and nonprofit sectors. One brief example—the giving practices of the United Way—illustrates this point. The United Way started in the 1920s as a federated fundraising organization for the leading nonprofit service agencies in local communities around the country. It was a membership-based organization that required member organizations to adhere to certain guidelines and restrictions. The members were rewarded with predictable increases in funding every year, with the amount of the increase dependent upon the success of the annual pledge campaign. The priorities of the United Way were decidedly private and separate from government, with a substantial focus on recreational services, counseling, child welfare, and emergency assistance. Most of the United Way agencies did not receive any public funds.

In the 1960s and 1970s, the federal government created an entirely new and separate universe of nonprofit service agencies outside the ambit of the United Way. For a while, these agencies were content to exist outside of the United Way membership circle. But in the 1980s, the devolution of some federal programs brought increased scrutiny of local philanthropic funding. At the same time, the competition for public and private funds increased. Consequently, more and more agencies demanded access to United Way funds.

This political dilemma pushed United Way chapters to open up its membership to newer, less traditional agencies. The initial response was tentative and limited. Separate funding streams were established to award small, time-limited grants to newer agencies, leaving the existing United Way system largely the same. But political pressure built over time and gradually United Way chapters responded by changing their membership rules to allow a broader, more diverse membership. Some chapters in major cities such as Washington, D.C. and Seattle eliminated membership entirely, essentially allowing funding applications from any local service agency.

To a varying extent, United Way chapters also adopted new program priorities, previously characteristic of the public sector. Traditionally, United Way chapters gave money to member agencies on an unrestricted basis. But now, United Way chapters typically identify areas of urgent needs in the community, such as services for at-risk youth, economic development, or AIDS-related services. These priorities look very much like public sector priorities. As part of this process, many long-time United Way agencies such as the Boy Scouts who provide programs outside this new program emphasis have lost United Way funding. Moreover, the United Way has now adopted many of the increased monitoring mechanisms typical of government officials contracting with private agencies, especially with a demand for performance measurement and outcome evaluation. Financial reporting expectations are also much more extensive.

Thus, the paradoxical effect of devolution was to push the United Way closer to the public sector. Many private foundations have experienced a similar shift, although foundations exhibit tremendous diversity so it is more difficult to generalize. Nonetheless, private foundations are under increasing pressure to help nonprofit agencies address pressing public issues. Many private foundations are even providing operating support to nonprofit service agencies, a sharp break with their longstanding practice of only providing short-term seed or project grants.

In a sense, the regulatory transformation of the state has been mimicked by the United Way and other private funders, albeit to different degrees across the country. These isomorphic tendencies (Powell and DiMaggio 1991)— that is, the trend to similarity among organizations in the same field—are offset to an extent by the ease of entry into the nonprofit sector and the diversity of private philanthropy. Nevertheless, the shift is quite striking. No longer does private philanthropy consider its mission completely separate and apart from the public sector.

The other paradoxical and unexpected impact of devolution on private philanthropy relates to the internal changes within nonprofit service agencies. Prior to the 1960s, most nonprofit service agencies did only very small scale fundraising, if at all. Most agencies were relatively modest in size and service expectations were not high. Thus, if an agency incurred a deficit, board members contributed their own money or conducted a special appeal. For eligible agencies, the United Way also filled an important fundraising niche. And due to United Way restrictions, many agencies found it difficult to do fundraising outside of the United Way umbrella. The rise of federal funding allowed many service agencies to minimize their direct fundraising. But the failure of government funds to keep pace with rising costs has produced a marked, albeit variable, shift in attitude toward fundraising. Many agencies, even quite small ones, have hired development staff to work full-time on raising money to fund operations, capital projects, and to create or add to an endowment.

In the context of contemporary public policy, the evaluation of this new emphasis on fundraising is complicated and underscores the difficulty of making easy generalizations about the impact of devolution or privatization. From one perspective, the new fundraising represents the "capture" by private nonprofit, service agencies of private funds from individuals and organizations. But these private funds are being used to cross-subsidize activities by nonprofit service agencies supported or financed by the public sector. These funds, then, are being tapped in support of public activities and priorities.

To be sure, a fair number of nonprofit service agencies are not substantially dependent on public funds, relying instead on private donations or fees for service. But these agencies tend to be either small (such as a church-affiliated soup kitchen) or occupy a very specialized role (such as a provider of emergency assistance). The broad array of social service agencies with highly professional staff or extensive numbers of volunteers—from child welfare to mental health to domestic violence programs—tends to depend upon public funds. But as public funds have become more competitive and have failed to keep pace with inflation, these agencies have been forced to seek alternative sources of funds to support their operations.

In an important and underappreciated way, the challenges faced by many nonprofit agencies in developing adequate capacity and infrastructure also tend to create complications in their relationships with government, making the goal of independence and distinctiveness often quite elusive. In particular, the growing complexity of the nonprofit funding environment and the escalating expectations of public and private funders for accountability have placed vastly increased demands on the management infrastructure of nonprofit service providers. Nonprofit social service agencies are pressed to invest in management information systems and improved technology in order to be able to respond to the greater demands for accountability. Performance contracts require the agencies to provide detailed data on clients and programs. New accounting standards impose extensive record-keeping requirements on nonprofits. And the competition for funds means that nonprofit staff and boards need much better financial and program data in order to assess their present and future needs.

Often the expertise and resources necessary for an adequate management infrastructure are in short supply. This is particularly true of smaller community-based agencies, which have grown and evolved by obtaining legal status and modest public and private grants. But many of these agencies are highly dependent on a very narrow range of funding. Many of the new community agencies in areas such as AIDS, immigrant services, housing, and emergency relief are almost completely dependent on public funds. Many of these agencies often lack sophisticated management and have weak board structures. And problems with board governance can often contribute to the already difficult challenges facing the agency in attracting and keeping qualified staff, raising private donations, and developing community and political support. These serious and ongoing problems then can make it very difficult for these community organizations to resist government or donor pressure on programmatic issues.

The funding and regulatory role of government also calls attention to the importance of political institutions in shaping the nonprofit sector. In recent years, many scholars have called attention to the vital and central role of political institutions in influencing civil society, including the actions and goals of voluntary associations and groups (Evans, Rueschemeyer and Skocpol 1985; Powell and DiMaggio 1991; Steinmo, Thelen and Longstreth 1993; Peters 2000). As it pertains to our understanding of the government-nonprofit relationship, the institutional perspective suggests that the prevalence and vitality of nonprofit organizations is a product of the political, legal, and institutional environment (Woolcock and Narayan 2000). As such, weak and ineffective governments, a lack of public funding or appropriate tax incentives, and poor public leadership will profoundly affect the nonprofit sector (see Tendler 1997). Oppressive or inappropriate government regulations can in turn undermine nonprofit organizations and directly affect the willingness to form nonprofit organizations or participate in these organizations as staff and volunteers.

Two important variants of this institutional perspective are particularly relevant to understanding the government-nonprofit relationship and the debate about the independence and distinctiveness of the nonprofit sector. First, Theda Skocpol (1999) has argued that voluntary associations thrive in tandem with active government, that government support for voluntary organizations is critical to the growth of the sector. This point is also made by many other scholars including Jeffrey Pressman (1975), Robert Salisbury (1984), and Jack Walker (1988), who have all emphasized the important role of government in spurring nonprofit activity and encouraging the formation of nonprofit advocacy and service organizations.

Nonprofit advocacy organizations expanded greatly in number in the post-sixties era, fueled by the expansion of the federal government. At the national level, most advocacy organizations are indirectly or directly tied to the federal government. Some national advocacy organizations are funded through member dues but their members are heavily dependent upon federal funds or subject to federal regulations. To be sure, the creation of nonprofit advocacy organizations may be due to a foundation grant or the collective response of concerned advocates to a pressing social problem such as poverty or health care. Yet, the expansion of government provides the organizational impetus for the increase in nonprofit advocacy and a focus for their advocacy efforts (Stewart 1975; Heclo 1980; Salisbury 1984, 1990; Walker 1988 ; Berry 1989). Estelle James (1987) has made a similar point in her comparative research on nonprofit organizations in which she observes that government funding and nonprofit organizations have grown in tandem. Judith Tendler's (1997) recent work on NGOs in Brazil also supports this overall perspective.

Of course advocacy groups could increase due to the increasingly prominent role of government but still be independent of government. Indeed, this is the point made by many scholars who have studied social movements, who have called attention to the importance of many social movements, including the civil rights movement, the women's movement, and the AIDS movement, in changing government policy. Further, as Skocpol (1999) notes, social movements of the 1960s such as the women's movement and civil rights movement prompted the establishment of innumerable nonprofit organizations. However, she also contends that without the ultimate change in government policy, these social movements would not have been able to sustain their momentum. Government sometimes offered direct and indirect funding. And the big increase in government policy initiatives related to civil rights, for example, prompted a tremendous incentive for the formation of nonprofit advocacy organizations.

Tendler's work also underscores another key point regarding the role of political institutions broadly defined in shaping nonprofit organizations. She found that often personnel from NGOs went to work for the central government and vice-versa. Indeed, the success of NGOs in Brazil hinged, in part, on the networks created by professionals who crossed the "public-private divide." Put another way, there existed a notable lack of distinctive differences between government and NGOs, in part, due to these networks. So-called independent nonprofit organizations outside this orbit were actually quite weak because they were politically isolated and organizationally fragile and unstable.

Significantly, Tendler's work indicates that blurred public-private boundaries may actually be helpful to nonprofit effectiveness because it may enhance opportunities for cooperation and resource development. She also calls attention to the point made by others (Rein and Rainwater 1986; Smith and Lipsky 1993) that seemingly private behavior may in fact be quite public in nature. Nonprofit agencies are often founded as a result of a community of interest focused on addressing an issue of mutual concern. As a first priority, those getting involved tend to strive to be responsive to this community, broadly defined. But government is often motivated by equity concerns, so nonprofit agencies accepting public funds often have to shift their focus and adopt broader priorities. This can also be reflected in the political activity of nonprofit service agencies, which tends to concentrate on issues of public funding and regulations. They take their cues for their advocacy from public sector decisions and concerns (Smith and Lipsky 1993).

Sectoral decisions reflect political choices. The decision to incorporate as a commercial theater or a nonprofit one will be directly affected by government policy, including tax incentives and funding opportunities. Or the decision to convert from a nonprofit hospital to a for-profit hospital will inevitably be affected by tax and regulatory considerations. A nonprofit art museum is not necessarily a reflection of market failure, but rather of the incentives provided by government to incorporate as a nonprofit.

The importance of institutions has direct implications for the ongoing debate on privatization and devolution. One perspective on privatization suggests that less government will mean more voluntary action through nonprofit organizations. Yet, the work of Rein (1986), Gronbjerg (1993), Smith and Lipsky (1993), Skocpol (1999), Salamon (2002), and Smith (2002) and and others would predict that a withering of the public sector might actually lead to a withering of the nonprofit sector. Thus, the public and nonprofit sectors are interdependent. Further, the growth of the nonprofit sector—and people's reliance upon it for services—will likely invite public regulation and monitoring. It is for this reason that the Bush administration's Faith-Based and Community-Based Initiatives might actually invite more intervention by public entities in the affairs of churches and faith-related organizations than ever before.

Inattention to the complex interconnections between government and nonprofit organizations risks undermining the contributions of nonprofits to citizen participation and policy reform, as well as reducing the effectiveness of government and nonprofit programs. Peter Evans (1996) and Woolcock and Narayan have studied the community development field, including the role of NGOs in the developing world. They propose a "synergy view" which emphasizes "dynamic professional alliances and relationships between and within state bureaucracies and various actors in civil society" (Woolcock and Narayan 2000).

Central to the synergy perspective is the idea of complementarity and embeddedness. The former refers to mutually supportive relationships between public and private actors. For instance, the nonprofit sector cannot exist without a supportive legal framework. Russia is a case in point: Weak political institutions and deep cleavages between the public sector and civil society organizations can lead to political instability and a fragile, weak nonprofit sector (Rose 1998). In the United States context, many federal social programs fail to sustain themselves because of poor political leadership and a lack of cooperative social networks at the local level (Pressman 1975; Smith 1998). Mark Warren (2000) also concluded that community organizing was unlikely to be effective unless cooperative social networks existed within a structure of supportive political institutions.

The concept of embeddedness directly relates to the lack of distinctiveness between sectors. For instance, the relationship between government and nonprofit social welfare agencies can often be considered a "contracting regime," characterized by regularized interactions between the public and nonprofit actors and governed by a set of norms regulating behavior (Smith and Lipsky 1993). Wagner (2000, 542) observes that nonprofit organizations should be viewed "not so much as forming a specific institutional sector but as part of a complex network of organizations." Elinor Ostrom (1996) reached a similar conclusion in her study of development in Brazil.

She argued that the successful projects were the result of "co-production" in which the public sector "co-produced" an improved sanitation system with local citizens who often participated through local associations. Albert O. Hirschman (1984) noted in his study of grassroots organizations in Latin America that the pluralist politics of Colombia, Peru, and the Dominican Republic were reinforced and supported by a dense network of grassroots movements and social activist organizations. The external ties of these community agencies to state actors were a critical determining factor to effective community mobilization (O'Rourke 2001). Warren (2001) found the same dynamic in his study of the Industrial Areas Foundation in Texas and the Southwest.

Looking Ahead

The vision of an independent sector has been very attractive throughout American history. Unlike many other advanced industrial countries such as Germany and the Netherlands, we have not had a long tradition of extensive government support for nonprofit organizations. Americans also tend to be very suspicious or skeptical of government, except in times of crisis. Nonprofit community organizations can be a valuable source of citizen participation, community building, social capital, and pluralism. But the vision of independence has had a number of unintended and inadvertent consequences for nonprofit organizations themselves.

Many nonprofit organizations are small and undercapitalized with weak governance structure and unstable leadership. They need long-term technical assistance and adequate public and private funding for their operations. Because of their capacity limitations, they are also very susceptible to donor or grantor pressure and influence. If they are to become sustainable entities, they need a lot of help and support from government and the local community. They cannot exist as independent entities.

In addition, nonprofit organizations are unlikely to be sustainable and effective in promoting citizen participation if they do not have a web of cooperative social networks that transcend their own community and include networks and ties with government officials. Even nonprofit agencies without substantial government funding may need government assistance and responsiveness from public officials. Neighborhood associations, for example, will not be very effective or sustainable if city hall is unresponsive to their concerns and issues. Advocacy groups will not flourish in an environment of restrictive tax laws and regulations.

Government is also in a very difficult and complicated relationship with nonprofits. Government often provides direct and indirect funding. Increasingly, government officials also couple this funding with extensive evaluation and accountability standards. But these standards can often conflict with the goals and mission of nonprofit organizations. Balancing the need for accountability with the legitimate desire of nonprofits for programmatic autonomy and discretion is challenging, and one of the central issues facing government and nonprofit organizations as they strive to find the right balance in their ongoing relationship.

In sum, if we as a society want nonprofit organizations that are sustainable and vital, we need to be prepared to invest in both the public and nonprofit sectors and squarely address the challenges in managing the relationships across sectors. We also need to shift away from the discourse of independence and discuss the many important ways that public policy can help promote and facilitate voluntarism, citizen participation, and the overall health of the nonprofit sector.

2

Social Welfare Organizations, Politics, and Regulation

Elizabeth Reid

Early social welfare groups were membership organizations, such as Moose lodges, yacht and country clubs, or police and firefighter benefit associations. Today, however, social welfare organizations have broadened and diversified to make distinctions between social welfare organizations and other nonprofit organizations less obvious in practice. Advocacy organizations, in particular, make up a small, but important, part of those nonprofits classified by the Internal Revenue Service (IRS) as 501(c)(4) social welfare organizations.

Some of the most visible and politically active nonprofit organizations in the United States are 501(c)(4) social welfare organizations. The National Rifle Association, National Organization for Women, American Civil Liberties Union, The National Right To Life Committee, and Sierra Club, for example, are large, high-profile 501(c)(4) organizations that are active participants in the nation's public policy process. Some advocacy organizations are stand-alone organizations, but many are linked with related 501(c)(3) organizations to maximize advantages of tax and political regulation.

Several factors warrant further investigation into the interaction between regulation and practice in social welfare organizations. Little information exists on social welfare organizations as a class of tax-exempt organizations and on its subset of advocacy organizations, inviting faulty characterizations of their activities and finances. Public awareness about the role of nonprofits in policymaking and elections is increasing, along with questions about the legitimacy and accountability of advocacy nonprofit organizations. Tax and political regulation guiding the practices of these organizations is in the process of change as a result of recently enacted campaign finance reforms.

In light of these shifts, the following questions demand our attention:

- What are 501(c)(4) social welfare organizations? How do they differ from 501(c)(3) charitable organizations? Does the classification of social welfare organizations need clarification?
- How are social welfare organizations linked with 501(c)(3) charitable organizations and political organizations in law and practice? In what ways do their joint financial and program practices affect their advocacy activities?
- Do social welfare organizations with full-fledged members play a special role in policymaking and elections that should be encouraged in regulation and practice?
- What kinds of democratic rationales should inform regulation, and what kinds of policy reforms might be considered?

501(c)(4) Social Welfare Organizations

There are approximately 1.2 million tax-exempt (nonprofit) organizations registered with the IRS. Depending on an organization's purpose and mission, it is classified under one of 25 different tax-exempt categories. Those classified under Section 501(c)(4) are called social welfare groups. They account for 11 percent of all tax-exempt organizations (Independent Sector and the Urban Institute 2002). The IRS describes social welfare organizations as follows:

> To be considered operated exclusively for the promotion of social welfare, an organization must operate primarily to further (in some way) the common good and general welfare of the people of the community (such as by bringing about civic betterment and social improvements). An organization that restricts the use of its facilities to employees of selected corporations and their guests is primarily benefiting a private group rather than the community and, therefore, does not qualify as a § 501(c)(4) organization (Internal Revenue Service [IRS] Website/Social Welfare Organizations 2002).

Civic associations, community associations, and volunteer fire associations are examples of social welfare organizations, according to the IRS. A small subset of 501(c)(4) social welfare organizations are called "action organizations," or more commonly, advocacy organizations.

Curiously, the IRS publication "Tax-Exempt Status for Your Organization" does not discuss action organizations as a type of social welfare organization (IRS 2002). Nor does the IRS suggest that the 501(c)(4) exempt category was formed to accommodate groups organized to do policy and electoral advocacy, though elsewhere, the IRS does advise groups doing substantial lobbying to organize as 501(c)(4)s.

However, IRS regulations that describe 501(c)(3) charities make direct reference to 501(c)(4) social welfare groups: "An action organization . . . , though it cannot qualify under 501(c)(3), may nevertheless qualify as a social welfare organization under Section 501(c)(4) . . ." (Treas. § 1.501(c)(3)-1(c)(3)(v)). Similarly, the regulations describing 501(c)(4)s make direct reference to 501(c)(3) charities: "A social welfare organization will qualify for exemption as a charitable organization if it falls within the definition of charitable . . . and is not an action organization . . ." (Treas. § 1.501(c)(4)-1 (A)(2)(ii)). Thus, IRS definitions, while not rigorously defining the positive attributes of social welfare organizations, suggest they are similar in ways to both exempt organizations with members as primary beneficiaries and those with charitable purposes and public beneficiaries.

Data from the Urban Institute's National Center for Charitable Statistics on 501(c)(4) social welfare organizations indicate that a diverse group of organizations have come to rest in this tax-exempt category.

- In 2000, there were approximately 22,000 social welfare organizations, almost half of which are small organizations with under $50,000 in annual expenses (Krehely and Golladay 2002).
- In 2000, the activities of social welfare organizations included inner-city and community activities: sports, recreational and social activities, education, training and health services, and many more (Krehely and Golladay 2002).
- In 1998, social welfare organizations received government grants accounting for 3.3 percent of their annual revenue. Those most likely to receive government grants were classified as public safety, human services, and employment related organizations (National Center for Charitable Statistics [NCCS], Statistics of Income File [SOI] 1998).

Distinguishing Social Welfare Organizations from Charitable Organizations

These definitions and data trigger questions about the rationale for IRS classification of organizations as either social welfare or charitable organizations. Is there a distinction between the public purposes of charitable and social welfare organizations? Do social welfare organizations have more in common with each other or with charitable organizations? Except for a small number of "action" social welfare organizations that distinguish themselves from 501(c)(3)s by the level and kind of their political activity, the classification of organizations as 501(c)(3)s and 501(c)(4)s is a matter of degree. For charitable organizations, the IRS defines the activities in detail that qualify it as a 501(c)(3) organization:

An organization will be regarded as "operated exclusively" for one or more exempt purposes only if it engages primarily in activities which accomplish one or more of the exempt purposes specified in § 501(c)(3) . . . . [Those exempt purposes set forth in § 501(c)(3) are] charitable, religious, educational, scientific, literary, testing for public safety, fostering national or international amateur sports competition, and the prevention of cruelty to children or animals. The term charitable is used in its generally accepted legal sense and includes relief of the poor, the distressed, or the underprivileged; advancement of religion; advancement of education or science; erection or maintenance of public buildings, monuments, or works; lessening the burdens of government; lessening of neighborhood tensions; elimination of prejudice and discrimination; defense of human and civil rights secured by law; and combating community deterioration and juvenile delinquency (IRS Website/Charitable Organizations 2002).

Charitable organizations receive the most favorable tax status of all tax-exempt organizations, qualifying for both an exemption from paying federal income taxes and the ability to receive tax-deductible contributions from the public. Charitable groups agree to limit the amount of time and money they may devote to lobbying as part of the bargain for eligibility to receive tax-deductible contributions. Charities are further prohibited from partisan activity in elections at the local, state, and national level, and from directly affiliating with or donating to political action committees (PACs), which are used to financially support political parties and candidates for public office.

In IRS definitions and in organizational practice, it is sometimes hard to distinguish exempt purposes or activities of 501(c)(3) charitable organizations from those 501(c)(4) social welfare organizations. Even the IRS acknowledges definitional issues: "Social welfare is an inherently abstruse concept that continues to defy precise definition"(IRS 1981). One distinction between charitable and social welfare organizations, for example, is based on the perceived beneficiaries of the organization's activities. It suggests that charitable organizations benefit the "public writ large" or society, because of the obligation of society to care for its poor and the other regarding nature of charitable acts. In contrast, social welfare organizations benefit the "public writ small" or communities, based on the mutual self-help affiliation of members. The IRS notions of community reduce the scope of the public benefit offered by social welfare groups.

The term community generally refers to a geographical unit recognizable as a governmental subdivision, unit, or district thereof. Whether a particular association meets the requirement of benefiting a community depends on the facts and circumstances of each case. Even if an area represented by an association is not a community, the association can still qualify for exemption if its activities benefit a community(IRS Website/Social Welfare Organizations 2002).

Many of the early social welfare groups were membership organizations, but operated for the common good by serving communities. Moose lodges, yacht and country clubs, police and firefighter benefit associations, medical societies, and other economic associations in cities and counties were among the 533 organizations formed before 1940 now classified as social welfare organizations (NCCS/Core Files 2002). Today, the scope of work by social welfare organizations extends well beyond conceptions of community or the common good, and its earlier association with self-help and civic betterment is weaker. Social welfare organizations now include diverse groups, such as The Over the Hill Soccer League, The Cat Fanciers Association, The Georgia Amateur Wrestling Association, The Beavercreek Popcorn Festival Corporation, The Lumberjack World Championships Foundation, The United States Open Sandcastle Committee, and many other disparate entities.

Why some organizations are classified as charities and some as social welfare groups is not readily apparent. The Racing Association of Central Iowa tops the list of groups of big spenders, with $2.7 billion in annual expenses for 2000 (Krehely and Golladay 2002). Also of note, some of the largest 501(c)(4) groups are health insurance providers, such as Delta Dental of Pennsylvania, Security Health Plan of Wisconsin, and the Health Plan of the Upper Ohio Valley. Interestingly, some of the largest 501(c)(3) groups are health insurance providers as well, including the Health Insurance Plan of Greater New York, Iowa Health System, and the Group Health Cooperative of Puget Sound.

Some organizations ended up as social welfare organizations, because they no longer qualified for 501(c)(3) status. Groups that originally began as charities, for instance, must convert to social welfare organizations if they begin to devote a more than insubstantial amount of time and money to lobbying, as was the case with the Sierra Club in the 1960s. In addition, groups that miss the deadline for or have problems in applying for 501(c)(3) status may temporarily register as 501(c)(4)s, recoup some of the income tax expenses they may have incurred while in limbo, and later reapply for 501(c)(3) status.

Indeed, leading legal scholars, Hill and Mancino (2002) state that, "Section 501(c)(4) has become the Internal Revenue Code provision that the IRS uses to address difficult issues without making difficult choices." Fishman and Schwarz (2000) state that, "As a practical matter, apart from its role as the Code section of choice for advocacy groups, § 501(c)(4) has become the 'dumping ground' for organizations that fail to make the grade as a § 501(c)(3) charity but nonetheless provide a substantial public benefit."

Is something to be gained by converting nonadvocating 501(c)(4) organizations to 501(c)(3) charitable organizations, or to one of the other twenty-five tax-exempt categories of organizations with which they may have a greater affinity, such as social clubs or labor and agricultural organizations? In considering reorganization, what are the resulting tax and fiscal benefits for an organization and regulatory barriers to collective expression and participation in policymaking and elections? In effect, social welfare groups reorganized as charities would widen the eligibility of groups and activities for tax deductible contributions while narrowing the scope of permissible political activities and expenditures for groups reclassified as charitable organizations. However, the fiscal benefit to other social welfare organizations reclassified into other non-501(c)(3) exempt categories would be minimal, as would the impact on their permissible political activities.

Acknowledging classification problems, scholars have begun to more critically examine the research frameworks that derive from describing and classifying 501(c)(4) organizations. A common misconception in nonprofit research equates the entire class of social welfare organizations with "action" or advocacy. Lester Salamon (1999) refers to social welfare groups as "public-serving organizations heavily engaged in direct political action (campaigning and lobbying for legislation), for which a special section of the tax code [Section 501(c)(4)] exists." It turns out, however, that a surprisingly small number of social welfare organizations actually describe themselves as having an advocacy role.

In conclusion, charitable and social welfare activities have broadened and diversified and in some ways converged to make distinctions in the tax code less obvious in practice. In addition, some social welfare organizations are organized to take advantage of more relaxed standards for political advocacy. These changes raise issues for researchers and regulators about the ways in which to clarify the classification of 501(c)(4) organizations.

Politically Active 501(c)(4) Social Welfare Organizations

As mentioned earlier, a small but significant part of the 501(c)(4) social welfare organizations are action or advocacy organizations. They are distinguished from other 501(c)(4)s and 501(c)(3)s in large part by their levels of political engagement. Action or advocacy social welfare organizations may engage fully in lobbying, as long as the lobbying serves to further their exempt purposes. They may have affiliated PACs, through which they can contribute to campaigns and parties. Also, they may contact their membership to advocate directly for the election or defeat of specific candidates for public office. Rules for lobbying and election-related activity grew out of an earlier recognition that civic and political betterment required involvement with local authorities over such matters as zoning (Hill and Mancino 2002). Subsequently, the class of social welfare organizations has expanded to include large interest groups influential in national politics.

How many 501(c)(4)s are advocacy organizations? Do these advocacy organizations have a different relationship with government and market institutions and with citizens than do charitable organizations? What advantages arise when advocacy organizations are linked financially and administratively to a 501(c)(3) organization? Data from the NCCS give us a starting point for profiling advocacy organizations. In working with these data, it is difficult to sort out advocacy organizations from the bulk of social welfare organizations, as few report advocacy or social action as the primary, secondary, or tertiary activity on their annual IRS Form 990. Nevertheless, data on self-selecting advocacy organizations indicate the following facts:

- Just 2,582 or 12 percent of social welfare organizations identified "advocacy or attempts to influence public opinion of specifics issues" as an organizational activity. However, 1,800 of them were Lions and Rotary chapters (Krehely and Golladay 2002).
- The 818 self-identified advocacy organizations that were not Lions or Rotary Clubs tend to be midsized groups with $50,000 annual expenditures. The most prevalent advocacy issues mentioned were human and civil rights, environment, and abortion. About 60 percent of these advocating social welfare organizations formed after 1980 and more than half were membership organizations (Krehely and Golladay 2002).
- These advocacy-related social welfare organizations were more reliant on income that is considered "unrestricted," such as general contributions and member dues revenue, than were all 501(c)(4)s (Krehely and Golladay 2002). Also these groups are less reliant on program-specific revenues and government grants (NCCS/SOI 1998).

In addition to those who self-identify as advocates, a rough estimate using NCCS data indicates there are nearly one hundred additional high-profile advocacy organizations with over $1 million in annual revenue that are classified as social welfare organizations (NCCS/Core Files 2001). These groups, such as the National Rifle Association, are consistently in the public eye, expend large amounts of money, and use sophisticated tactics to influence public opinion and mobilize voters.

Perhaps the most dramatic finding from these data is that there are so few readily identifiable advocacy organizations among social welfare organizations. At this stage in nonprofit research, there are few data sources against which to check this finding or from which to produce a fuller picture of the activism, ideologies, and partisan preferences of 501(c)(4) organizations. Survey data on organizational finances and activities, structures and governance, and membership affiliation in social welfare organizations are needed, although several studies of environmental and civil rights organizations have made inroads into these dynamics (see Shaiko 1999; Boris and Krehely 2002).

Additionally, these data tentatively suggest that the relationship between social welfare organizations and government may be different than that of charitable organizations. Social welfare organizations have a lower reliance on government as a source of funding than charitable organizations and are more likely than charitable organizations to have members. Both these factors combine to suggest that advocacy 501(c)(4)s may have a more contested relationship with government, different from the partnership between charitable organizations and government.

Presently, social welfare organizations that engage in advocacy may play important intermediary roles between government policymaking and civic expression. Again, more research is necessary, but at first glance these data appear to indicate that social welfare organizations are more likely than charitable organizations to have members. Advocacy organizations with members, it might be argued, exemplify some of the celebrated democratic virtues of Tocquevillian civil and political organizations. These members meet and express common interests toward social and political ends and have the financial independence to voice opposition to government policy. Large membership organizations also derive a substantial portion of their income from dues, monies that are less restricted for use for advocacy activities.

How organizations affiliate their constituencies and fund their political activity potentially affects their relationship with government. Government funding to charitable social service organizations has grown since the 1960s as the government has become increasingly reliant on the nonprofit sector. This has led Lester Salamon (1995) and others to conclude that the relationship of government and charitable organizations can best be characterized as a partnership in the delivery of social and other services. Smith and Lipsky (1993) have further suggested that public funding may alter the kinds of issues and strategies of action undertaken by organizations in the political arena, predisposing them to incremental adaptation to policy rather than policy change.

Social welfare organizations, however, are not immune to pressures of patrons and members. Members may on occasion slow or prevent progress on policy positions supported by organizational leaders. Large private and institutional funding may affect the issues and tactics of social welfare organizations. Some recent evidence indicates that corporate and political interests may be forming and using 501(c)(4) organizations to adjust to regulatory changes in campaign financing (Edsall 2002).

As institutional channels for broadening and deepening expressive activities of citizens, how should regulatory policy design and organizational practices of social welfare organizations reflect these participatory values? Which advocacy organizations operate with sound democratic values and practices? How are they funded and how do they use their money in the political system? Whom do they represent, how do they make decisions, and do their organizations have roots in communities and among the "body politic"? Do tax and election regulations offer incentives or create obstacles for groups to engage the public in policy debates and elections?

Rising public sentiment for transparency and accountability of both commercial and nonprofit corporate finances and activities has led to greater public scrutiny. However, private, nonprofit organizations historically have been separate from government in part to protect civil society's role as a check and balance on government in American democracy. The privacy enjoyed by nonprofits makes questions of legitimacy and accountability hard to answer. In the next several sections, the chapter addresses these concerns.

Election-Related Advocacy in a Changing Regulatory Environment

Elections are the fundamental arena in which citizens exercise their sovereign authority to constitute their government. In addition to their lobbying and policy advocacy, some 501(c)(4) advocacy organizations attempt to influence election outcomes for public office, raising private dollars to educate the public on issues, register and turn out voters, and build electoral majorities in coalition with others.

Social welfare advocacy organizations have shaped regulatory policy changes and adapted their advocacy to new conditions and rules in the political environment. With creativity, efficiency, and political expediency, they have gradually expanded their role in national politics. These advocacy organizations are pivotal, along with political parties, in expanding the kinds of activities used to shape public attitudes and influence policy and election outcomes. They developed a repertoire of activities to shape public opinion and voter behavior, including activities that fall outside of regulatory strictures through niches in tax law on reportable lobbying expenditures, and election law on reportable partisan contributions and expenditures.

One of those, issue advertising, became a contested practice of organizations and political parties (Krasno and Seltz 2001). Issue ads, funded by soft money, replaced a direct message to vote for or against a candidate (a reportable partisan expenditure to the Federal Election Commission [FEC] known as express advocacy) with highly suggestive images and language linking policy issues with candidate performance, while leaving little doubt among those watching as to the merit of voting for or against a candidate (a nonreportable activity). Moreover, huge infusions of soft money into the political system through political parties, corporations, and nonprofit organizations left the public wary of the conduct of groups, businesses, and politicians during elections.

New rules under the Bipartisan Campaign Reform Act (BCRA) sought to address public concerns over these issues. Prior to the passage of BCRA in 2002, expenditures in social welfare organizations for issue ads were largely unregulated unless they were direct partisan communications. BCRA brought to light the question, among others, of which political activities need further regulation and why? Under a new electioneering communication law, social welfare organizations will be prohibited from using their treasuries to finance certain types of issue advertising prior to an election. Electioneering communication is defined as "any broadcast communication which (1) refers to a clearly identified candidate for federal office, (2) is made within 60 days before a general, special, or runoff election or 30 days before a primary or caucus, and (3) is targeted. Specifically, the bill defines 'targeted electioneering communication' to mean a federal candidate-specific broadcast communication that can be received by 50,000 or more persons in the congressional district or state in which a candidate is running for Congress or Senate, as applicable" (Campaign Finance Institute 2003). New disclosure laws also require that political ads be subject to increased disclaimer requirements. However, those social welfare organizations with a connected PAC can use PAC funds to sponsor political ads.

Membership Organizations or Special Purpose Organizations?

Close organizational links with the citizenry are one important measure by which groups are extended credibility as representatives in the political process. By examining membership structure and involvement, it may be possible to distinguish whether members have strong or weak ties with social welfare organizations, and to determine which social welfare organizations build popular political will and link it to public decisions, and which tend to be special purpose social welfare organizations representing a small number of large corporate and individual contributors.

Generally speaking, *membership* is a term widely used to describe the relationship between individuals and their associations. The term *member* suggests a stronger identification with an organization, than does *donor* or *constituency*, because members have made the explicit decision to join with others under an organizational banner. Membership interaction in organizations can build shared meaning and solidarity, strengthen social capital and collective action, and lend to bargaining clout on policy when groups mobilize their members to vote as unified blocks in elections.

Social welfare organizations with members enjoy special regulatory advantages when it comes to politics. Using their organizational funds, they may contact their members with information urging the election or defeat of a candidate. While laws and regulations use membership as a qualifier for tax and political advantages, the definitions of membership are imprecise. The IRS uses facts and circumstances to determine who is a bona fide member, and virtually permits anyone to be called or counted as a member. The FEC requires groups to solicit and acknowledge members, and to have members pay dues annually or have participatory rights, or have a significant financial attachment to the organization (Reid 2003). In general, as long as a member can voluntarily enter and exit the association, the state has little interest in the governance structure or the extent of members' voice in the internal governance of the organization (Brody 2001).

Thus, the structure and character of membership affiliation in a social welfare organization may vary widely. Organization trustees and boards largely determine organizational formation and operation, including governance restrictions and membership protections. Member-organizational relationships vary, for example, as to whether the membership is exclusive or inclusive, individual or organizational, or whether the member is simply a donor or has formal rights to elect leaders or to give input into the direction of the organization.

Membership also comes at a cost to organizations. Additional resources and management skills are needed for the increased time and costs associated with maintaining membership lists, raising money in small denominations, communicating with members, chairing internal deliberative discussion, and creating governance procedures and using them in ways that include member voice in the internal affairs of organizations. Thus, many charitable organizations and some social welfare organizations have limited roles for members in organizations, other than as donors.

The same legal space that provides flexibility in structuring social welfare organizations also opens a door for these groups to become *special purpose* social welfare organizations. Special purpose social welfare organizations, in contrast to organizations with broad and diverse membership bases, are often organized by campaign wizards or political consultants, and comprise a small number of widely influential elite voices from corporate or political classes. Special purpose social welfare organizations may make bold claims to represent the public or the grassroots, even though their income is largely derived from a few large corporate or individual contributors with well-defined political agendas. They are not likely to have, or be connected to organizations with, grassroots membership, especially membership with voting rights and representation on standing committees, such as the American Association of Retired People or the National Rifle Association.

A particular form of special purpose organizations, so-called "astroturf organizations," have the trappings of a grassroots constituency, but in reality are a marketing scheme for mobilizing individuals on policy issues. Organized business interests have established Citizens for Sensible Control of Acid Rain and the National Wetlands Coalition that appear to have a grassroots constituency sympathetic to environmental regulation, but in fact do not (Boris and Krehely 2002). Without additional information on members, donors, or policy positions, organization names can be misleading to the public. Indeed, social welfare organizations appear to be a ready-made alternative channel for special interest soft money, a troubling prospect for those who see nonprofit organizations as structures for citizen participation.

These trends raise questions. What is the basis of organizational legitimacy and power? Are nonprofit groups rooted in the Tocquevillian idea of a "nation of joiners," or are they captives of special interests? Should organizations with members, especially those with constitutions spelling out member rights in organizations, be allowed more autonomy in their political affairs and be subject to different kinds of reporting and disclosure regarding their members? How can we define and clarify which groups are genuine membership groups from those that are marketing shams?

In considering future tax and campaign regulatory reforms, regulators and organizations should consider strengthening definitions of members and membership organizations. Clarifying the difference between members and contributors will link an important associational attribute to financial and other incentives to encourage groups to affiliate their constituencies as members, broaden the base of small contributions to organizations, and confer with members in their organizational decision making. These three organizational factors would help ensure that social welfare organizations are firmly rooted in and supported by the body politic and that they adhere to the democratic practices in their organizational decision making that provide citizens with democratic experiences and skills transferable to public life. They would also tamp down the increasing tendency to use social welfare organizations for special purposes.

Advocacy Organizations Embedded in Complex Organizational Structures

Politically active social welfare organizations are often part of a larger complex of organizations. Separate tax-exempt organizations, related through overlapping boards and shared administrative and fundraising costs, form complex organizational structures in response to incentives in the tax system. In the case of politically active organizations, they are created to permit them to use additional resources and activities in the political system. Generally speaking, larger groups that are policy players in Congress and federal elections are most likely to use complex organizational structures.

One of the more familiar arrangements used to increase policymaking influence is a combination of a 501(c)(3) charity, a 501(c)(4) social welfare organization, and a Section 527 political organization that is registered as a connected PAC with the FEC. Sierra Club, for example, a 501(c)(4), may conduct unlimited lobbying and engage in limited partisan communications with its members. Sierra Club Foundation, a 501(c)(3), which can receive tax-deductible contributions, may engage in public education and also lobby within some limits. Both of these groups report information to the IRS and are subject to IRS constraints on their financial and political activities. Sierra Club Political Committee is a PAC established to contribute to candidates for federal office. While incorporated as a tax-exempt political organization, it is subject to FEC regulations and reporting but can receive support from the 501(c)(4) for certain administrative and fundraising costs.

These arrangements are entirely within the law and this discussion should not discourage groups from taking full advantage of the opportunities provided under the law. Individual nonprofit organizations that are part of a complex organizational structure cannot share control of day-to-day activities, but they often share advocacy goals, collaborate on strategies of action, and manage their resources in strategic ways to achieve political ends. Confusing tax and election laws, a lack of transparency about organizational finances, and diverse data from the IRS, FEC, lobbying reports, and other sources make it exceedingly difficult to determine which organizations are related to one another and how money moves through the organizations and into politics. Nevertheless, a rough match of 501(c)(3)s and 501(c)(4)s in the NCCS data indicates that approximately one in eight social welfare organizations is connected to a charitable organization (Krehely and Golladay 2002).

When social welfare advocacy organizations team up with charitable organizations, limited advocacy activities engaged in at the greatest tax benefit can be combined with the most aggressive advocacy activities to obtain the broadest range for advocacy efforts, presumably at the most efficient cost (Reid and Kerlin 2003). This can be achieved through transfers of organizational money as long as resources from one nonprofit are not used elsewhere to subsidize activities that it cannot conduct itself (Schadler 1998). A 501(c)(3) can transfer money to a 501(c)(4) for lobbying activities, within IRS-established limits. Similarly, a 501(c)(4) can transfer funds to a PAC, again within IRS-established limits. A 501(c)(4)-PAC transfer would also be subject to FEC reporting requirements.

In an examination of five environmental groups with complex organizational structures, Reid and Kerlin (2003) found four models of organizational interdependence, all with potential effects for financing advocacy activities in social welfare organizations. These relationships are characterized as follows:

- *Autonomous*: A 501(c)(3) and 501(c)(4) may relate, yet remain relatively separated financially and programmatically. While autonomous at times, the two entities nevertheless represent dormant organizational capacity. The organizations are structurally poised to shift funding and programs should conditions arise in the political environment that would make closer interaction practical.
- *Program Reliance*: When a 501(c)(3) transfers a large portion of its revenue to its 501(c)(4) partner, it becomes reliant on the 501(c)(4) to conduct its charitable programmatic activity. In this case, the charitable organization acts as a fundraising arm for programmatic activity that is centered in the parent 501(c)(4) organization. Additionally, the social welfare organization can offset its lobbying expense with this money and raise addi-

tional money for more rigorous political activity not allowable with tax-deductible money.

- *Financial Reliance*: A 501(c)(4) may rely in large part on a 501(c)(3) transfer of revenue, even though the 501(c)(3) transfer may be only a portion of the charitable arm's revenue. In this case, the charitable organization is likely to retain substantial programmatic activity while transferring money to the 501(c)(4). Again, the transfer may partially offset lobbying expenses and thus free resources for more rigorous political action.

- *Dependence*: In some cases, the charitable organization may transfer the bulk of its revenue to the social welfare organization and the social welfare organization may be heavily reliant on this source of income. As a result, the social welfare organization could do little more in law and practice than what the charitable organization could do alone. Without growth of the social welfare arm, both arms of the complex organization are constrained by the charitable organization's lobbying limit.

Few in-depth studies assess the costs and benefits of complex organizational structures to give us a glimpse of how organizational structures contribute to political practice. In fact, most groups that create such structures likely assume—without conclusive evidence—that a series of interrelated organizations will expand their advocacy capacity by enlarging opportunities for lobbying and political activity, and by efficiently allocating organizational resources toward meeting advocacy goals.

More research is needed to address questions raised by this form of institutional structuring for nonprofit activists, boards, and for the public at large. Does one arm of the complex organizational structure insulate another from the risks of political controversy? What is the "division of labor" among components of the complex organizational structure? What kinds of complex organizational structures represent "best practices" for civic and political engagement? Are donors given a clear picture of the different types of organizations and activities that exist within the auspices of one larger organization? How do complex organizations differ from coalitions?

New rules under BCRA apply strict regulations to the sponsorship of nonprofit organizations by political parties, candidates, and federal officeholders. The act specifically "prohibits national, state, district, or local political party committees from directly or indirectly soliciting funds for or making or directing donations to (1) a tax-exempt [501(c)] organization . . . which makes expenditures or disbursements in connection with an election for federal office and (2) a Section 527 political organization" (Mayer 2002). It also prohibits "candidates and federal officeholders from directly or indirectly soliciting contributions to fund federal election-related activities (except for hard money contributions)" with a few exceptions (Mayer 2002). Campaign finance reform also provides a new definition for coordination between nonprofits and political parties. It views "any expenditure made in cooperation, consultation or concern with, or at the request or suggestion of, a national, state, or local committee of a political party as made in coordination with the political committee and therefore as a contribution to that committee" (Mayer 2002). New definitions under BCRA have implications for how much of a 501(c)(4)'s activities are counted against their election-related limits as set by the FEC and tax on expenditures made for political activities.

At the same time, BCRA restrictions on the use of soft money by political parties may provide an incentive for political activists to use nonprofits as new conduits of soft money to indirectly promote party agendas. Under BCRA, shadow political parties might emerge as 501(c)(4) social welfare organizations as political activists look for new conduits to channel soft money. Republican and Democratic groups are already severing ties with national parties or establishing separate organizations to raise soft money for certain activities. The Democratic National Committee—the Association of State Democratic Chairs—is establishing a separate Democratic State Party Organization for this purpose and both Democratic and Republican governors' associations have cut ties with their corresponding national party committees for certain activities (Edsall 2002).

Indeed, 501(c)(4)s may become the nonprofits of choice among political parties, because they are not required to publicly disclose details on funding sources or expenditures as PACs are, yet they are able to take on more advocacy activities than 501(c)(3)s. Ironically, supporters of the law worry that such use of 501(c)(4)s "might undermine the purpose of the law by creating new conduits for soft money that require less public disclosure than was required before the legislation was enacted" (Edsall 2002). Progress for America, with its close ties to the Republican Party, is an example of this type of newly emerging special purpose social welfare organization. Progress for America's chairman is Ken Adelman, a top arms control officer in the Reagan administration, and it operates out of the corporate offices of Tony Feather, political director of the Bush-Cheney 2000 campaign (Edsall 2002).The group raises millions of dollars from corporations and individuals to support the Bush agenda, but does not disclose either funding sources or expenditures (Edsall 2002).

Is Disclosure the Answer?

There is no clear-cut answer as to what types of disclosure are beneficial, but regulators and nonprofits must balance concerns about individual privacy, organizational autonomy, and public accountability in deciding what is necessary to report and disclose to the public. Aggregate-level data from the NCCS cannot provide organizational-level data on contributors because of long-standing prohibitions on the public disclosure of member and donor identity and gifts. Further, contributions to nonprofit organizations from private institutions, such as corporations and foundations, and from individuals are not enumerated, but rather are lumped together as public support-income on the annual IRS Form 990.

However, other aspects of nonprofit financial operations are subject to substantial disclosure to government officials and the public. The Supreme Court has recognized the need to disclose hard money contributions or contributions made directly to candidate campaigns and other PACs. Using standard First Amendment tests, the Supreme Court has held that Federal Election Campaign Act (FECA) laws are constitutional if they are "narrowly tailored" to advance a "compelling public interest" (Campaign Finance Institute 2003). In key cases such as *Buckley v. Valeo, Nixon v. Shrink,* and *Missouri Government PAC and Colorado Republican Party v. FEC,* the Court found that combating "corruption or the appearance of corruption" was compelling enough to limit contribution levels and in some cases require disclosure. In 2001, Congress required public disclosure of contributor information from tax-exempt organizations that were formed for political purposes under IRS Section 527, but were not required to register or report to the FEC. New BCRA rules, implemented after the November 2002 elections, created new levels of disclosure for "electioneering" activities.

Members' privacy—the right to associate without disclosing members' names to government authorities—is also a protected element of civic participation. This is because a valued aspect of civic culture is its ability to place demands on society and government that challenge norms and create controversy. The Supreme Court in *NAACP v. Alabama* held that the state of Alabama could not require the NAACP to disclose its members as a condition for its registering as a corporation under state law. The Court held that such disclosure would be inconsistent with the First Amendment's guarantee of "the right of the people freely to associate" and only necessary in the face of compelling state interest. Contributor anonymity, nonprofit sector leaders further argue, has allowed individuals and institutions to give substantial sums of private money to tax-exempt organizations without public notoriety.

Disclosure is a difficult issue, but one that is not going away. The use of exempt organizations to circumvent the intent of campaign finance reform can be expected to continue as a matter of sheer political expediency. Nonprofit sector leaders and policymakers will need to consider whether and what kinds of private institutional and individual resources should be permitted to remain anonymous in advocacy groups that apply these resources toward political activities other than lobbying. Greater disclosure will be contested in the Courts and raise concerns about its impact on nonprofit fundraising.

Some nonprofit organizations have already instituted voluntary disclosure to assure the public and their donors that their organizational activities and finances are representative of civic interests, and that their political messages are rooted in the preferences and sentiments of their members and missions. Voluntary disclosure by social welfare organizations is a step that would begin to isolate those who find organizational opacity, not civic participation, the most attractive feature of the nonprofit forms they are adapting to their own uses. To do nothing about these practices poses the risk that the public will come to equate nonprofit organizations with deception in politics and with instruments for undermining campaign finance reform.

Conclusion

In summary, many regulatory issues play out in the tactics and strategies social welfare organizations use in a democracy, in the movement of money in and out of politics through these organizations, and in the ways social welfare organizations link citizens to policy decisions and the election of representative government. Reformers might well ask whether the state has the right to limit speech and expression at all, even when organizations receive benefits from the state. Regulators might consider revising their definition of membership to better distinguish between members and contributors, thus allowing for greater disclosure of contributions while protecting the privacy of members.

When the relationship of nonprofit groups to the state is mediated through the system of taxation, questions arise about the degree to which tax policy should be a determinant in regulation affecting political expression. Should tax incentives, designed to attract private resources to the nonprofit sector, be a basis for limitations on the political activities and expenditures of organizations? Should the state constrain the political activities and expenditures of those nonprofit organizations that partner in programs funded by the government to deliver services to the public through private organizations?

When the relationship of nonprofit groups to the state is viewed through the processes of democracy, other questions arise about the degree to which the rules of political engagement build legitimacy among citizens, organizations, and elected representatives in the political system. Is more transparency in the political affairs of organizations necessary in order to restore legitimacy to politics and build participation in the political life of the nation? Should groups with members be given more tax incentives to affiliate members, build citizenship skills, and engage the public in society and politics?

In considering future reforms to tax and election law, policymakers should calculate how regulatory changes will affect civic and political association and the role of groups as representatives of civic interests and preferences. Civil society groups should play a major role in shaping public outcomes, and regulation should strive to strengthen their contributions to democracy. Reforms need to create conditions that ensure the legitimacy of private associations as public actors in policymaking and elections. Regulatory policy, however, should not complicate associational affairs to the point that it discourages use of nonprofits for popular political expression. Instead, regulation should ensure that the legitimacy of groups is rooted in civic culture through their membership and governance structures, create accountability through financial transparency, and provide the latitude for organizations to be fully competitive players in the political system.

3

What Is the Political Role of Nonprofits in a Democracy?

Mark E. Warren

The question, "What is the political role of nonprofits in a democracy?" does not admit of a simple answer, if only owing to the sheer variety and complexity of the nonprofit sector. Independent Sector's taxonomy of tax-exempt entities lists 654 subgroups, excluding religious organizations (Hodgkinson et al. 1996, 271–309). But answer we should, if only because the nonprofit sector is a growing presence in our political system, both in relative and absolute terms. When religious organizations are added, Independent Sector counted 1.19 million organizations in 1997, up from 739,000 in 1977. From 1982 to 1997, revenues grew from $212 billion to $665 billion, or from 6.4 to 6.7 percent of the national income. When the estimated value of volunteer labor is added, the figures swell from $2.7 trillion to $7.3 trillion over the same time period (Hodgkinson et al. 1996, 23–54). More recent data indicate that these trends have accelerated, with now approximately 1.8 million nonprofits registered with the Internal Revenue Service (O'Neill 2002). We should answer for another reason as well: The nonprofit sector does not exist in a vacuum, nor does it grow spontaneously. It is something we—that is, our society—have engineered into our social and political system—not directly, of course, but through laws, policies, and protections that have enabled and encouraged nonprofits as ways of getting things done. So, ideally, if we can figure out what these impacts are, then we can also ask whether they are desirable impacts. And we should be quite deliberate about relating these justifications to the ways we decide to make collective decisions and to organize collective actions. We should, in other words, have good reasons for policies that cultivate some kinds of nonprofits and not others, and for the regulations that limit their political activities, or affect their internal workings.

The justifications I emphasize here are those having to do with democracy. There could be and are other justifications: those that focus on the efficiency of serving public purposes, or freedom of association, or pluralism in society (see, e.g., Gutmann 1998; Rosenblum 1998). These goods are not incompatible with democracy, rightly understood (Warren 2001, 21–29). Even if we were to measure policies toward nonprofits by this one metric, democracy, it would turn out not to be a single metric, but rather a multidimensional one. Democracy, as it has evolved in the advanced industrial nations, turns out not simply to be a kind of electoral process, occurring within constitutional frameworks, but a messy ecology of institutions, organizations, dispositions of citizens, and cultures, which, if they complement one another in appropriate ways, serve to enhance the basic norm of democracy: that individuals should have equal chances to influence those collective decisions that affect them (cf. Habermas 1996, 107; Held 1996, 324; Dahl 1998, 37–38; Young 2000, 23; Warren 2003).

The possible roles nonprofits might play within a democratic ecology are extensive. Conceived schematically, there are three broad classes of conditions that democracies need to function (Warren 2001):

- The first class involves attributes of the individuals in society. In principle, nonprofits might serve to *develop the democratic capacities of citizens.* They might do so by providing information and educating citizens, developing their sense of political efficacy, cultivating capacities for deliberation and problem solving, and developing civic virtues such as tolerance, reciprocity, and trust.
- The second class of attributes has to do with a society's capacities to make public judgments in ways that are both deliberative and broadly inclusive. Nonprofits might serve these *public sphere* functions by developing and communicating information to the public, providing groups in society with a public voice, and, more generally, providing representations of difference and commonality in ways that underwrite and focus public deliberation.
- Third, nonprofits may serve *institutional* functions, by providing representation and voice within the institutions of government, means of resistance when formal representation breaks down, alternative venues of governance (or venues for *subsidiarity*, to use a recently revived Catholic concept), and even serving as alternative venues of politics by serving to resolve conflicts and coordinate policies across sectors and even across national borders.

Just listing these functions makes the point that we should not expect any one kind of nonprofit to serve every possible democratic role, and, accordingly, there will be no one-size-fits-all policy that will enhance their democratic functions as a whole. So there is no answer to the question, if we are looking for something simple. But it may be possible to take a slightly different tack. We might be able to develop a theoretical description of the landscape, which in turn might generate some rules about how the boundaries between government and the nonprofit sector might be regulated so as to enhance their democratic roles.

The conventional designations of the nonprofit sector don't give us the tools we need to conceive such a strategy. Why? The nonprofit sector is not really a sector, but rather a residual category. It consists of organizations that are neither government nor for-profit business. The residual nature of the term plagues similar designations: The concepts of an independent sector, a third sector, a voluntary sector, and civil society, are no more helpful. While the most interesting and rich of these concepts is the notion of civil society, the notion of an "independent sector" overlaps most closely with the topic in this instance, and has the virtue of an operational definition. The organization, Independent Sector, uses the tax code, defining the sector as being made up of 501(c)(3) organizations or charitable institutions, and 501(c)(4) organizations, or those with social welfare purposes (Hodgkinson et al. 1996, 23–24).

Charitable institutions include all those organized to serve a public benefit, such as education, science, health, animal welfare, religious organizations, and so on. Their tax status allows them to receive tax-deductible contributions, but they are forbidden to lobby. Social welfare organizations are those constructed for the sake of public purposes as well, but they cannot receive tax-deductible contributions, and so face fewer restrictions on activities intended to influence government policy. Together, these two tax categories comprise the bulk of nonprofits, and these are really the ones we are talking about when we equate nonprofits with the independent sector, the third sector, or the voluntary sector. Following this same logic, a more expansive conception of the independent sector might include all organizations with similar purposes, whether or not they have an income: reading groups, groups that arise in response to political issues, and so on.

Unfortunately, this way of thinking about the independent sector is not quite what we need to frame the question about the political role of nonprofits in a democracy. The reason, simply, is that the tax designation is a purpose-based designation—a designation that is inadequate in two ways. The first inadequacy has to do with the question of residual categories: The independent sector includes every kind of purpose that doesn't involve profit making or depend directly on the powers of the state. Thus, the Veterans of Foreign Wars is lumped in with AIDS prevention groups, animal shelters with universities, the National Association for the Advancement of Colored People with the Michigan Militia, the Kiwanas with the Sierra Club, and Catholic hospitals with the National Rifle Association. The second inadequacy has to do with the fact that purpose-based schemas don't really tell us what we want to know anyway. We need functional designations. We want to know what the effects of organizations are within the democratic system, not just what purposes they have (Warren 2001, 37–38, 140–42). Thus, an organization can seek to serve purposes that are not especially public at all, much less democratic: Religious organizations, for example, may seek to save their members' souls. But in so doing, these organizations may teach individuals the habits of association that de Tocqueville, for one, saw as essential to the democracy-sustaining habits of citizens. It is not their purpose to teach these habits, but this is their effect. On the other hand, an organization may be quite public spirited, benevolent, even internally democratic, and yet accumulate powers and capacities that allow them to do things with little or no democratic accountability to the people affected. Universities, for example, can often behave in such ways toward their surrounding neighborhoods.

Moreover, the functional questions about democracy presuppose that we have workable structural designations. In general, I think the common three-sector models are workable—that is, the models that distinguish state, markets, and civil society, or, if you prefer, government, business, and the third sector (Cohen and Arato 1992; Habermas 1996). But it is difficult to get here from the purpose-based designation, because so many organizations blend government and business resources to achieve their purposes. So many governments farm public purposes out to third sector organizations, such as universities, urban hospitals, welfare groups, private licensing groups, and now religious organizations (Van Til 2000). In fact, government sources accounted for 31.3 percent of independent sector income in 1992, almost as much as income derived from dues and private payments for services (Hodgkinson et al. 1996, 159–161). Moreover, businesses set up nonprofits to lobby, and community development groups become closely involved with businesses. Purposes are not irrelevant to democratic roles and functions, but they should not be confused with the structural distinctions we need to identify these roles and functions.

Because of such difficulties, I think we need to begin with a different question. What means do societies have to make decisions and organize collective actions? What means do societies have available to make decisions and organize collective actions? In principle there are only three "media of operational organization" of a society, to borrow from Talcott Parsons (1971). First, societies can organize through *power*, and rules can be enforced by power. States are centered on this medium of organization. Second, societies can use *money*, so that organization and coordination are unintended by-products of individual exchanges—that is, organization through markets. Third, societies can organize though the social resources of custom, traditions, norms, discussion, and agreement about common purposes—a medium I shall call *norms* for the sake of simplicity. Associations such as churches and families are formed through normative agreements and organized through the reciprocity and trust these agreements make possible.

The various dimensions of democracy inhabit each of these media of organizations. Power is important for democracy, since it enables organizations, particularly governmental ones, to provide public goods and overcome collective action problems. Without power, there can be no collective action of certain kinds—particularly the kinds that are susceptible to free riders, like public health, security, an educated labor force, environmental integrity, and so on. Without state power, a people will have no collective agent to act on its behalf. On the other hand, power is dangerous, so it is important that it be limited and held accountable. This is, of course, the key justification of institutionalized democracy within the state sector. The forms democracy takes are both of the traditional kind—electoral and representative institutions— as well as of newer kinds, such as interactive policymaking (Warren 2003).

Markets manage and aggregate billions of decisions, enabling forms of economic organization whose complexity far outstrips the planning capacities of the state. For many reasons, much organizational capacity within today's liberal democracies is market-driven. Markets are not, however, responsive to democracy. They are simply structures of supply and demand, mediated by money. But markets can be indirectly responsive, if money is channeled through the state so as to impose public purposes on businesses or nonprofits, or if associations exist to align consumer choices with public purposes (the green certified forest products movement, for example), or to direct investments in ways they serve, say, the goals of community development (such as Community Development Corporations).

But the most interesting medium of social organization is that of norms. People can, simply, agree to associate to serve whatever purposes they choose, and organize their interactions through norms. Many of the ideals associated with democracy are centered on this medium of organization and its vitality within democratic societies: Here, freedom, commitment, uncoerced social relations, and collective action coincide. The associational way of organizing common purposes is inherently legitimate, since people choose their collective projects and willingly engage with others. Implicit in associational logic is a certain element of choice and equality: In a pluralistic society, individuals can choose their identities, their goals, their norms, and associate with like-minded people to achieve their purposes. Coercion, where it exists, is tempered by voluntarism: Individuals can, as it were, vote with their feet.

Citizens can learn the habits of association, collective self-reliance, and in so doing accumulate the precursors of association, the dispositions of reciprocity and trust—what many now call "social capital." Moreover, associative organization exemplifies the positive dimensions of politics. Politics, especially democratic politics, is not just about managing conflict in the face of power (although it is always that), but is also about deliberating over and deciding, to borrow from Max Weber, what we should do and how we should live. Such deliberations cannot be organized by power since coercion is never friendly to deliberation, although it requires an atmosphere protected by state-enforced rights in order to exist. Nor can deliberations be organized by markets, which, having no location or agency, also lack brains and speech. The deliberative elements of a democracy can only be organized along associational lines, and the deliberative publics can only emerge where there exists social basis in voluntary associations (Cohen and Arato 1992; Habermas 1996; Young 2000).

These observations give us a partial answer to the question of the political role of nonprofits in a democracy. Because of their medium of organization, they enable people to collectively self-organize, to pursue collective purposes, and in so doing they teach the habits of political agency, and the virtues of cooperation, trust, and reciprocity. They provide conduits of information for citizens, and may provide organizational and political skills. In addition, nonprofits provide voice and stimulate public debate. They provide the social bases for communication and deliberation, and in this way enable public opinion to form and guide public policies. Because democratic governance needs an active, self-confident, and informed citizenry, democracies need to maintain institutional boundaries between these media of power, money, and norms. In this way, each medium can do what it does best: Power deals with collective action problems, money with complexity, and norms with social goods and common purposes. If we were to idealize the three-sector model of society, we would say that the state centers on power, businesses on money, and voluntary associations on norms.

We can recognize these idealizations in much of the talk about the good of nonprofits: Capacities and virtues that attach to the normative medium of organization are read onto the sector and the organizations that inhabit it. If businesses serve individual interests of profit, and government is somewhat clumsy because, well, power is a clumsy way of getting things done, the third sector draws people toward public purposes and benefits, engaging them with the subtlety that voluntary motivations make possible.

These conclusions are not wrong, but they do over generalize. They are sometimes the result of reading an abstract characterization of media onto actual organizations, and sometimes the result of generalizing to all nonprofits the good works of a few. The problem is not just that ideal types are just that—ideal—but also that only half the conceptual work has been done. When societies differentiate media and lodge primary responsibility for these media in different kinds of organizations (governments, businesses, and civil society associations), they produce problems of coordination among sectors (Van Til 2000). It is here, of course, that the problems of regulation and interrelations arise—not just in the ways organizations relate to one another externally, but in their very constitution. So actual institutions and organizations are neither pure expressions of their primary medium, nor of their relative virtues. Even ideally, they are blended and ambiguously located, often by design, so that the downsides of each medium do not become objectionable.

In the case of the state, for example, the dangers of power are moderated not just through checks and balances, and elections, but also by inserting associative relations, and therefore capacities for normative direction, into the heart of the state itself (Habermas 1996). Traditionally, of course, these appear as deliberative bodies: the legislature, courts, and juries. Less traditionally, governments have developed, and continue to develop, associative venues in the form of public hearings and stakeholder deliberative processes. The dangers of markets are also well known: They provide neither public goods nor public direction, while they do provide incentives for organizational irresponsibility in the form of cost shifting onto workers, the public, and the environment. In market contexts, costs incurred on behalf of public goods, common concerns, environmental integrity, worker safety, and all other nonmarketable goods is usually a recipe for business suicide. This is also true, by the way, of those nonprofits, such as hospitals, that work in a market environment. For these reasons, markets can be aligned with democratic collective choice only through high-level binding impositions by states or state-like bodies.

This is all familiar territory. I mention it to highlight the fact that we rarely pose the same kind of question—the question of dangers—of the independent sector, no doubt because it has for the most part been uncritically associated with the virtues of its associative medium of organization (Portes 1998; Chambers and Kopstein 2001). The question is not entirely parallel. The dangers are mostly not inherent in the associative medium, but rather result from the blending of this medium with power and money, so that specific kinds of nonprofits acquire the inherent dangers of states and markets. Still, there are some inherent dangers, made more dangerous, perhaps, because they are often masked by the association of the nonprofit sector with the virtues of its medium of organization. We justify nonregulation of voluntary associations, for example, just because they are voluntary. Its members can leave if they don't like the way things are done. But not all normatively organized associations are voluntary. Families and churches, for example, are not voluntary for at least some of their members—particularly children. Another inherent danger is that the other face of voluntary association is exclusion. Unless members can exclude those they don't want to associate with, the notion of "voluntary" association has no meaning. Sometimes, exclusion is just exclusion. But sometimes, exclusion can lead to unjustifiable economic marginalization, as when the local Junior Chamber of Commerce serves as a normative gatekeeper to local business success, as Sandra Day O'Connor noted in her concurring opinion in *Roberts v. Jaycees* (486 U.S. 609 [1984]).

This last example points toward a second set of dangers, and this is really where we find the most interesting problems. The dangers reside in the blending of normative means of organization—the means of the third sector—with power and money. These are interesting dangers, however, because the blending is at the same time essential to the coordination among spheres in general, and crucial to what I referred to above as one of three sets of democratic functions of the nonprofit sector—its institutional functions. Public opinion formed outside of government needs conduits into government through representation. Governments often find they can deliver services better, or even resolve problems of conflict and coordination, through nonprofits. Very often they farm out regulatory functions to nonprofits—such as the American Bar Association. Ideally, these blends enable governments to benefit from the virtues of associations, while nonprofits connect government to society and provide for its normative directions.

But with these blended functions come at least four kinds of dangers, each of which is exemplified with the U.S. political system. By calling these dangers, I am suggesting that nonprofits can damage democracy, or at least not improve it, and that these are target areas for democratic reforms.

First, there is the problem of nonprofits taking on public powers without a parallel accountability to the public. This danger is the kind of danger that can occur when governments seek to privatize public services and regulatory functions. Contracting for government services is, of course, a key area for corrupt dealings by businesses and nonprofits alike. HUD and Medicare, for example, are structured in ways that produce maximum opportunities for businesses and nonprofits alike to gratify their own interests with very little accountability to the public purposes they are supposed to serve. Lack of accountability need not involve only finances. It is equally insidious to democracy when nonprofits pursue well-meaning but sectarian missions when empowered to provide public goods. When a Catholic hospital is the only local provider of Medicaid services—as happens in inner cities—it can impose its norms of reproductive medicine on its clientele. It does so at public expense for a public purpose, but is accountable neither to its clientele, nor to the public, but only to the Church.

Second, when governments try to capture the virtues of nonprofits by farming out public functions, there is the danger of inequity in the provision of public goods and services. Especially in health and welfare, the general rule is that those locales that are richer in education and wealth also tend to be richer in nonprofits. Within the District of Columbia, for example, most community-based nonprofits are centered on the 16th Street corridor in Northwest, where they are badly needed. But these kinds of nonprofits are virtually absent in disadvantaged neighborhoods in Northeast and Southeast, where they are needed much more. Nonprofits simply lack the capacities to compensate for inequalities in health and welfare, and so government devolution of public responsibilities to nonprofits can reinforce existing inequalities and cleavages.

Third, when governments give money to nonprofits—to universities and health care providers, for example—they help to bring interest groups into existence. These groups can then exercise enormous influence over government policy. The result is one in which the public pays, in effect, to generate a covert form of corporatism that is no more democratic than the sort practiced by the business sector.

Finally, it is often said that 501(c)(4)s (and, increasingly, 501(c)(3)s) provide a voice for those who would otherwise not have a voice within government. Many nonprofits, however, are the lobby arms of business and other special interest groups, there to ensure influence for the wealthy and powerful. They use their relatively privileged market positions to short-circuit democratic processes in ways that corrupt rather than strengthen democracy. So it could be that one of the overall effects of nonprofits in American democracy is to amplify the influence of the privileged. There exists no aggregate level research, however, that measures the relative impact of differing kinds of nonprofits on the political system.

How, then, do we capture the democratic virtues of nonprofits while avoiding dangers such as these? The ways and means are likely to be highly variable, but I think some general rules can be derived from the broad theoretical point I have tried to make: Namely, that we shouldn't mistake the virtues of normative means or associative means of organization for the virtues of nonprofits in general. It is true that the independent sector makes greatest use of associative media, and so we are likely to find many nonprofits that exemplify its virtues. But a differentiated society must have many organizations situated at sector boundaries. They will, out of functional necessity, be media-blended organizations.

It follows that we may be able to generalize about the nature and desirability of policies that create, limit, and regulate nonprofits according to the state and market powers with which they blend, as well as the power they can generate over their members if they are less-than-voluntary. The general principle is that as nonprofits accumulate power and wealth, they should be limited in what they can use their powers for, and they should be accountable for the effects. There are many different ways of achieving accountability, most of which we already use, if in ways that are inadequate. These include limiting political activities and campaign contributions, cultivating organizations to provide voice for those who are normally not represented in the political system (as many philanthropic foundations now seek to do), requiring financial audits, and imposing democratic procedures. The general rule, however, is that the means used should conform to the generalization that the more power or wealth an organization has, the more attentive we should be to its possible negative effects on democracy, and—where we find them—the more we should seek to counter these effects.

We can formalize the generalization somewhat by asking two questions about state and market power, questions I portray as dimensions of the independent sector space in table 3.1. First, how easy is it for individuals to exit the organization or association? Clearly, the less easy it is for individuals to exit, the greater the justification for external regulation. In the case of families, we generally hold that because of the vulnerability of children, the broader society ought to ensure that families provide the basic conditions of physical and intellectual development. This principle might be extended to low-exit nonprofits. It is not easy, for instance, for many urban residents to exit from a Catholic Medicaid provider, if there are no other providers in the area. Regulation or other means for producing accountability are, in such cases, justified. In contrast, there are no democratic reasons to regulate nonprofits with easier exit, such as most civic groups, social groups, hobby clubs, and the like. Here, we do our best by democracy by leaving voluntary associations alone to serve their latent democratic functions.

Table 3.1
Interventions According to the Exit and Power Characteristics of Organizations

Ease of exit	Media of organization		
	Normative	**Norms blended with state or market power**	
Higher	1 Social clubs, civic groups, hobby clubs	2 Professional and business associations, CDCs	Protection, cultivation
Lower	3 Families, schools, encompassing religious communities	4 Hospitals, scientific establishments, quasi-governmental regulatory bodies	↑↓

Protection, cultivation	←——→	Regulation, power balancing

Second, what kinds of resources can the association or organization deploy? The greater the capacity to make consequential decisions and impose them on others, the greater the justification for interventions on behalf of democracy. What this suggests is that associations that work primarily through normative attachments—social clubs, churches, various citizens groups, and the like—ought to be protected but otherwise left alone. But institutions that control needed resources, such as jobs, medical care, professional certification, or land, can use their resources in ways that damage democracy. In these cases, policies that limit the damage are appropriate.

Conclusion

The bottom line is organizations that are social and voluntary should be encouraged, protected, and cultivated. The more blending there is between associative media and state or market powers, however, the more likely organizations are to generate effects that corrode rather than complement democracy. In such cases, there is justification for regulation, intervention, and selective support on behalf of democratic goals.

Part 2

Nonprofits and Business:
Blurred Boundaries

4

Sector-Bending: Blurring the Lines Between Nonprofit and For-Profit

J. Gregory Dees and Beth Battle Anderson

Traditional sector boundaries are increasingly breaking down (Weisbrod 1998a; Ryan 1999; Young and Salamon 2002). Everyone has seen the headlines about nonprofit hospitals, HMOs, or health insurers converting to for-profit status, and in some cases being acquired by for-profit chains. But many individuals could not tell you whether their own provider is a nonprofit or a for-profit entity. Most have heard about Edison Schools, a public corporation that manages 150 public schools in twenty-three states and Washington, D.C., but few know that Nobel Learning Communities has started a chain of independent, for-profit schools, operating 179 private schools in fifteen states. And while for-profit health clubs try to stir up controversy over unfair competition from suburban YMCAs, Pioneer Human Services, a Seattle nonprofit serving substance abusers and ex-convicts, quietly provides metal bending operations for Boeing as a means of training and employing their at-risk clients. Further south in Los Angeles, students at Crenshaw High School planted a community garden, began selling produce at the local farmer's market, and now sell all-natural salad dressings and applesauce in regional supermarkets and via mail order. Company profits provide college scholarships for the student owners, and 25 percent of the produce is donated to the needy in their community.

What is going on here? On small and large scales, in local communities and across the country, for-profits and nonprofits are moving into new territories and exploring uncharted waters. While this kind of sector-bending is not entirely new—remember Goodwill Industries and Girl Scouts Cookies—it is certainly growing in popularity. Increasingly, we are turning to business methods and structures in our efforts to find more cost-effective and sustainable ways to address social problems and deliver socially important goods. Should we be troubled by this behavior? We should not. As with any new development, this one has its risks, but these can be identified, evaluated, and managed. We have entered a very healthy period of experimentation. Some of the experiments will fail, but others will succeed. These successes should allow us to use resources, particularly scarce philanthropic resources, more effectively to serve public purposes. In this way, boundary-blurring activities have the potential to increase the "independence" of the "independent sector." They may even lead us to change the way we think about "sectors." Instead of emphasizing legal forms of organization, such as nonprofit, for-profit, and governmental, perhaps we should focus on communities of practice that include different organizational forms serving a common purpose, such as the improvement of elementary and secondary education or the preservation of biodiversity.

The Definition of Sector-Bending

Before exploring some of the potential benefits, it is important to understand what we mean when we talk about "sector-bending." Sector-bending refers to a wide variety of approaches, activities, and relationships that are blurring the distinctions between nonprofit and for-profit organizations, either because they are behaving more similarly, operating in the same realms, or both. Some behaviors are more widespread than others, several have been a reality of the social sector for generations, and others represent relatively new phenomena. For simplicity, we define sector-bending around four broad types of behavior: *Imitation, Interaction, Intermingling,* and *Industry Creation.* Just as the boundaries between sectors are blurring, the lines between these categories are indistinct. In fact, behaviors falling within one category quite often lead to or are part of activities associated with another.

Imitation and Conversion

Nonprofit organizations are increasingly adopting the strategies, concepts, and practices of the business world. Anyone working in this field sees it regularly. Organizations in which "customer" and "marketing" once had negative connotations are hiring marketers or consultants, identifying their target markets, segmenting their customers, and developing competitive strategies. Tools developed specifically for use in the business world, such as Porter's Five-Forces strategy framework (Porter 1980) or Kaplan's Balanced Scorecard (Kaplan and Norton 1992), are being adapted and adopted by nonprofit organizations. As successful business entrepreneurs become increasingly interested in bringing their skills, as well as their wealth, into the social sector, this trend should continue. Even highly charitable, community-oriented organizations such as Habitat for Humanity have been influenced by the business experience of its founder Millard Fuller, a marketing entrepreneur and self-made millionaire. Habitat builds houses for those who otherwise could not afford a home of their own, but it requires its new homeowners to repay a modest mortgage. Many other nonprofits have become more businesslike by finding ways to generate fees for services rendered. In the most extreme case, nonprofits are actually converting to for-profit status. This practice is most prominent in health care (Goddeeris and Weisbrod 1998), but it also happens elsewhere. For instance, America Works, a welfare-to-work training program, started as a nonprofit and later converted to for-profit status (Boschee 1995).

Interaction

Another kind of blurring occurs as nonprofits and for-profits increasingly interact with each other as competitors, contractors, and collaborators. Many of these interactions stem directly from public policy shifts away from grantmaking toward contracting and reimbursement. But private innovations, such as private health insurance, have also played a major role as nonprofits are finding new corporate markets for their goods, services, and assets.

Competitors: For-profits are playing a greater role in arenas formerly dominated by nonprofit and public sector organizations, while nonprofits are entering the domains of business. In the former category, health care provision provides the most obvious example, though even there, the average observer may underestimate the extent of the activity. How many know that the largest single provider of hospice care in the United States is VITAS, a for-profit that started as a nonprofit (Boschee 1995)? But the emergence of for-profit players extends beyond the health care arena to a wide range of social services, including education, day care centers, rehabilitation services, affordable housing, and even welfare-to-work. Anywhere a savvy business entrepreneur can find a way to make a profit in a market dominated by nonprofit or public agencies we can expect to see for-profits enter and compete directly with nonprofit providers.

In return, nonprofits are competing head-to-head with businesses. Much of this activity is not new. Sheltered workshops have long provided services and produced goods in competition with business suppliers. This concept is being extended as many social services organizations are starting businesses to provide employment and training opportunities for their clientele. These nonprofit-run businesses range from manufacturing to bakeries, restaurants, grounds maintenance, and translation services. Larger nonprofits are moving more aggressively into ventures that compete directly with businesses. The American Association of Retired People offers an alternative to for-profit insurance companies. Harvard Business School Press broke with the image of an academic publisher to aggressively compete with for-profit publishers of business books. The National Geographic has moved beyond the production of branded tour books and maps to having its own cable television channel, competing directly with the Discovery Channel as well as with one of its longtime distributors and collaborators, the nonprofit Public Broadcasting System. Museum catalogues and Web sites compete directly with businesses selling similar items.

Contractors: Given that nonprofits are engaging in more "businesslike" activities, it is not surprising that for-profits are contracting with nonprofits for both "nonprofit-like" goods and services as well as goods and services that were traditionally provided by other businesses. Universities are contracting with corporations to conduct research (Powell and Owen-Smith 1998). Xerox Corporation hired the nonprofit Family Service America, now known as The Alliance for Children and Families, to provide family counseling services to its employees (Johnston 1999). For-profit players who have become social services providers are also contracting with nonprofits to access their expertise and community relationships. For instance, after winning one welfare-to-work government contract, Lockheed Martin hired nearly thirty nonprofit agencies to supply various services (Ryan 1999). In other arenas, Bay Area business parks, commercial developments, and public facilities contract with Rubicon Landscape Services, an operation run by a nonprofit agency providing employment, job training, and other social services for the economically disadvantaged. Similarly, nonprofits are outsourcing the provision of specialized or capital-intensive services to for-profit providers. Nonprofit charter schools contract with for-profit education management companies to run the whole school or just provide administrative services. Universities contract with technology companies to transfer curriculum to media suitable for distance learning.

Collaborators: Nonprofits and for-profits are entering into strategic partnerships and joint ventures that aim to be mutually beneficial to both parties. The Nature Conservancy partners with Georgia Pacific to manage forestlands in environmentally sensitive ways (Austin 2000). City Year, a youth-service nonprofit, helps teach Timberland employees about team building and diversity and provides an outlet for employee community service, while Timberland offers City Year business expertise, funding, and uniforms. Together they developed a new Timberland product line called City Year Gear (Austin 2000). Share Our Strength, an anti-hunger organization, entered into an agreement with American Express to market and raise money for both organizations via a cause-related marketing campaign called the "Charge Against Hunger" (Andreasen 1996).

Intermingling

A step beyond the interaction of independent nonprofit and for-profit organizations is the intermingling of organizational structures that occurs in "hybrid organizations." Hybrid organizations, as we are using the term, are formal organizations, networks, or umbrella groups that have both for-profit and nonprofit components. For-profit organizations may create nonprofit affiliates, and nonprofits sometimes establish for-profit subsidiaries or affiliates. Nonprofit affiliates of for-profits usually serve purposes and conduct activities that do not fit neatly into a for-profit structure. For instance, two prominent community development financial institutions, Grameen Bank in Bangladesh and Shorebank Corporation in Chicago, were set up as for-profit organizations but over time created nonprofit affiliates and for-profit subsidiaries to attract and deploy resources most efficiently. More recently, soon after its launch, CitySoft, a for-profit Web development and management firm committed to hiring predominantly lower-income urban adults, realized that existing training programs were not effectively preparing urban adults for success in high-tech careers. Thus, the firm spun-off a nonprofit called CitySkills to partner with training organizations and employers to create the necessary infrastructure and "labor pipelines" for recruiting, training, and placing inner-city residents in upwardly mobile information technology jobs. On the other side of the equation, some nonprofits have been looking for for-profit business opportunities explicitly to help generate income for the nonprofit. For this reason, Children's Home & Aid Society of Illinois (CHASI) launched Ask4 Staffing, Inc., an affiliated for-profit corporation that provides staffing solutions to social service organizations (Anderson, Dees, and Emerson 2002).

Industry Creation

Finally, as these various forms of sector-bending have evolved, a few relatively new sector-blurring fields of practice have emerged or at least have taken on a distinctive identity. The emerging industries of community development finance, welfare-to-work training, eco-tourism, charter schools, and alternative energy production are all populated by for-profit, nonprofit, and hybrid organizations looking to harness market forces for social good. The charter school movement provides an interesting example. Charter schools are independent public schools that are run and managed by parent-teacher partnerships, community-based nonprofits, universities, for-profit companies, or hybrid forms of organization. Some charter schools are new schools while others have been converted from traditional public schools. In return for demonstrated results, these schools are granted the autonomy and flexibility to operate outside of the traditional rules and regulations of the public school system. This independence will ideally spur innovation while enhancing accountability and providing choice and competition that will lead to reform and educational improvements in the K–12 system in the United States.

Potential Benefits of Sector-Bending

Many have raised concerns about the increasing popularity of boundary-blurring activities, though few have explained the potential benefits. This situation is not surprising given the relatively early stage of many of these experiments, the challenges of performance measurement, and the complexity of the issues. Only time will tell whether and to what extent these benefits will be realized, but the potential benefits of new social innovations and experiments are great and should not be neglected.

More Effective and Appropriate Resource Allocation

Both the emergence of for-profits delivering social goods and services and the increase of nonprofits generating earned income can lead to better resource allocation and more effective use of scarce philanthropic funds. At the sector level, the presence of for-profits can allow for a greater division of labor. If for-profits can generate even a minimal profit by serving clients who are willing and able to pay (directly or through a third party), then donor-supported nonprofits can concentrate on serving those who need philanthropic subsidies to cover the costs of serving them. In essence, for-profits would be freeing charitable dollars to be concentrated on those who need them most. This overall market structure functions more efficiently and encourages innovation amongst both for-profits and nonprofits. For-profits have the profit incentive to provide better services to those who can pay. If their quality declines too dramatically due to cost-cutting measures, the nonprofit offers an alternative. For nonprofits, the threat of losing profitable customers to for-profits should also enhance their performance and innovation.

Moreover, in health and human services industries, research has shown that nonprofits appear to be slower than for-profits both to grow to meet demand and to contract in response to changes in the environment and declines in demand (Hansmann 1996). Thus, perhaps we need two layers of providers in these industries—for-profits to ensure responsiveness to market changes and nonprofits to preserve access for all, with limited wasted resources overall. Admittedly, for certain capital-intensive industries, there may not be room in some markets for more than one provider, whether for-profit or nonprofit. Hospitals in smaller communities provide a good example. In these cases, it may make sense for the leaders to consider hybrid structures, such as a for-profit hospital with an affiliated nonprofit clinic, to attract the necessary resources and meet the full spectrum of community needs.

At the organizational level, for nonprofits earning more commercial revenues, the revenues can serve as a source of leverage for philanthropic donations. Not only should donors not want to subsidize customers who can pay (either directly or through an interested third party), but they also should be attracted to the possibility of their dollars having greater social impact when combined with the revenues from earned income activities. Ideally, a greater pool of funds will be available to provide social goods and services for which nobody is able or willing to pay, either because these are true public goods or the clients are economically disadvantaged. And if a nonprofit organization can support all or the vast majority of its social mission activities via earned income, donors should shift their charitable dollars to other causes that are more in need of philanthropic subsidy. Again, a more efficient allocation of resources results in maximum social value creation overall.

Furthermore, the use of appropriate business tools has the potential to improve the effectiveness of nonprofit organizations. The discipline of identifying customers, defining how you will create value for them, developing strategies that reflect the organization's competencies and the competitive environment in which it operates, and pushing for more careful tracking of impact can have a very healthy impact on organizational performance even in philanthropic organizations. Of course these tools can be misused, as can any tools. Nonetheless, the potential for improving organizational effectiveness by importing and adapting tools from the business world is great.

More Sustainable Solutions

The blurring of sector boundaries has been accompanied by an increased interest in finding systemic and sustainable solutions to social problems. It is difficult to say which trend is driving the other, but they are certainly intertwined and complementary. Where appropriate, social entrepreneurs are looking to address underlying problems rather than meet needs, empower individuals rather than provide charitable relief, and create sustainable improvements rather than short-term responses. Business methods and approaches provide valuable tools for achieving these goals. Habitat for Humanity requires its new homeowners to pay mortgages. Grameen Bank provides small business loans, instead of grants, to economically disadvantaged villagers in Bangladesh. Pioneer Human Services employs ex-convicts and recovering drug addicts in various enterprises. Each of these approaches requires the individuals receiving help to take an active role in improving their own lives. They need not feel like objects of charity. Even providing social services through employers enhances the potential for positive, lasting social impact. While the workers do not pay directly for services, they feel a sense of entitlement when these services are included in their benefits package. Covered workers are likely to be more comfortable seeking help for their troubled teen, failing marriage, or alcohol abuse problem than they would if they had to find an appropriate agency on their own, and either pay for the care out of pocket or request charitable assistance. The spread of employer-sponsored social services programs represents a systemic approach to addressing a variety of underlying problems. All of these businesslike strategies empower the individuals and increase the chances of lasting social impact, giving them an advantage over charitable efforts that offer temporary assistance to those willing to accept charity.

When it is possible, aligning social and economic value creation through business approaches provides the most sustainable kind of solution. This principle is not limited to human services. Many environmentally concerned for-profit and nonprofit organizations have recognized the value of this alignment. For instance, The Nature Conservancy has shifted from just buying and preserving lands to finding ways to generate both economic and social value through sustainable harvesting techniques and environmentally conscious development. Some of this work is done in partnership with corporations that are working to find sustainable ways to harvest timber (Howard and Magretta 1995). While these types of initiatives are challenging to implement and require a real sensitivity to the tensions between economic and social goals, they provide valuable opportunities for experimentation and learning. A small number of successes could easily make up for a number of failed ventures.

Increased Accountability

Shifting from a charitable to a customer relationship improves accountability and can bring increased market discipline to the social sector. Paying customers are more likely than nonpaying clients to hold organizations accountable by providing direct feedback, expressing their complaints publicly, or taking their business elsewhere. Even third-party payers can provide greater market discipline than most donors. They have greater legal standing to complain and often have greater incentives to hold providers accountable and better information on performance. They tend to have a more direct obligation to and relationship with the service recipients, and the recipients themselves have a sense of entitlement, since the service was paid, not charitable. Thus, employers can act based on input from their employees on the value and quality of the social goods and services delivered: Public agencies can expect the same from their constituents.

This improved (though still imperfect) market discipline clearly holds true for for-profits and for nonprofits charging fees for the delivery of social goods and services. For other nonprofit activities, market discipline is only beneficial if the earned income strategies are aligned with effectively serving the organization's mission. The success or failure of a hospital gift shop, a Save the Children brand tie, or a co-branded Starbucks coffee sampler from countries in which CARE operates reveals nothing about the nonprofit organizations' ability to achieve their social missions. These ventures are all subject to market forces, but the market is responding to products and services that are distinct from the organizations' mission-based activities. While these ventures may contribute value to the organizations in other ways, the market feedback will not help them assess or improve their creation of social value. In other cases, the benefits of market discipline can extend into more commercial activities such as nonprofits' operating businesses to employ their clientele. The success or failure of these businesses, and the feedback from customers, can provide valuable information regarding the effectiveness, strengths, and weaknesses of their job training and employment programs, much more so than merely asking the trainees if they were satisfied with the training. Thus, for mission-related activities, the value of market feedback can help overcome some of the performance measurement and accountability concerns in the nonprofit sector.

Greater Financial Strength and Capacity

Boundary-blurring activities have the potential to help build a social sector with greater financial strength and capacity than currently exists. For-profits entering the social sector increase the sector's access to capital, allow for faster growth and increased flexibility, and increase the capacity of the sector overall. For nonprofits, if earned income and other business methods can provide more diverse and sustainable revenue streams, then the financial strength of the organization will be improved. Granted, earned income streams are not necessarily more sustainable than donations or grants, and diversification can lead to fragmentation and loss of focus. But developing an appropriate earned income strategy can free up and even create new capacity, in the form of both financial and human resources, to be dedicated to direct delivery on the mission.

Overall, healthy competition among organizational forms has the potential to improve the effectiveness of the social sector. The diversity of options gives clients, paying customers, and funders a choice. Keeping in mind the following genuine risks outlined, we should let these experiments flourish and have the participants decide what works best for them. Some of the experiments will fail, and others may even prove detrimental in the short term. We should work to reduce the chances of irreparable harm, but acknowledge that progress has its costs. We must allow enough time for learning and for making adjustments.

Risks and Concerns

Though we are attracted to the potential benefits from sector-bending activities, we are not endorsing all activities or encouraging every organization to pursue sector-bending approaches. Bridging sectors is challenging and necessarily creates some tensions within organizations and the sectors. Increased commercial activity is not appropriate or feasible for every nonprofit, nor is a shift to providing social goods and services suitable or desirable for every for-profit. Not every individual or organization, no matter how successful and competent in certain arenas, will be adept at merging social goals with business activities or at operating in different political and cultural environments. In addition to the practical challenges, sector-bending activities pose some inherent risks. Without addressing the specific risks associated with each type of activity described earlier, we have identified three broad categories of significant, cross-cutting concerns: threats to direct social performance, potential loss of indirect social benefits, and further bifurcation of society into haves and have-nots. As we move forward with this boundary-blurring experimentation, these areas must be vigilantly monitored and managed.

Threats to Direct Social Performance

Perhaps the greatest concern about the blurring of sector boundaries is that, despite the potential benefits previously mentioned, these activities will actually result in a decline in social value created (James 1998). Three specific concerns pose potential threats to direct social performance: Business approaches may cause mission drift, profit emphasis may lead to lower quality services overall, and blurring of sectors may provoke a decline in advocacy by nonprofits.

Mission Drift: Business structures and methods could pull social-purpose organizations away from their original social missions (Weisbrod 1998b). Social services organizations that intended to serve the very poor may find it is easier to generate fees or contracts by serving clients who are less disadvantaged, than to raise funds to subsidize their charity work. Similarly, a homeless shelter that starts a business to train and employ shelter residents may find that it is too difficult and costly to make this option available to the homeless who are hardest to employ. An environmental group that wants to produce products using nuts from a rain forest cooperative may discover that the cooperative cannot deliver enough high-quality nuts to meet demand and switch to other suppliers (Welles 1998). A university attracted by lucrative funds from licensing practical developments emerging from its labs may shift resources away from the humanities and basic sciences toward applied sciences. Though, in theory, generating this kind of fee income should help an organization serve its intended audience through cross-subsidy or just by covering overhead expenses, the relative ease of bringing in commercial fees or the market pressures exerted on earned income activities may slowly draw an organization away from its mission. On a practical level, it may be easier to grow and fund an organization by giving up on its original mission and target audience. Strong leaders, engaged funders, active boards, and clear mission statements should help keep organizations focused, but these mechanisms are not perfect and mission drift could well occur despite them. The situation is made worse by the lack of clear performance measures in this sector, as it is difficult for customers, payers, donors, and sometimes even board members and managers to recognize when certain activities are actually causing a decline in social impact.

Lower Quality Services: Many people worry that the presence of a profit motive or a strong emphasis on efficiency will lead service providers to cut corners, lowering both costs and quality (Steinberg and Weisbrod 1998). Various studies have looked at this issue in sectors in which nonprofit and for-profit players compete directly. The results are inconclusive, as some studies have found differences in quality while others have not (Hansmann 1996; Sloan 1998; Ryan 1999). However, even if research overwhelmingly found lower quality of care on average in for-profit versus nonprofit providers of health care and social services, one could not fairly conclude that having for-profit players is a bad thing, unless the industry has excess capacity or the service quality has fallen below some morally acceptable minimum. For instance, we are familiar with a small nonprofit hospice for people with AIDS that offers very high quality care and is reluctant to expand for fear the quality will decline. Yet many people in that community are on waiting lists for AIDS-related hospice care. Is it better to maintain very high quality and stay small, or would it be more socially desirable to lower quality but expand capacity to serve more of the people in need? If a for-profit enters the market and offers to provide a lower quality of care but serves the unmet need, is that a bad thing? It is bad only if the quality is so low that the customers would have been better off receiving no care at all. When quality is costly, as it is in many social services, providers may have to make a trade-off between the quality of care provided and the number of people served. While a profit incentive may pull a for-profit provider towards quantity rather than quality, if demand is greater than current supply, this bias may actually be socially desirable and superior to offering high quality care to a small number of people, while others get no care at all.

Charter schools represent a case in which quality is more crucial. These schools are replacing existing capacity rather than serving an unmet need. Thus, the question is whether these schools improve on the public schools they replace. We must monitor this situation with careful oversight and standards. Even so, we need realistic benchmarks. These experiments should be judged a failure only if they are not successful at delivering a better education than the existing alternatives. Since for-profit charter school operators want to maintain their contracts and even expand their markets, they have every incentive to perform at a high level and should be expected to do so. The challenge, again, is in finding the right measures, but parents and school boards face this same challenge in assessing public schools. Quality measurement problems should not automatically wed us to the status quo or rule out experimentation.

Decline in Advocacy by Nonprofits: Advocacy is one of the crucial functions that nonprofit organizations can play. It is natural to worry that if nonprofits are contracting and collaborating with for-profits, it may compromise their roles as advocates and critics (Ryan 1999). Yet nonprofits have been striking this balance for quite some time when receiving corporate donations, gifts from wealthy individuals with their own business interests, or even grants and contracts from government agencies. Very few nonprofits are supported totally by grassroots fundraising. It is a matter of selecting the right partners and being clear on the terms of engagement. It is possible that nonprofits that have traditionally engaged in both service delivery and advocacy may have fewer resources to dedicate to advocacy if they are trying to compete with for-profit service providers or develop other streams of earned income. However, if successful, earned income activities should actually generate or free up other resources for advocacy activities. And even if there is some decline on these fronts, nonprofits dedicated solely to advocacy will not face these concerns and may even gain from a greater perceived need for their presence.

Corporate collaborations such as McDonald's and the Environmental Defense Fund working together to address waste management issues have raised concerns that nonprofits are jeopardizing their legitimacy as watchdogs and social advocates by becoming too cozy with the business sector (Reinhardt 1992). But we cannot have it both ways. We cannot urge businesses to be environmentally conscious and socially responsible and then deprive them of access to the best resources for addressing our concerns. Groups particularly concerned about their independence need to limit their financial dependency on the corporations they should be watching and tailor their sector-bending activities to avoid conflicts of interest. Some nonprofits will, and should, always exist as advocates primarily working outside of and against the system. But as long as it is done carefully, having some advocates also work across sectors with for-profits and government agencies should enhance the success and overall social impact of their efforts.

The risk of reduced social impact is real, but it is unclear how serious it is. Little empirical data is available to help us assess the potential magnitude of this problem. Do new commercial revenues help an organization achieve its social objectives, or do they pull the organization away from its mission, provide incentives for objectionably low levels of quality, and undercut its role as an independent advocate? We do not know for sure. However, we do know that these risks are not unique to boundary-blurring activities. Mission drift is a real issue for philanthropic organizations as they work to attract and satisfy different donors with agendas that may not perfectly match their original mission. We also know that donor-supported nonprofit organizations can be slow to respond, inefficient, and wasteful. Is the risk worse with sector-bending activities? The answer is unclear. Finally, we also know that many nonprofits do not serve the most needy or address the toughest social problems. It is an open question whether boundary-blurring activities will pull those who do away from these difficult populations and issues. But while these concerns are legitimate and need to be monitored and managed, in some instances, sector-bending activities' risks to direct social impact have been exaggerated. In others, it is just too early to tell.

Undermining Indirect Social Benefits

In addition to directly serving social objectives, many nonprofit organizations facilitate the creation of social capital in communities, and the nonprofit sector provides an outlet for expressing charitable impulses. It is conceivable that sector-bending activities on the part of nonprofits endanger both of these roles.

Nonprofits as Creators of Social Capital: Community-based nonprofits, particularly those with high levels of volunteer involvement, can serve as vehicles for building social capital—trusting connections between community members who might otherwise not have any contact with one another (Putnam 1999). Some observers are worried that sector-blurring activities in nonprofits will change the character of the interactions they spawn in a way that undermines social capital creation. Goodwill and mutual concern will be replaced by more arms-length business relationships. On a more practical level, as business skills become more valued, the level of volunteer engagement may decline, as might the diversity of the volunteers and board members (Backman and Smith 2002).

While social capital should not be undervalued, one must consider how organizations create social capital and the types of organizations that create significant amounts before expressing major concerns about the effects of sector-bending activities on this front. Organizations can create social capital by offering a venue for members of the community to get acquainted through some common interests or activities. Only a small proportion of nonprofit organizations do this now. Many nonprofits are professional organizations with limited volunteer activities. These professionally staffed nonprofits may not play this role any better than, or even as well as, a local grocery store, diner, neighborhood bar, or professional sports team. Nonprofits that do create a great deal of social capital include membership organizations, clubs, churches, amateur sports leagues, and service organizations with large numbers of volunteers. For many of these organizations, sector-bending is not a serious risk and is unlikely to drive out their social capital building activities. Will the local Rotary Club, Junior League, or little league become too businesslike and drive out voluntary participation by their members? It seems unlikely. They may try to generate revenues through quasi-commercial events, such as candy sales or auctions, but these events are unlikely to undermine their capacity to build social capital.

Nonetheless, for the few organizations in a community that create social capital broadly, it is possible that moving away from a charitable economic model to one based more on business principles could result in a change that reduces the opportunities for volunteers and others to interact. However, such a consequence is certainly not inevitable. A church that uses business methods to start a day care center to serve its members may create new social capital by inviting members to volunteer at the center or bring their business knowledge to a diverse board that includes some of the parents served. A for-profit charter school can still have an active PTA that facilitates interactions between parents and teachers. Habitat's mortgage requirement does not reduce the social capital created by a house-building project. The sale of Girl Scouts cookies, if handled well, can foster positive relationships amongst the girls, their parents, and their neighbors (and sometimes even between parents and coworkers!). Furthermore, the intelligent adoption of business practices could make many nonprofit organizations even more effective in creating social capital. For instance, marketing techniques may allow an organization such as an art museum to reach new audiences, increasing the diversity of participants and improving its social capital creation. Professionalization, the increasing emphasis on placing credentialed professionals in key service positions, is probably a greater threat to social capital creation than is commercialization (McKnight 1995). It would be a mistake to conflate the two, especially given that many social sector professionals, such as teachers, social workers, doctors, nurses, and environmental scientists, have been vocal opponents of bringing businesses or business methods into their domains.

The Charitable Character of the Nonprofit Sector: The nonprofit sector provides a variety of ways in which people can express their charitable impulses. If it became sufficiently widespread, sector-bending could reduce the opportunities to give back by leading organizations away from relying on donations and volunteers. However, we need to be careful. The nonprofit sector has long been dependent on fee-based income for much of its revenue. Of course, the prevalence of fees varies widely from one subsector to another. However, if charging fees is corrupting to the charitable character of the sector, we have already crossed that bridge. Imagine colleges being prevented from charging tuition or performing arts groups being prohibited from charging for tickets. Could they raise enough in donations to provide the quality of services that they now provide? It seems unlikely. In any case, many nonprofit organizations, such as major universities, have found ways to blur sector boundaries and still provide opportunities for alumni to get involved and to give back.

Admittedly, some studies have suggested that increases in earned income tend to slow the growth rate in donations and, in extreme cases, may lead to a decline in donations (Segal and Weisbrod 1998). While intriguing, this finding should not be worrisome. This correlation is open to a number of explanations. It could reflect a conscious decision by the organization to pursue a strategy of being less dependent on contributions. The shift to earned income could also be designed to compensate for the anticipated loss of a major grant that was due to expire. The leaders of the organization may have had less time to dedicate to fundraising as they were launching an earned income strategy. Or they may simply have failed to market their new earned income plans effectively to their donors. In any case, at the sector level, increased earned income by some organizations should result in more efficient use of donations overall. If one organization successfully shifts to a heavy emphasis on earned income, its donors can shift their funds to other organizations that require a greater philanthropic subsidy. Neither the rise of earned income nor the entrance of for-profits into the social sector has reduced the number of nonprofits looking for donations or volunteers. Vast opportunities still exist for donors and volunteers to experience the psychological benefits of supporting their favorite causes. Moreover, the rise of "venture philanthropy" and other forms of engaged philanthropy that explicitly draw on individuals' business skills and expertise appears to be attracting a new breed of donors to the sector who are interested in contributing significant time and money to generating social impact. These donors do not seem to be discouraged by earned income strategies. Indeed, many of them welcome such approaches.

It would also be a mistake to assume that charity is somehow morally or socially preferable to commerce. Being the recipient of someone's charity can be demeaning, making recipients feel helpless and powerless. Many individuals are too proud to seek or accept charitable assistance except as a last resort. By comparison, as we described when discussing the potential benefits of sector-bending, treating clients as customers can be empowering, giving them standing to complain and a sense of ownership and accomplishment. Protecting the charitable purity of the sector is not necessarily a good thing.

The blurring of sector boundaries does not have to undermine the indirect social benefits associated with the nonprofit sector. In fact, in some cases, these types of activities may actually enhance them. Yet given the concerns that have been expressed regarding the decline of social capital in U.S. communities, social sector leaders should pay close attention to the indirect social impacts of boundary-blurring activities and consider these effects as they pursue the direct creation of social value.

Bifurcation into Haves and Have-Nots

With respect to sector-bending activities, one of the powerful benefits mentioned above was the potential unbundling of activities to allow philanthropic resources to be devoted to programs and individuals that are in the greatest need of charitable support. However, this benefit has a potential dark side. It could result in two classes of service in the social sector: one for those who can pay or are eligible for third-party payment, and the other for those who need charitable assistance. This could reinforce class differences in society at large. Again, this is not a necessary consequence of sector-bending activities, but it is a possible consequence. Creative social sector leaders can take steps to avoid this consequence, using some of the very business structures and methods that might have contributed to it. Better marketing to those who are willing and able to pay can increase the amount of money available to cross-subsidize those who cannot afford to pay. Clients can be offered the same services with a sliding price scale or with "scholarship" opportunities. Thus, sophisticated sector-bending organizations may be able to use business methods to improve their ability to serve all of their clients seamlessly, without any publicly apparent difference between those who can and cannot pay. However, this will require a diligent effort. Social entrepreneurs, funders, and public policymakers must be careful to consider and monitor all of the effects of these activities to assure that sector-blurring does not lead to greater class divisions.

Given that many of the effects of sector-bending activities are uncertain, the impact of business practices on the decisions and activities of nonprofits should continue to be monitored closely in hopes of developing better mechanisms for measuring social performance and assessing the impact of various innovations. In fact, business methods may actually be able to help address some of the challenges of managing and measuring these risks. As we have already described, marketing techniques can help nonprofits attract resources and penetrate target markets more effectively. Accounting tools may be adapted to measure performance and developing customer, as opposed to charitable, relationships should enhance market discipline and accountability. We are not proposing that business methods are the ultimate solution for addressing some of the shortcomings already inherent in the nonprofit structure, and we recognize that the adoption of business techniques will cause additional complications and implementation issues. But we are not convinced that sector-bending activities significantly increase the risks of poor performance, declining societal benefits, or further class division. We embrace transparency and evaluation as tools to help us assess these experiments, but do not see a case for inhibiting activities that further blur the lines between nonprofit and for-profit.

Pitfalls to Avoid in Making Assessments

Though the risks are real, they seem manageable if we are realistic in our assessment of them. In evaluating the potential social impact and assessing the risks of sector-bending activities, we encourage researchers, public policymakers, and sector leaders to be careful to avoid three very natural pitfalls.

Focusing on Individual Organizations Rather than the Sector or Society

What happens within individual firms is certainly relevant to assessing the impact and risks of sector-bending activities. Understandably, much of the research takes this organization-level focus. However, for policy purposes, the emphasis should be on the overall performance of the sector and the overall impact on society, not just on performance by individual organizations. As we pointed out above, the fact that donations decline in a nonprofit organization that increases its earned income does not imply that donations decline overall in the sector. The donations may just flow to a more appropriate use, an area of greater need. This outcome represents a positive result. If for-profits or more commercial nonprofits are shown to offer lower quality services than more philanthropic nonprofits, this finding does not imply that users of the services are hurt by the presence of these lower quality providers. Lower quality services may serve excess demand that cannot be served by the limited capacity of high-quality providers. They may even represent a more cost-effective way of serving an unmet need. Not every car needs to be a Rolls Royce, and not every drug rehabilitation center needs to be comparable to the Betty Ford Center. Finally, a study may show that a hospital provides less charitable care or does less research or provides less education after it converts from nonprofit to for-profit status. This conclusion neglects the fact that at the time of conversion, a fair price must be paid for the net assets of the nonprofit hospital and the proceeds must stay in the nonprofit sector. Usually a new health-related foundation is created. The social impacts of the old nonprofit hospital should be compared to the performance of the new for-profit hospital in combination with the new foundation that has been created. The issue is whether the conversion served society well, not whether the new for-profit hospital alone serves society as well as its nonprofit predecessor.

Assuming What Is Must Be

Another danger is to assume that the kinds of average differences that are documented in descriptive studies must be the case. Consider again the decline in donations that may accompany an increase in fee-based revenue. If the organization could still put donations to good use, this may just reflect poor marketing to donors. Better marketing might correct the situation. This kind of effect may also reflect the tendency of major donors, such as leading foundations, to move on after a certain period of time. That practice could be changed, not by the nonprofit, but by the foundations. Similar reasoning applies to the issue of quality differences. Even if we found that on average nonprofit hospices provide better care than for-profits, we should not assume that this must be true in all cases. In many samples, even with statistically significant differences, the comparison groups will overlap. Some for-profits are likely to out-perform some nonprofits, despite the statistical differences. If we believe it is socially desirable to improve the performance of for-profit hospices, we might look at the high performing for-profits to see if there are practices that can be profitably transferred to those that are not performing as well. Indeed, we could do the same across high performing and low performing nonprofits. We cannot neglect the different incentives and operating environments associated with different organizational structures, but we should use research findings productively to help improve overall performance. Structure does matter, as we will acknowledge in what follows, but it may not alone determine behavior and impact.

Comparing New Forms Against a Fictional Ideal

Finally, it is natural to compare some of the new sector-bending structures to some kind of ideal organization built on principles of charity and funded exclusively through philanthropy. As we already mentioned, the nonprofit sector was never purely charitable. Many of the sector-bending changes are simply extensions of past behaviors into new arenas. It has been argued that people can trust nonprofits more because of the "non-distribution constraint"—nonprofits cannot pay profits out to those in a controlling position (Hansmann 1980). However, this constraint is a crude and often ineffective instrument. It may inhibit certain forms of self-enrichment, but it is no guarantee against corruption and it does not ensure effective performance. We have enough examples of corrupt behavior in the sector to recognize that corruption is not unique to the for-profit sector (or government). The non-distribution constraint eliminates an incentive to maximize profits, but it does not replace that incentive with anything in particular. Power, politics, and money play important and potentially corrupting roles in any sector. People are people. No one sector is morally superior. The attitude of moral superiority sometimes apparent in the nonprofit sector just serves as a barrier to creative problem solving. Because of the non-distribution constraint, complacency, inefficiency, and waste can be serious problems in nonprofit organizations. At least for-profit organizations depend on the voluntary choices of customers to pay for their product to help assure they are creating value in an efficient way. In the more "pure" philanthropic nonprofits, donors are the primary payers, and they are rarely in a strong position to evaluate the efficiency and effectiveness of the organization. Few of them invest any serious effort in an assessment process. A nonprofit can survive, even thrive, and yet be very inefficient and ineffective in creating social value and serving its mission. In the absence of reliable impact measures, a common condition, who would know? In comparing sector-bending activities with more "traditional" nonprofits, we need to use an honest benchmark, not some ideal.

Implications: Organizational Structure Still Matters

If nonprofits and for-profits are engaging in increasingly similar activities and practices, are we moving into a world in which organizational structure doesn't matter? Not at all. Nonprofit and for-profit organizations will continue to coexist and have distinct characteristics (Hansmann 1996). Every social sector actor should be aware of these differences, and the associated strengths and weaknesses, in order to choose the best structure or combination of structures given a particular mission and operating environment. Different structures are tools with different qualities. Following are a few of the central distinctions:

1. Potential Profitability: For-profits are limited to engaging in activities that will yield sufficient profits for their investors. Even social-purpose businesses that raise funds from socially oriented investors must have an economic model that can generate at least modest profits to be sustainable. Nonprofits are not only freed from this constraint but are actually prohibited from distributing any profits. Surpluses can be created by nonprofits, but they must be used to further the mission of the organization.

2. Access to Resources: For-profits can use equity ownership to raise capital and reward performance, are generally better able to access debt markets, and if successful, can be "self-sustaining." Nonprofits can solicit donations and attract volunteers, but they have fewer options for incentive pay, no access to equity, and limited access to debt.

3. Market Discipline: Both for-profits and nonprofits are subject to market forces, but capital and consumer market discipline is much stricter and more effective in the for-profit sector. Nonprofits cannot create wealth for investors, and their missions often cannot be served by simply creating consumptive value for customers. Donors are rarely in a position to assess value creation or efficiency. Moreover, social performance is hard to measure in timely and reliable ways and is also subject to differences in individual values, further blunting the effects of market discipline for both for-profit and nonprofit operators who truly have a social mission.

4. Governance and Control: Boards of directors govern both for-profits and nonprofits, but investors own for-profits and, at least in theory, control the boards. Given the absence of investor-owners, the lack of strict market discipline, and the difficulty of performance measurement, the accountability of a nonprofit rests heavily on their boards and managers. For-profits are directly accountable to their investors. They can curb profit maximization and pursue social objectives if they maintain control by seeking out socially oriented investors and keeping their business closely held. Many businesses operate in this manner, although this approach greatly restricts the pool of available capital, offsetting some of the benefits of being a for-profit.

5. *Culture and Norms*: While not mandated by the particular organizational form, there are certain norms associated with each sector. Many nonprofit employees, and even some donors and volunteers, are uncomfortable with the language and practices of business and may be skeptical of the values and motives of people trying to introduce business concepts. Nonprofits often rely heavily on "psychic income" to compensate for traditionally lower salaries. The sector overall also seems to have a bias towards smaller organizations, local autonomy, and consensus-driven decision making.

6. *Taxes*: Under current tax laws, for-profits are generally subject to both income and property taxes on both the state and federal levels. Nonprofits are broadly exempt from these taxes as long as the property is used primarily for the nonprofit's social purposes and the income is generated from activities related to their primary mission. Nonprofits are subject to Unrelated Business Income Tax (UBIT) for ongoing activities that are not substantially related to their social purpose, though it is often difficult to differentiate taxable and nontaxable activities, and even then, there are significant opportunities for cost and revenue-shifting to minimize taxation.

We mention taxes here because current tax policy creates distinctions between nonprofit and for-profit structures that cannot be ignored. However, the complex interactions between tax policy and sector-bending activities are beyond the scope of this paper. That said, we are compelled to address briefly the common complaint that tax exemptions and ease of avoiding UBIT give nonprofits engaging in business activities an unfair competitive advantage (Cordes and Weisbrod 1998; James 1998). These concerns are exaggerated. Most nonprofits have inherent disadvantages with regard to social mission costs, size inefficiencies, difficulty attracting people with valuable business skills, and limited access to capital. We suspect these inefficiencies more than make up for the difference in tax status. If for-profits find that nonprofits have a clear competitive advantage, then perhaps the for-profit competitor has chosen the wrong organizational form. Indeed, if nonprofit status provides such an advantage, why haven't we seen more for-profits converting to nonprofit status to gain this advantage? Conversions, in fact, usually run in the other direction. Nonprofits should not be prevented from engaging in potential socially beneficial businesslike activities merely because we have not determined how to monitor and tax them effectively. In any case, the limited profitability of many nonprofit business activities is unlikely to generate significant taxes. Moreover, any tax losses from nonprofit business activities could be made up by for-profits entering the social sector. They are bringing social sector activities into a taxable structure. All things considered, sector-bending could well increase overall tax receipts.

Given the previous distinctions and the abundance of social issues and problems that need to be addressed, it is reasonable to assume that a diversity of organizational structures will both continue to be necessary and evolve as time progresses.

The Road Ahead

What lies ahead? We aren't sure exactly, but we hope the emphasis will be on social performance and finding the best organizational structures to serve as a means for achieving maximum positive social impact. Perhaps we will see an increasing number of hybrid organizations that seek to take advantage of the strengths of both organizational forms, while allocating resources efficiently to create social value. Even further, maybe we will see more incidence of "industry creation," with social entrepreneurs employing for-profit, nonprofit, and hybrid structures in the pursuit of social impact in distinct arenas. In time, we may actually even move beyond talking about "sectors" based on legal forms of organization and begin focusing on "communities of practice." Actors in these communities will cross traditional sector lines in their efforts to harness market forces and supplement them with the necessary charitable impulses to effect social change, address the root problems in society, and empower individuals, communities, and society-at-large. This envisioned world may be blurry and indistinct, and even uncomfortable for some who are used to characterizing the business world as greedy and the nonprofit sector as pure and altruistic. And creative new approaches will certainly pose some taxation and regulatory challenges. We should be mindful of the potential for abuse and misuse, but these false characterizations and operational hurdles should not prevent us from embracing new ideas, experimenting with different structures, and striving for a reality in which progress is not needlessly impeded by policy. At the same time, we recognize that sector-bending will not be appropriate for many organizations, and we hope each one will assess the potential carefully before jumping on this bandwagon.

5

Commercialism and the Mission of Nonprofits

Estelle James

In recent years, growing commercialism among nonprofit organizations has blurred the boundaries between nonprofits and for-profits and raised important questions about the appropriate public policies toward nonprofits. Examples of these blurred boundaries are:

1. Nonprofits carry out a mix of profitable and loss-making activities—the former cross-subsidize the latter (most successful nonprofits do this).
2. Nonprofits have for-profits as affiliates, subsidiaries, partners, and spin-offs (university collaborations with biotech companies are good examples).
3. Nonprofits and for-profits compete with each other in a number of key industries, including some cases where for-profits are moving into traditional nonprofit areas (education, child care, nursing home industries).
4. Nonprofits are converting into for-profits, especially in the health industry (hospitals and HMOs).

These blurred lines take on increased importance as industries in which nonprofits and for-profits coexist are growing as a share of the economy (education, health, biotech research). Does commercialization of nonprofits matter? Does it distort the mission of the nonprofit sector, or provide the resources that enable it to perform its mission better? Who benefits from "mixtures"? How should public policy respond? A public interest clearly exists because tax advantages and special access to subsidies create wealth for nonprofits. Examples of these privileges are: tax deductibility of contributions, tax exemption of property and net income, and the requirement of nonprofit status to be eligible for public grants. These tax expenditures and other privileges are presumably given to increase the provision of "charitable" goods beyond the level that we would otherwise have, so as a minimum, this criterion needs to be revisited and tested in cases in which the nonprofit–for-profit line has become blurred, to ensure that this public policy purpose has not been subverted. Note that in this chapter the term charitable means services that qualify the organization for special tax treatment because of its supposed public purpose. It does not necessarily mean services that primarily benefit the poor, as many nonprofits provide services that primarily benefit the middle class and rich.

Cross-subsidization is a key fact of life for nonprofits, enabling them to grow and become more diversified, less dependent on government grants and private donations, therefore less at risk and more sustainable. Nonprofits charge fees and earn profits on one part of their activities, including activities that add little value to the core mission of the organization, in order to generate revenues that help them to carry out their preferred activities that earn losses. Their ability and incentive to do so stems from the fact that many nonprofits produce public or quasi-public goods together with private goods. The losses may stem from the organization's inability to charge fees on their core activities, because they are public or quasi-public goods from which exclusion, hence price finance, is difficult. The profits stem from the goods that generate private benefits, for which price finance is feasible. As private donations and government grants decrease, which has happened in recent years in some organizations, the incentive to generate commercial revenues (fees) to cross-subsidize core activities increases.

So long as the charitable goal of the nonprofit remains the driving force, such commercialization has a positive impact on the finances and long-term stability of the organization and the sector. However, dangers arise if the values of the nonprofit converge toward the for-profit's values, if the profit-making activities become large relative to and conflict with the core charitable activities, and if public resources are diverted to private gain.

The more extreme examples of commercialism, such as the partnerships between universities and the biotech industry, and the recent spate of conversions of hospitals and HMOs to for-profit status, are not explained by the cross-subsidization hypothesis, but require a deeper explanation that derives from theories about how institutional form is chosen in the first place and why it changes.

Why Nonprofit Rather than For-Profit?

Nonprofits cannot distribute a monetary residual and do not have owners who can sell their stock and garner capital gains. So, when an organization becomes a nonprofit, it loses access to equity capital and financial markets that for-profits enjoy. Why, then, does an entrepreneur choose the nonprofit form? Nonprofit theories suggest at least three answers:

1. Nonprofits get exclusive access to private donations, because they are considered more trustworthy than for-profits by potential donors. Donations are needed, in particular, when services are provided that cannot be effectively fee-financed, hence will not be profitable and able to attract equity capital in the for-profit marketplace.
2. Governments sometimes use the nonprofit sector as a preferred mechanism for delivering quasi-public services, so nonprofits get special access to public grants and tax privileges. This is most likely to occur in heterogeneous societies, where people disagree about which services should be provided and about the (religious, linguistic, ideological) flavor of the service that they want to consume.
3. Closely related, nonprofit founders often have religious or other ideological objectives, which are more likely to be pursued and preserved if the nonprofit form is used.

Based on these theories, we would expect the nonprofit form to be used in industries in which capital requirements are modest, exclusion and fee finance are difficult for some products, trustworthiness is important to encourage private donations, government grants are available to nonprofits as a way to accommodate heterogeneous preferences, and the entrepreneur has strong nonpecuniary ideological motivations. When these conditions change, the relative advantage of being a nonprofit also changes, and institutional transformations may occur.

Ideological Motivation of Nonprofit Entrepreneurs

It is well to remember that every organization has to be started by someone, and that many nonprofit organizations were started by individuals or by other "parent" organizations with strong ideological motivations—often designed to promote a particular religious, linguistic, or political point of view. To these founders, profits are not the objective, and using the nonprofit legal form helps ensure that profits will not be the objective of successor boards and managers, also.

Governments sometimes grant tax exemptions for donations to and income of nonprofit organizations that produce quasi-public services, as a way to let people vote with their dollars about which service should be financed. This approach may be favored in heterogeneous societies in which we do not all agree about which "public" goods should be produced, how much of each, and are they really good or bad? (For instance, are family planning, abortion pills, and stem cell research good or bad, and should they be supported by public funds? Not everyone agrees.) Indirect support via tax deductions and exemptions, rather than direct support, helps avoid social conflict on this type of issue. This heterogeneity in values is characteristic of the United States, which may explain why we use tax and other privileges for charitable organizations as a way to determine our product-mix of quasi-public goods, while more homogeneous European countries are likely to use direct allocation of public funds.

Closely related, provision of services through nonprofits can be a subtle way of dividing consumers of services into more homogeneous groupings and providing the ideological or cultural "flavor" that each group prefers. For example, Jewish and Catholic day care, old age facilities, and schools may be legally nonsectarian but they signal to and attract different constituents. This division would not be feasible or likely in pure public organizations or in profit-maximizing organizations. Sometimes government grants and tax privileges are a political response to pressure from the ideologically motivated nonprofits that provide these services to their constituents, so it is hardly surprising that nonprofit status is a condition for receiving this money. In the Netherlands, provision of educational and health services through nonprofits, financed largely by the state, has been institutionalized as a response to historical religious schisms. In Australia, large voucher-like subsidies to private nonprofit schools were introduced in the 1960s as the Catholic population grew and demanded access to their preferred educational system. Separation of church and state in the Australian Constitution was interpreted to mean equal treatment for secular and religious-based schools. In the United States, separation of church and state, as assured in the Constitution, has been interpreted to require tax exemption for diverse religious organizations, and for schools, hospitals, and social services organizations that had religious origins—but to prohibit direct government aid to some religious organizations, especially schools. This interpretation is currently under review.

Unobservable Characteristics and Trustworthiness

Important characteristics of some services are unobservable—for example, some quality components of child care and nursing homes are difficult to observe and measure. When individuals contemplate donating to such organizations because they care about these services, it is difficult to monitor directly how the money is actually spent—did output or quality really increase as a result of the donation? Nonprofits may be more trustworthy and less likely to economize on these characteristics that cannot be easily observed, since entrepreneurs and managers face less incentive to increase profits which cannot be distributed to them. This is the basic reason often given for private donors' preference for nonprofits, and it also helps explain public donors' preference for nonprofits—a scandal is less likely to arise.

Further underlying the trustworthiness theory is a belief that entrepreneurs and managers with different objectives flock to different kinds of institutions as a result of a self-selection process. Not only are the incentives different once you get there, but knowing this in advance, different people are attracted to nonprofits and for-profits, helping to make nonprofits more trustworthy. In particular, people with strong pecuniary objectives are likely to flow to for-profits, while those with social or ideological goals would choose nonprofits. Donors can then choose organizations whose managers are likely to have congruent objectives, so monitoring is less essential.

But three caveats are immediately suggested:

1. If these characteristics are unobservable to donors, they may also be unobservable to researchers. Therefore it is difficult to test this hypothesis and many empirical studies (e.g., in the hospital industry) have not found differences.

2. We need to observe and count in order to make nonprofits accountable. This is especially true when public funds are involved—measurement of achievement is essential to justify these advantages. But if everything were observable and could be counted, we could reward both nonprofits and for-profits according to their outputs and would not need to favor nonprofits. Increasing accountability—in education (number of students, test scores, value added), in hospitals (such as number of admissions and patient days by diagnoses, mortality rates)—driven in part by the desire to make public and nonprofit organizations accountable, also reduces the need to give any particular organizational form favored treatment.

3. While differentiation of trustworthiness may be true at the extremes, I suspect we would find a large overlap in the middle. Nonprofit managers undoubtedly have nonpecuniary objectives, but many also have an undeniable interest in money (most people do) and similarly, managers of for-profits pursue nonmonetary goals such as power and prestige. In fact, this creates a principle-agent problem in for-profits (managers may pursue their own diverse goals instead of shareholders' profit-maximizing goal) as well as in nonprofits (managers may pursue their own monetary goals instead of donors' philanthropic goals). Moreover, blurred boundaries between the sectors may reduce this selection effect, even if it existed before. Differences in entrepreneurial and managerial objectives, and how they respond to incentives in the nonprofit versus the for-profit sector, constitute a fruitful topic for further empirical study.

Blurring Boundaries—Why Is This Happening?

The above discussion suggests that a sharp line might exist between nonprofits and for-profits, as a result of differing entrepreneurial and managerial objectives and incentives. Yet, we observe these lines becoming blurred in recent years, with nonprofits exhibiting more "commercial" proclivities and for-profits providing similar services. Why is this happening?

My earlier work, and later work by Weisbrod and others, shows that cross-subsidization is a key fact of life for nonprofits, enabling them to grow and carry out activities they consider worthwhile although not financially viable on their own. Nonprofits earn profits on one part of their activities, including activities they find distasteful, in order to generate revenues that help them to carry out their preferred core loss-making activities. The loss-making activities are often public or quasi-public goods from which it is difficult to price and capture the full social benefit. Usually the profit-making activities involve goods and services that can be sold for a fee, and the fee exceeds marginal production costs. This ability to earn profits may arise because their reputation creates barriers to entry, or because economies of scope and complementarities give them cost advantages over new for-profit firms that might otherwise enter the industry and through competition force prices down.

As other sources of revenue diminish, the incentive to undertake profit-making activities, to cross-subsidize preferred loss-making activities, increases. This is often given as the rationale for increased commercialism. Well-known examples are the cross-subsidization of university research by undergraduate tuition or by adult education classes and gift shops run by museums, hospitals, and other institutions. Other examples of increased commercialism may be found in public (nonprofit) radio, museums, and zoos, as a response to increased scarcity of resources relative to demand. Cross-subsidization may occur within a single nonprofit organization or through the use of for-profit subsidiaries. But so long as the goal of the nonprofit dominates, I would argue that it has a positive impact on the finances of the sector. It increases the organization's resources and decreases its dependence on public or private donations, while of course increasing its dependence on market forces—but diversified dependence is much less risky than concentrated dependence.

Basic Changes in Institutional Form

When an organization becomes a nonprofit, it loses access to equity capital and financial markets—so if much capital is needed, the for-profit institutional form is likely to be chosen. In exchange, nonprofits gain access to private donations and public privileges. These are particularly important in situations where fee financing is problematic, because exclusion of nonpayers is not feasible or because the target clientele cannot afford to pay a fee that covers its cost. Additionally, adoption of the nonprofit form makes it more likely that the ideological values of the founders will not be driven out by monetary objectives of subsequent managers. This is important because, historically, many of our nonprofit universities, schools, and hospitals had religious origins. I would hypothesize that, as capital requirements and access to fee finance increase, and as ideological motivations weaken, the balance would shift toward the for-profit form—or toward partnerships that attempt to have the best of both worlds.

Indeed, this appears to be happening now. The biggest examples of commercialism (mergers, partnerships, conversions) are occurring in industries (health, education) in which:

1. Capital intensity and economies of scale or scope have increased.
2. Institutional or technological change has made exclusion and price financing (through patents and fees) more feasible.
3. Legal regulations that, in the past, constrained the ability of nonprofits to earn profits, have been lifted.

Under these circumstances, it is more advantageous for nonprofits to act like and to become for-profits, and many do so. I would argue that increased cross-subsidization through profit-making subsidiaries may be a response to marginal changes in financial positions, but mergers, conversions, and close partnerships with for-profits are a response to global changes in incentives, opportunities, and constraints that change the cost-benefit calculus regarding institutional form.

In hospitals, for example, high-tech medicine has increased capital requirements. Broad insurance coverage, including Medicare, has made fee financing the norm. Charitable or free hospital care is rare. The consequence is widespread conversion to for-profit status. In the academic-biotech revolution, expensive laboratory or computer research imposes heavy needs for up-front funding. Simultaneously, in the 1980s, federal regulations were changed to permit patents to be taken out by universities that had received federal funds (previously this had not been permitted), and to include collaboration with private for-profits as a positive input into the grantmaking process. Whereas previously a choice had to be made between access to government grants for basic research and profitable fees from the development and sale of research results, under the new regime nonprofits had access to both through strategic alliances with for-profits. The consequence is that such partnerships are now commonplace on the university research scene and private industry is the fastest growing source of research and development (R & D) financing at universities. Concomitantly, for-profit spin-offs of university research, jointly employing university students and faculty, are common. In both the health and education industries, access to venture capital became more important while legal and institutional changes altered the ability of universities and hospitals to sell their products, thereby enabling and encouraging them to form partnerships with or to become for-profits.

The initiative may have come from the for-profit world. Indeed, mergers and conversions can be viewed as a capital market response to potentially profitable nonprofit organizations. In the for-profit world, financial markets provide discipline and limit the proclivity of managers to pursue their own welfare at the expense of shareholders. If the manager does not maximize the firm's profits, it is eventually taken over in the financial market by another organization that will—the new company offers shareholders a higher stock price than the current market rate to accomplish the takeover. Similarly, if a nonprofit has large potential profits that it is not exploiting, the financial markets will attempt a takeover. The for-profit entrepreneur must then convince the nonprofit's directors and managers to merge, but this may be easier (may cost less) than convincing numerous stockholders.

The success of such takeovers, and the conversion of nonprofits to for-profits generally, are likely to be less in organizations whose directors and managers have a strong ideological (religious, cultural) bias. Such entrepreneurs and managers would place a heavy weight on retaining control and would be willing to forego monetary gain to do so. One might, therefore, expect the surviving nonprofits to be relatively more ideological in industries in which conversions and close inter-sectoral collaborations are occurring. This hypothesis is empirically testable.

The fact that nonprofits specialize in industries that generate both private and public benefits also helps explain why these industries are often mixed. In these cases, we would expect subtle differences in product-mix. The for-profits emphasize products that yield private benefits in which fees can be charged to cover costs. We would also expect for-profits to produce goods and services whose quantity and quality are more easily measured. As nonprofit educational and health organizations have been pressed in recent years to develop measurable accountability indicators, for-profits have sprung up, using these same measures to "prove" their reliability. The argument for using nonprofit status as an indirect signal of trustworthiness falls, when direct measures are available. Viewed from this perspective, it is not surprising to see for-profits hired to carry out responsibilities that previously would have been the domain of nonprofits. One example is the Edison School project, in which a for-profit educational firm, competing against nonprofits, has managed to sell its services to public school systems on grounds that it will meet certain observable measurable criteria regarding student performance.

Potential Dangers of Blurred Boundaries

Are these developments problematic or beneficial? Commercialism is socially desirable if it increases access to fee revenues and capital markets so that scarce donations and grants can be allocated to services in which these other revenues sources are not available. This can, potentially, enable greater output of goods with "public" characteristics and more equitable distribution than would have occurred otherwise. The most efficient institutional form changes over time, for reasons we have already spelled out. However, problems can develop, against which both the nonprofit sector and policymakers need to guard. The chief dangers involve value convergence of the nonprofit toward for-profit values, misallocation of tax privileges, and diversion of public resources to private gain when institutional form changes.

As people are hired to whom monetary goals and skills are relatively more important, to pursue the "profitable" activities of the nonprofit, it is possible that the ethos and value structure of the entire organization will change. The objective of the organization, as an example, may become wealth accumulation and income growth, rather than service provision. Psychological theories of cognitive dissonance, sociological theories of status and imitation, and economic theories of labor mobility are all relevant. According to the concept of cognitive dissonance, attitudes follow behavior. If people are hired to earn a profit, they will come to believe that earning a profit is important, to justify their behavior. The more successful they are at earning a profit, the higher their status and the more other people will emulate their values and behavior. Labor mobility theory tells us that if the nonprofit sector hires managers from the for-profit world, who expect to move back some day, they will try to build evidence of their ability to earn profits, which may require displacing other objectives to a subsidiary role. Workers who are hired jointly by nonprofits and for-profits (as in the biotech-university alliances) may carry with them the values of the latter, which offer greater monetary rewards.

Do we find a value and behavioral convergence between nonprofit and for-profit managers, and is this convergence greater in industries in which the lines between the two are more blurred and inter-sectoral mobility is greater? If pecuniary goals take on greater importance, how does this affect the output and pricing decisions of the nonprofit organization? How have organizations guarded against undesirable changes in values and behavior? These are all-important researchable issues—difficult ones because they require us to define the counterfactual (what would have happened otherwise) as well as to measure and explain what actually did happen. The danger is that, if value and behavioral convergence occurs on a large scale, the nonprofit form is no longer a good signal of trustworthiness, so access to public and private donations may fall or the donations may fail to be used in the desired way.

Are Tax Privileges Misallocated?

In principle, tax advantages are given in order to induce behavior that otherwise might not occur—for example, lower prices that enable access to low-income groups, greater output, and higher quality. In mixed industries, however, it is possible that public money may simply be financing goods that would have been produced anyway. In such industries, consumers apparently feel they can observe, measure, and pay for the outputs they want, so the need for donations and the use of signals of trustworthiness are less important. Day care and assisted living facilities, for instance, provided by for-profits and nonprofits can be directly compared by consumers, who then make a choice.

If this is the case, should special tax privileges be given to nonprofits in mixed industries? What do we get in return? Do we get a product mix with more public elements, lower prices for the poor, or other features we are willing to pay for socially? Or do nonprofits drive out potential for-profit firms because of their lower costs stemming from tax advantages, with no corresponding welfare gain? These are vexing questions because if the marginal impact on social welfare is small it is possible that scarce tax dollars have been misallocated. Even more troubling are the cases in which joint costs and assets are allocated between nonprofit and for-profit affiliates in such a way as to maximize the value of the tax advantages, rather than the value of the joint outputs and the equity of its distribution.

How common are these phenomena and do they suggest that rule-changes are needed regarding access to tax privilege in mixed organizations and industries? Should institutional form be the basis for tax advantages and for special access to public grants in situations in which outputs have now become relatively observable and measurable, or should grants be awarded on the basis of measured performance, on the same basis for for-profits and nonprofits? In the educational field, we are moving in that direction. These questions, pertaining to the relevance of institutional form as the basis for tax privileges and public grants, constitute some of the key research and policy issues regarding nonprofits in mixed industries.

Diversion of Public Resources to Private Gain When Institutional Form Changes

The most dramatic examples of partnerships and close inter-sectoral collaborations are found in the R&D field. A university provides the skilled human resources and access to federal funds for basic research, while the for-profit provides additional venture capital and develops the research product for the marketplace. What does each party get from this arrangement and is it socially beneficial? The university gets capital to carry out its research activities, while the for-profit gets exclusive access to new discoveries (e.g., a nonprofit research institute develops a drug in collaboration with a pharmaceutical company that utilizes a profit-maximizing pricing and output strategy). Possibly an arms-length competitive bidding process ex post would have resulted in more money to the research institute or a lower price to the consumer—but the university would not have gotten its venture capital ex ante and might not have been able to pursue the research.

More disturbing is the question of how the terms of trade were determined, as well as the possibility that the surplus from this arrangement might go disproportionately to the for-profit party, and to the university faculty and administrators who helped to negotiate the deal and then split their time between the two organizations. Also troubling is the conflict between the norms of academia and the private marketplace. Publication and dissemination of the research results will be delayed until patented, in the interests of monetary gain—a clear conflict in the modus operandi of the two sectors. Similar conflicts of interest in other industries occur when the managers of nonprofits benefit personally from their business dealings with for-profits, by receiving commissions and other perks—a form of disguised profit distribution that is difficult to monitor or when these nonprofit managers receive a large bonus for negotiating a successful takeover with a for-profit.

In all these cases, the nonprofit sector lacks the business analysts and securities markets that impose discipline by constantly evaluating the net worth of for-profit firms. (Of course, these monitors sometimes fail in the for-profit sector, too, as the Enron case demonstrates.) The danger is that some of the public grants and private donations will be siphoned off from the original charitable purpose and used instead to increase profits or personal compensation. Who is monitoring the monitors of the nonprofit resources when their goals and allegiance change?

Change in institutional form from nonprofit to for-profit status is sometimes efficient, as the advantages of access to equity capital outweigh the loss of donations, tax exemptions, and ideological purity. The board of the nonprofit must make this evaluation carefully. However, if they take into account their personal gain rather than the gain to society as a whole, the outcome can be problematic. For instance, managers may prefer to be part of a larger and wealthier organization, as a source of power and prestige. Insiders may purchase converted nonprofit assets at a low price, cut out the loss-making public services of the new organizations, and raise their perks and salaries. When new charitable foundations are required to be set up with some of the proceeds of the conversion, the old managers may benefit from the power over large funds, without being careful to carry out the public purpose of the original organization.

How are these potential principle-agent problems averted, who should be permitted to acquire the assets of the converted nonprofit, by what procedures, and how should society be compensated for the past tax advantages that generated these assets? These are some of the challenging questions that courts have had to face in controversial conversion cases, in which nonprofit managers have been accused of deriving private benefits from their public trust. This, too, would be worthy of further research exploration.

Concluding Thoughts

I have tried to elucidate some of the causes, effects, and potential dangers of blurred boundaries between the sectors, as well as the empirical research that might help us understand what is happening and how policies can shape these happenings constructively. I argue that cross-subsidization is a fact of life for successful nonprofits, and the recently growing cross-subsidization among numerous nonprofits may be a consequence of scarce grants and donations relative to needs. However, the more extreme examples of partnerships and conversions are a response to basic changes in economic and legal conditions that alter the benefits and costs of becoming and remaining a nonprofit. In particular, fee financing and performance measurement have become more feasible in parts of the education and health care industries, at the same time that access to capital has become more essential, shifting the tide toward the for-profit form. Commercialism and change of institutional form increase the resources available to nonprofits but pose the danger of changing managerial values, misallocated tax privileges, and a diversion of public funds into private gain. Both the sector and policymakers need to reevaluate public policies toward nonprofits in light of these benefits and dangers, and careful empirical research can help to point us in the right direction.

6

How Important Is a Nonprofit's Bottom Line? The Uses and Abuses of Financial Data

Mark Hager and Janet Greenlee

Over the past decade, the multiple stakeholders of nonprofit organizations, including clients, donors, and government, have become increasingly enamored with the idea of measuring nonprofit performance. Sometimes it is to determine which nonprofit to rely on for services, while other times it is to determine which organizations to support financially with grants or contributions. In almost all cases, the desire to measure performance comes down to an interest in making the nonprofit sector more accountable and businesslike in its operation, and to use measurement as a way of bringing some discipline to a sector that for many years has operated without many controls. In the business world, after all, information about the performance and financial condition of firms is bountiful and, until the recent accounting scandals, thought to be very reliable. Business has a bottom line and measuring the financial performance of a firm comes down to using a set of time-tested metrics to see how well a company has performed. In the nonprofit sector, the achievement of mission is a far harder thing to assess. Still, using data to assess the performance of nonprofit is an idea whose time appears to have come.

In this chapter, we consider the special dynamics of assessing the financial performance of nonprofit organizations. We argue that the use of financial proxies for real measures of program effectiveness has given some the illusion that the nonprofit sector has finally found its own bottom line, but in reality it has led to some important distortions and omissions.

A Giving Story

Some people give small amounts of money to charity throughout their lives, carving their contributions from their limited incomes and establishing a relationship with a variety of worthy causes. Others come upon the behavior later in life, after they have established themselves and have a steady flow of disposable income. This is the case for the person in the story told in this chapter, a person we refer to as the Donor. After several years of setbacks, the Donor's small business was finally getting on its feet. The Donor was now in the position of paying down his debt and thinking about his role in the community. Consistent with his new attitude and station in life, he earmarked $2,000 to contribute to a charity. While the Donor had a vague sense that he should give money to a worthy cause, he had no idea to whom he should give the money. It makes sense to him that the money should go to a good charity—one that does good things for people that need help. Beyond that, however, he is at a loss. How can the Donor find a worthy recipient of his hard-earned cash?

The financial windfall from his newfound business success means that the Donor is also getting familiar with ways he can invest some of his profits. One mutual fund company's materials advertise its program for charitable giving. According to the literature, the Donor can put some money in a fund and then designate how the funds can be dispersed to various charities. But which ones? Luckily, the company advertises a Web site which will allow the Donor to "access a Web-based philanthropic community" in which he can quickly find specific causes worthy of his contributions. He follows the links, and is introduced to GuideStar, a site that features the forms that nonprofits file with the IRS every year. The Donor looks through a few of the entries and looks quickly through some of the returns, but finds that he still doesn't know which organizations are the best ones to give his money. He needs more help.

In an Internet search for "charity rankings," the Donor stumbles upon Charity Navigator. "Thank you for choosing Charity Navigator to be your guide for intelligent giving," reads the Web site. "We are a nonprofit organization dedicated to helping you find a charity which best matches your interests and beliefs." Pleased with his find, the Donor digs further into Charity Navigator. The site makes it easy for him by rating different charities from one to four stars. The Donor quickly discards those organizations with one, two, or three stars, and starts making a short list of four-star organizations with interesting names. That night, he showed the list to his wife. "These are all organizations that Charity Navigator says are really good charities," the Donor tells his wife. Impressed with her husband's research skills, she voices support for one of the animal sanctuary organizations that made the Donor's short list. The Donor picks out a cancer research center, and writes two $1,000 checks, one for each of the two organizations.

The Donor never gets to see what happens to his money, but he has no reason to doubt that it was used to improve the world somehow. In addition, he got to take a $2,000 charitable deduction when tax time rolled around.

"Not only am I a successful business owner," the Donor thinks to himself, "I'm a shrewd researcher and an informed philanthropist as well."

Comparing Charities

All givers must make their giving decisions somehow. Many people have connections to their communities that make giving to a specific church or popular community organization an obvious choice for their charitable dollars. Others give to well-known organizations such as the American Cancer Society or the American Red Cross. Some give to charities that happen to call on the phone, knock at the door, or send solicitation letters in the mail. Some rely on the guidance of materials provided by a federated campaign, news story, or Web site. For the latter group, some assessment of which charity is better than other charities may play a substantial role in deciding to which organization they choose to give.

While givers may assume that rating the worthiness of charities is a simple task, it turns out to be a very complex task. In most people's minds, the best measure of the quality of a charity is how well it carries out its social mission. That is, the organizations with the best programs are the ones that should get the high ratings and the majority of charitable contributions. After all, all else being equal, who wants to give to a charity that does not do its job very well? Traditionally, program evaluation and outcome management have focused on an organization's instrumental outputs. The measures that come closest to tapping into effectiveness and performance are those that reflect program outcomes, such as successful training, appropriate distribution of services, happy clients, or quality performances. Hatry (1999) opens his book on performance measurement by specifically referring to measurement of the "efficiency of services or programs" (Hatry 1999, 3), effectively excluding evaluation of nonprogram activities in his scope of study. In short, program outcomes resonate with most people's conceptions of what counts in assessing the quality of a nonprofit organization.

However, the goal of rating charities based on program outcomes runs immediately into two problems. First, organizations with different missions have no common yardstick for evaluating which is doing better than the other, and which is thereby comparatively more worthy to receive charitable donations. Consider a homeless shelter and a youth soccer league. Both are nonprofits that rely on volunteers and contributions to carry out their social welfare missions. However, the measures by which we might conclude that the shelter is effective in its program delivery are different from the measures by which we might judge the effectiveness of the soccer league. If you think you can come up with some common measures, ask yourself if they also work for evaluating the local orchestra or nonprofit publishing company. They likely will not work.

Even if we could effectively compare the programs of all nonprofits that compete for contributions, a second problem exists. Regular evaluation of programs is expensive, time consuming, and idiosyncratic. It requires expertise to do it well, and many nonprofit organizations lack both the expertise and the desire to take time from programs to do outcome evaluations. Further, there is no central repository that attempts to amass outcome evaluation data for even a small percentage of several hundred thousand charities in the United States. If one could compare program outcomes directly and amass the findings into a giant comparative database, the ability to make intelligent giving decisions would take a huge leap forward.

We probably do not have to tell you that the Donor introduced earlier did not find any kind of real program effectiveness data in the database he consulted when he was deciding how to best distribute his $2,000 in contributions. The evaluation methods used by Charity Navigator are not much different from those used by GuideStar, another national online purveyor of financial data related to nonprofits. Nor are the ratings that much different from the grades assigned to charities by the American Institute of Philanthropy, yet another charities information and rating service. Nor even are they different from the summary statistics provided to potential givers in the Combined Federal Campaign. None is based principally on program effectiveness. All are primarily based on the financial information that nonprofits provide to the IRS each year.

These data can tell us something about the administrative efficiency and financial health of a nonprofit organization, but they say nothing about effectiveness.

Research on Nonprofit Financial Data

In the absence of a way to compare the quality of the programs of nonprofits, an alternative mode of measuring performance had to be conjured up to fill the void. This alternative turned out to be how nonprofits spend their money. This approach is not completely outlandish—people are legitimately interested in giving to charities that spend their money wisely (Doble 1990; Glaser 1994; Stehle 1998). Charity watchdog organizations, such as the Better Business Bureau's Wise Giving Alliance, emphasize financial ratios in their field standards. Indeed, some people are more concerned with the efficiency and financial accountability of potential recipients of their contributions than they are with how well nonprofits are delivering their programs. Certainly, financial ratios have taken center stage in recent years and taken the spotlight away from the murkier topic of effectiveness (Lammers 2003). A recent public opinion poll by Princeton Survey Research Associates (2001) asked Americans what kind of information is most important when making giving decisions. Nearly half of the respondents focused on how the organization uses its money. In contrast, 13 percent focused on an organization's legitimacy or reputation, and only 6 percent cited fulfills a genuine need or makes a difference as the primary impetus for giving.

Although donors may indicate a desire for financial information when making giving decisions, studies examining the impact of this information on actual decisions have found mixed results. Some (Steinberg 1986; Greenlee 1993) found no impact, while more recent studies (Greenlee and Brown 1999; Tinkelman 1999) have found that financial information plays a significant role in the allocation of donor resources. Thus, while program performance is important, a charity's financial performance may well play a large role in its reputation and ability to garner future resources. In the current environment, program excellence may take a backseat to financial responsibility, at least among some stakeholders.

While working conditions and benefits may matter to workers and community-friendliness may matter to neighbors, businesses are judged primarily on their profits, stock prices, efficiencies, and returns to investors. Is it reasonable to judge charities by a similar yardstick? The answer is far from clear.

Researchers have begun to take stock of some of the financial measures of nonprofit organizations, especially in relation to the quality and sustainability of their overall operations. Several scholars used financial measures to assess the health of nonprofit organizations in the 1980s (Cleverly and Nilson 1980; Chabotar 1989). However, much of the current work takes an early article by Howard Tuckman and Cyril Chang (1991) as its starting point. Whereas previous works relied on small samples of nonprofits in particular subsectors, Tuckman and Chang took advantage of new access to research databases of variables collected from Form 990, the form that nonprofits with more than $25,000 in gross receipts file with the IRS each year. Analysis of Form 990 data opened a new era of benchmarking in the nonprofit sector, since researchers could compare the same financial information across many thousands of organizations. Greenlee and Bukovinsky (1998) described twelve financial ratios that could be used for benchmarking purposes, and many are used by watchdog and information agencies in their assessments of individual charities.

The work by Tuckman and Chang is notable because it describes an effort to investigate the relationship between financial measures and the overall health and flexibility of a nonprofit. They hypothesized that four financial measures, calculated from information readily available from Form 990, could be used to indicate the comparative vulnerability or flexibility of a nonprofit organization. Despite the appeal of these measures to nonprofit watchdog groups, most nonprofit scholars in the United States initially paid little attention to them. Researchers in Australia (Kent 1993; Buckmaster, Lyons and Bridges 1994; Worth 1996) made the first attempts to translate Tuckman and

Chang's theory and measures to nonprofit benchmarking exercises, but the growing American focus on performance measurement has still paid little attention to Tuckman and Chang's financial measures.

Ten years after Tuckman and Chang's work, Greenlee and Trussel (2000) and Hager (2001) revisited these measures in an attempt to make them relevant to ongoing discussions of nonprofit performance and accountability. Greenlee and Trussel focused on whether Tuckman and Chang's measures could be used to predict a decline in program expenditures over a three-year period. They used variations of their ratios to separate "financially vulnerable" from "not financially vulnerable" nonprofits, and developed a model that individual organizations could use to determine which category the measures placed them in. They then expanded this model to include a financial risk rating system that gives managers, board members, and potential donors one way to benchmark organizations within broad sectors and to assess financial risk.

Hager argued that the Tuckman-Chang measures are likely to differ substantially not only between sectors, but also within sectors. He focused on nonprofit arts organizations, many of which are notoriously unstable financially and display higher mortality rates than other types of nonprofit organizations. Instead of focusing on declines in program expense or equity balance, Hager looked over time to see if financially flexible nonprofits display a greater likelihood of survival. He found that different measures are useful for different types of arts organizations, and that for some types of arts organizations, the Tuckman-Chang measures could not be used to differentiate the successes from the failures. Nonetheless, he concluded that the measures hold substantial promise for predicting the outcome for some types of arts nonprofits.

Whether these respective works will spark renewed scholarly attention to the financial characteristics of nonprofits is yet to be seen. If givers such as the Donor make their giving decisions based on ratings of nonprofit financial efficiency and accountability, then researchers and policymakers must have a clear understanding of the implications of such decision making. Overall, scholars have lagged behind the field in coming to terms with how these financial measures work, how they are distributed, and how they are related to other measures of organizational performance.

Strengths and Weaknesses of Focusing on Financial Measures

As the business model of measurement is adapted by those in the nonprofit sector, it might be important to consider whether our primary assessments of charities ought to be based substantially on financial information. The question, however, is rendered moot by the widespread practice and lack of viable alternatives. That is, while the research community was trying to come to grips with whether financial measures should be used to evaluate nonprofit organizations, the practice field had already moved firmly into adopting the approach. Rather than complain about the practice, we offer an assessment of the strengths and weaknesses of the approach. We conclude with several ideas about how some of the weaknesses might be addressed.

Strengths

The strengths of an approach to measuring nonprofit performance that relies heavily on financial data are fairly clear.

Easy Access to Data: A decade of collaboration between the Internal Revenue Service (IRS) and the National Center for Charitable Statistics (NCCS) has made data from Form 990 widely available to researchers. Further collaboration with Philanthropic Research, Inc. (GuideStar) makes Forms 990 available to everyone with access to an Internet connection (Andrews 2002). These resources make it easy for researchers to better understand the finances of nonprofit organizations, as well as the relationship between finances and other organizational characteristics (Lampkin and Boris 2002). More importantly, these resources make it easy for people such as the Donor to learn something about each of the organizations that he might consider contributing money to. Researchers, journalists, watchdogs, institutional funders, and individual givers all have a common basis for rating and assessing charities.

Legitimate Comparison Across Many Different Organizations: Advancement of tools and techniques for program evaluation have been hampered not only by lack of availability of data, but also by simple differences between programs in organizations that do very different things. Recall the example of the homeless shelter and the youth soccer league that we gave earlier. While each might be independently evaluated on its own merits, there are few meaningful programmatic comparisons that would help the Donor think about which of the two programs is the most worthy recipient of his funds. In contrast, organizations of all types speak a common financial language. Although their accounting practices may differ, they account for many common elements, such as revenue sources and amounts, expenditures categories and amounts, assets and liabilities. These financial elements provide a commonality of comparison that is frequently lacking in studies of capacity and effectiveness of nonprofit organizations. The homeless shelter and the youth soccer league both have a track record of raising and spending money, and givers may be justified in looking to those track records as a means of making giving decisions.

A History of Established Procedures to Build On: While only a few scholars have used financial ratios and other indicators to shed light on the management practices of nonprofit organizations, the use of these kinds of measures to assess the condition of businesses is well established. Such measures as stock prices, earnings per share, the price to earnings ratio, and net asset values have become almost as common to average investors as they have to professionals who use them to assess investment decisions every day. While benchmarks established in the for-profit sector will almost certainly not translate meaningfully to nonprofits, the procedures by which the benchmarks have been established will. Like businesses, nonprofit organizations have revenues and expenses, assets, liabilities, and fund balances. Nonprofit scholars have a rich tradition of financial analysis from the corporate world to draw upon in designing their studies.

A Recognizable, Practical Application with a Hungry Audience: Individual donors and institutional funders care about how nonprofit organizations spend their money. Individual givers such as the Donor benefit from information that helps them decide whether a particular nonprofit organization is a worthy recipient of their contributions. Even though he might not have dug deeply enough into Charity Navigator to realize how nonprofits on the site are evaluated, the financial language he did see resonated with his understanding of investments. Administrative cost ratios and operating margins are a practical way to evaluate whether a particular charity might be the kind of organization that will be a proper steward of his money. Nonprofit information brokers have a hungry audience who want to know whether a candidate for their money is stable or unstable, usual or unusual, and efficient or inefficient in their financial arrangements. As long as reporting is reasonably consistent, benchmarking and financial evaluation of individual organizations provides this.

Weaknesses

While these considerations make the use of financial measures appealing, there are some notable problems with this kind of analysis. The weaknesses of using financial data to assess the performance of nonprofits are ultimately hard to ignore.

Accounting Problems: Currently, numerous nonprofit information brokers rely heavily on Form 990, financial statements, and grant reports as primary sources of financial information on nonprofit organizations. Despite reasonably clear and precise guidelines from the IRS and the American Institute of Certified Public Accountants, nonprofits account for fundraising and administrative expenditures in idiosyncratic ways. Noncompliance is widespread. As an example, nonprofits often ignore the rules for allocating expenses that have both programmatic and fundraising content, often charging no expenses to fundraising at all (Lipman 2000; Brostek 2002). To further complicate matters, audited financial statements are prepared according to Generally Accepted Accounting Principles (GAAP), which are promulgated by the Financial Accounting Standards Board (FASB). Forms 990 are prepared according to IRS regulations, which differ in some areas.

Focusing on Financials Sometimes Misses the Big Picture: Possibly the most important criticism of financial analysis of nonprofits is that it takes the place of trying to determine whether the organization is doing a good job of fulfilling its mission or not. When researchers (or donors) focus only on financial aspects of a nonprofit, they give short shrift to other dimensions that may ultimately be more important. That is, some unstable or inefficient organizations may be much more productive in terms of quality service delivery than a competing nonprofit that has its eyes more squarely on the bottom line (Schambra 2003). When financial analysis becomes the order of the day, we run the danger of no longer asking the important questions about program outcomes and performances.

The availability of financial data is a boon to nonprofit researchers, but it also conditions the kinds of questions they ask and seek to answer. In short, the current practice of financial evaluation of nonprofit organizations is driven by available data. We focus on things that we can know from the available data, rather than develop a means for measuring the hard-to-measure dimensions of an organization's program activities. If we stop asking the hard questions, we should not be surprised when we do not develop the means to answer them.

Focus on Large Organizations and Single Standards: A well-known limitation of Form 990 data is that analyses based on its data necessarily exclude organizations that are not required to file. Two major groups that are not required to file Form 990 are churches and organizations with low levels of gross receipts in a given year. Systematic exclusion of churches has an unknown influence on benchmarking in certain subsectors, especially social services. Systematic exclusion of the large number of small nonprofits means that our benchmarks are biased toward the activities of larger organizations (Smith 1997). Unfortunately, when charity watchdogs set standards and information brokers rate charities, they do so without regard for the differences between nonprofit sizes, types, places, ages, or other distinguishing characteristics. Standards that are reasonable for one set of organizations of a given size and mission may not be reasonable for a somewhat different set of organizations. While watchdogs and evaluators are quick to cede this point, standards still get applied uniformly to all sizes and shapes of nonprofits.

"Teaching to the Test": Establishing benchmarks and then introducing pressures to meet these benchmarks may introduce the unwelcome tendency for nonprofit organizations to superficially change their activities so that they score well against the established standards (Masaoka 2003). That is, the increased focus on financial information may result in the "window dressing" that is seen in the for-profit world, in which nonprofits might take advantage of the legal flexibility that exists in U.S. accounting standards to choose methods that "dress up" their financial reports and improve any ratios based on these reports. A nonprofit that feels pressure to look efficient may find

reasonable (or, possibly, unreasonable) ways to allocate more of its adminis-trative expenses to program expenses. As a result, the resulting financial data may not be as useful for comparison purposes as we hope. Financial ratios used in the business sector have, over time since introduction of sector aver-ages, tended to regress toward the mean of a given sector. We should not be surprised if similar regression is seen in the nonprofit sector. Widespread disclosure of financial reports is a giant step forward in accountability and self-regulation. However, it also provides the opportunity for nonprofits to make accounting decisions based as much on "impression management" as financial management.

The Future

Nonprofit organizations have a public obligation to be open and account-able (Independent Sector 2002). Because Form 990 is the only public docu-ment required of nonprofit organizations in the United States, the spirit of this obligation is fulfilled in careful and accurate reporting on this federal form. Such openness and accountability allows donors to evaluate charities based on consistent information. At present, however, a range of forces con-spire to compromise the quality of financial information and hampers the sector from achieving this consistency. Change in accounting and regulation can come on the heels of cataclysmic events, or it can come incrementally over a longer period of time. However, the prospect of a quick overhaul of the current system seems unlikely. One would be hard-pressed to imagine a more catalyzing event than that of September 11, 2001, when America's donors experienced firsthand their inability to judge the worthiness of charities that gathered millions of dollars for victims of the terrorist attacks. If ever govern-ment or the public had an opportunity to demand accountability of the non-profit sector, it was in the months following the flurry of donations and the inability of organizations to answer hard questions about how the money was being used. Instead, accounting, accountability, and the relative lack of regu-lation have returned to their pre-9-11 levels.

This lack of response to catalyzing events reduces the likelihood of whole-sale revisions in our approach to improving reporting and our ability to assess the worthiness of charities. Keating and Frumkin (2003) have sug-gested the founding of a nonprofit regulatory entity that would police non-profit organizations in much the same way that the Securities Exchange Commission polices America's businesses. While such a proposal has clear merits, the restructuring of the current regulatory environment would require a tremendous exercise of political will that may not be immediately forth-coming.

Consequently, we expect that change will be incrementally negotiated and implemented. Financial accounting will still provide important benchmarks by which we evaluate the worthiness of nonprofits, but accounting will improve. Already, with the availability of Forms 990 on the Internet, nonprofits are forced to answer hard questions from donors. While the Donor in our story was content to rely on a third party to help choose a recipient of his contributions, others take advantage of the new transparency to do their assessments of the worthiness of charities. With two different types of improvements, individual donors will be able to take better advantage of the information available to them. First, financial reporting must be accurate. Second, information needs to be timelier. How does the field make incremental improvements in the accuracy of reporting? For small organizations, it may be mostly a matter of education about essential accounting and reporting standards. Many nonprofits are not in compliance with IRS rules or GAAP because they are unaware of the rules and unmotivated to learn them. For organizations both big and small, the field could benefit from professionals who specialize in auditing tax-exempt organizations. Geary, Greenlee, and Trussel (2000) found that complicated audit requirements and low revenue potential cause CPAs to shy away from providing services to nonprofit organizations. Even when CPA firms accept nonprofit clients, these clients rarely get star treatment. As a consequence, audit quality suffers. However, a cadre of professionals who specialize exclusively in the nonprofit sector would be uniquely qualified to evaluate both the financial and nonfinancial aspects of these organizations. Such specialists would have to be well versed in both nonprofit accounting standards and nonaccounting program evaluation, but the benefits to the donor accountability would be tremendous.

Accuracy of reporting might also be enhanced by required audits of Forms 990. Nonprofit financial statements are frequently audited, but these are not publicly available. Form 990 is publicly available, but an audit of the Form is not required. An audit of the public form is likely to increase the accountability of filers with their constituencies.

What about timeliness of reporting? The Donor had no way of knowing it, but the assessments he read at GuideStar and Charity Navigator were based on Forms 990 that were three years old. Part of the time lag problem lies in the long leash that the IRS gives nonprofits in extending their deadline for filing an annual form, but more of it lies in the processing time required by the IRS, GuideStar, NCCS, and various watchdog groups to scan forms, distribute them through a reporting bureaucracy, and make assessments. Currently, most nonprofit organizations file their annual Form 990 with the IRS by amassing a pile of attachments and sending them to a central processing repository in Utah. While the process of filing individual and business tax forms has developed substantially in the past ten years, the regulatory environment for nonprofits has not created the same need for electronic filing of Forms 990. However, several forces are converging to create pressure for this need. First, as noted repeatedly throughout this chapter, individual givers are increasingly relying on the information in Forms 990 for making charitable giving decisions. Consequently, the demand for timely, accurate information will bring pressure on the data collections and aggregation process. Second, the number of charities continues to increase without attendant increases in IRS resources to police the nonprofit sector.

Electronic filing of Forms 990 will remove many of the steps that slow down the process of making the information in Forms 990 available to the public. Although the IRS is unlikely to shorten its reporting deadlines or remove the opportunities for extensions, electronic filing means that the tedious process of scanning and re-keypunching relevant fields will be eliminated. Since the information submitted by organizations will already be in electronic form, the time between submission and public scrutiny will narrow. Potential donors will get relevant information sooner. Whether this translates into better giving decisions remains to be seen. However, the lag between spending and public reporting of financial documents puts discerning donors in a poor position: They are making their assessments based on old information. More timely information gives donors the opportunity to make more honest assessments of an organization's worthiness for their charitable dollars. Electronic filing is an incremental change whose time has come, and we should expect its implementation in the coming years.

However, improved quality and timely access to financial reports will not answer the question of whether we should be using such information as our primary benchmark of the quality and donation-worthiness of charities. Financial information is an important dimension of a nonprofit organization's viability just as it is for business corporations, but donors and researchers alike receive only a partial picture of nonprofits when they look exclusively at the bottom line.

Part 3

Philanthropy and Volunteerism: New Practices

7

Inside Venture Philanthropy

Peter Frumkin

Discontent within organized philanthropy today runs deep in many quarters. For years, leaders in the philanthropic world have worried about the effectiveness of their work. Although the amount of money given away each year continues to rise, there are lingering doubts about what the billions of dollars backed by good intentions have ultimately produced. Of course, almost all foundations, corporations, federated funders, and major individual donors can point to some grants that have led to impressive results. It remains very difficult, however, to see how the many small and isolated success stories of donors around the country aggregate up into anything vaguely resembling a meaningful response to any of the major social problems—be it economic development in the inner city, access to health care, reduction in youth violence, or reform of public schools—that private philanthropy has long targeted.

Amid rising doubts about the impact of philanthropy's diverse and diluted efforts, many ideas have emerged about how the field might be strengthened. Some foundations have, for example, abandoned categorical grantmaking in fields such as education, health, and human services in favor of a geographical focus on a few specific communities (Showalter 1998). Other donors have fled from the limitations of direct service grantmaking in favor of a focus on changing public policy through public information campaigns, advocacy work, and ballot initiatives, all with the hope of seeing major change happen through politics and policy (Ostrander 1995; Collins, Rogers, and Garner 2000). Still other donors have sought to create funding collaboratives in order to pool resources and act in a coordinated way (McCaffrey 2002). Many of these ideas have been developed for and applied to the fields in which the need for broad system-wide change has forced donors to look for ways to increase the impact of their giving.

While efforts to increase effectiveness have proceeded apace (McIlnay 1998; Orosz 2000), it is fair to say that no idea for advancing the field of philanthropy has gotten more attention over the past five years than that of venture philanthropy (Letts, Ryan, and Grossman 1997; Morino Institute 2001). What exactly is venture philanthropy? What makes it different from traditional philanthropy? What innovations has it introduced into the field? To begin to answer these questions, it is important to step back for a moment to consider the political and intellectual context within which the idea of venture philanthropy emerged.

The Investment Metaphor

Over the past decade, two broad developments, one in business, the other in politics, have quietly elevated the word "investment" to new heights. The 1990s saw the rise of Silicon Valley and the vast fortunes that were made by the creators of new Internet and computer hardware and software companies. The technological revolution that was ushered in by these new upstart firms gave the old practice of venture capital investing fresh exposure and currency. The capital flows that fueled the high-tech boom came from a relatively small group of firms, many located in California, that brought to their work a set of practices designed to increase the odds of success for their young and often inexperienced investees. These practices included heavy amounts of due diligence during the screening process, long-term financial commitments designed to overcome the problem of undercapitalization that cripples many start-up firms, and extensive advice and consulting on how to develop and manage the new company. The ultimate goal of this investment process was to build large companies from scratch, take them through an initial public offering in as short a time as possible, and for all sides to make large amounts of money in the process (Lerner 2000).

The powerful pull of the investment approach to achieving results was impossible to confine to business and soon entered the political arena. Starting with the presidential campaign in 1991, the Democrats shifted the language of their party's policy arguments in a distinctive way. Rather than call for higher taxes and more spending, the rhetoric of the Democratic campaign, repeated constantly and consistently, was about the necessity of greater "contributions" to make possible higher levels of "social investments." Of course, the contemplated investments in education and health care were nothing other than greater levels of spending in longstanding domestic health and education programs. But the change in language ushered in by the New Democrats was significant: It represented a repudiation of the idea of wasteful government, and the rise of a new tougher, more savvy fiscal policy, one that would take a more rigorous, businesslike approach to public problems by making "critical infrastructure investments" that were capable of generating social returns.

The rhetoric of the New Democrats and the practices of Silicon Valley were ultimately wed together in the field of philanthropy, and the result is what is now generally termed venture philanthropy. It was a marriage made in heaven, in that sophisticated donors have long sought to turn their gifts and grants into something more concrete and scientific. Rather than simply being a purveyor of charitable funds for deserving organizations of all sorts, venture philanthropy promised to turn donors into hard-nosed social investors by bringing the discipline of the investment world to a field that had for over a century relied on good faith and trust. Two major differences still separated the new philanthropic investors from their government and business counterparts: (1) While government was able to make social investments that affected millions of people through the funding of entitlement programs, philanthropy searched for enough resources to have a major impact. (2) While business firms had a clear way of determining whether their investments pay off, namely return on investment, philanthropy struggled to develop performance measurement tools to assess the impact of grants. The search for solutions to the problems of impact and measurement have been at the center of the conversation about venture philanthropy, as the approach has taken hold and begun to spread, especially among younger donors who have made their money through entrepreneurship. The attempt to transfer wisdom across sectors galvanized a small group of individual and foundations donors who have now declared themselves to be "venture philanthropists."

Venture philanthropy's approach and language have penetrated the private and community foundation world, the small giving circles and clubs that help guide new donors, and the territory of corporate philanthropy. The idea of turning philanthropy into social investing has been tried in a whole host of fields, such as early childhood health, environmental protection, and community development, to name just a few. However, one of the most popular fields for venture philanthropy efforts has been K–12 education. Many businesspeople see the failure of large parts of the public school system as a crisis that has the potential to erode America's long-term economic growth potential. The challenge of getting public schools to perform better has been taken up by many of the high-tech entrepreneurs who have shown an affinity for the venture philanthropy model and for education reforms across the country (Finn and Amis 2001).

It is difficult to pinpoint the exact size of the venture philanthropy movement today, though recent surveys have variously estimated that there are some forty institutional funders committed to the approach, investing around $60 million a year. Although venture philanthropy remains small today, particularly when compared to the total $200 billion given away each year by all donors, its influence is considerable (Morino Institute 2001). It has been the subject of growing media attention and the profile of its early practitioners has risen within the field. Most significantly, several of the largest private

foundations have recently begun to experiment with the language and practices of venture philanthropy. Because of the powerful appeal of the metaphor on which it rests, it is critical to understand what the approach has to
offer philanthropy.

Getting to Scale

When one considers the roster of America's largest nonprofit organizations, one fact imposes itself immediately. Most of the organizations on the
list have been on the scene for decades or more: The American Red Cross, the
Salvation Army, and the largest private universities and hospitals all have
long and distinguished histories that are testament to the significance of their
missions and the strength of their reputations (Bremner 1988). The list does
raise at least one troubling question, however. Why have so few nonprofit
organizations of more recent vintage achieved scale? In asking this question,
venture philanthropy starts with the tenets that size matters in the nonprofit
sector, that achieving it is a sign of success and relevance, and that creating
organizations that go to scale is a legitimate and worthy goal for philanthropy. These basic commitments are grounded in the belief that philanthropic funds need to be applied to important social problems and that donors
must strive to maximize the public benefits of their giving. Faced with the
threat of irrelevance or invisibility, venture philanthropy has consciously
declared that getting tangible results—and getting them on broad scale—is a
central task of philanthropy.

To achieve scale, venture philanthropy has sought to move beyond the
tired idea of program expansion through government replication. For many
years, philanthropy has relied on the rather optimistic assumption that government would replicate successful nonprofit programs. In fact, the hope that
government would extend many philanthropically funded efforts gave rise to
a cottage industry in "pilot programs" and "demonstration efforts" aimed at
attracting the attention of government, which was in a position, in principle
at least, to place large amounts of money behind these fledgling ideas. Unfortunately, the list of nonprofit projects that were ever brought to scale by
government is short, and growing shorter every year as discretionary funds
available for new initiatives shrink at all levels of government (MacDonald
2000; Streeter 2001).

In place of wishful thinking about government replication, venture philanthropy has sought to build into the philanthropic process a surer way to
achieve scale. The nonprofits chosen by venture philanthropists for support
are assisted in their efforts to construct and execute strategic plans that will
lead to substantial growth and broad social impact. These plans are often
anchored in a franchise model in which a programmatic idea is packaged and
made available to other social entrepreneurs either through autonomous units

or through affiliated entities. In seeking to take control of the diffusion and expansion process rather than simply pass it off to government, venture philanthropy draws on many of the ideas and practices of corporate strategy focused on growing companies. A critical element of any effort aimed at scale is refining the underlying service model until it is fully developed, tested, and debugged. Only after this process is complete can the model be extended to multiple new sites (Conservation Company 1994).

A different idea for getting to scale has also emerged. It focuses not on building a model that is ripe for replication, but instead on building a powerful organization with a steady revenue stream behind it that can drive internal growth (Anderson, Dees, and Emerson 2002). Some venture philanthropists have focused on building the capacity within nonprofit organizations to design and deliver services for which there is a paying client waiting to consume the service. However, the problem with any nonprofit model that is built on a base of earned income is simple: Even when the fee schedule is a sliding one, commercialism limits the ability of the organization to reach disadvantaged populations that may not be in a position to pay. Thus, in its place some funders have looked at ways of helping nonprofits operate independent, nonmission-related ventures that generate revenue capable of giving nonprofits the funds they need to grow. No matter whether the earned revenue is generated by the programs or by the unrelated business activity, this approach to getting to scale is fraught with at least a little danger since it requires that nonprofits do more than simply charitable work: It requires that nonprofits also show enough entrepreneurial instinct to succeed in breaking even or even turning a profit that can be used to subsidize the mission of the organization.

Getting to scale either through franchising or commercialism requires a different kind of financial support than is usually provided by donors. Venture philanthropy has therefore developed tools that are aimed at increasing the likelihood of success. At its core, venture philanthropy can best be seen as a three-legged stool, each leg of which is seen as a solution to a problem in traditional philanthropy that has impeded nonprofit organizations. First, venture philanthropists believe that large blocks of capital delivered over an extended period of time are needed to build the capacity of nonprofit organizations. Second, these new donors believe that improving nonprofit strategy through management consulting is critical to lasting success. Third, venture philanthropists are committed to the goal of developing new metrics to measure organizational performance or, in their words, the "social return on investment." It is useful to examine each of these three legs—capitalization, engagement, and performance measurement—separately to see just how strong they are and whether they support more effective giving.

A New Form of Funding

From the vantage point of nonprofit service providers, private foundation and corporate donors have long engaged in any number of practices that seem counterproductive and designed only to frustrate grant recipients. High on the nonprofit list of grievances is the move to increasingly narrow circumscribed forms of project support, often delivered for short periods of time, and almost never for general operating support designed to build operational capacity (Orosz 2000; Grace and Wendroff 2001). In a search for greater levels of accountability, many institutional funders have in fact developed a strong preference for project grantmaking, in large part because they believe that these grants can be monitored more actively than unrestricted support. One problem with general operating support is that it has come to be associated with non-essential items like support staff, rent, and other basic operational expenses. Providing funds to cover these overhead expenses is less attractive to many funders because these costs seem extraneous to the core mission and public purposes of nonprofit organizations.

As a consequence, many institutional funders have come to insist on funding projects and activities, not organizations. In recent years, generating operating support has constituted only about 15 percent of all grants (Foundation Center 2000). Much of the rest is being disbursed as project-specific grants. To make matters worse, it is not uncommon for many funders to limit their project support of particular nonprofit organizations to two or three consecutive years. Fearing that they will create a dependence that cannot be sustained indefinitely, traditional institutional funders have settled on a short-term approach to grantmaking that allows them flexibility to change direction quickly should community condition or board interest change. The consequences for nonprofit organizations of this funding pattern have been predictable: financial instability, programmatic uncertainty, and wasted effort, all of which makes the achievement of real scale and impact very difficult.

Venture philanthropy has keyed on this pattern and come forward with a different approach to funding, one that builds on the venture capital model and offers longer term support and larger amounts of unrestricted financial support. Instead of pulling the plug quickly and moving on to fund other organizations, the venture philanthropy model emphasizes long-term funding commitments designed to help organizations develop and grow. Unlike grantmakers that trickle out support in small installments, the venture philanthropist seeks to get into projects with a large initial investment that signals real commitment. In New York, for example, the Robin Hood Foundation, an early venture philanthropy entrant, has long focused on building lasting relationships with the organizations it supports, with some engagements lasting up to a decade. In a few cases, this has translated into very large financial commitments, while in other instances the amounts have been more modest.

By providing large blocks of capacity-building support to nonprofits over longer periods of time, venture philanthropy believes that it will be possible to overcome one of the biggest drawbacks in the nonprofit sector: Namely, the inability of nonprofit organizations to achieve real scale and impact.

Before delivering large blocks of support and committing to an organization over the long haul, the venture philanthropists engage in heavy doses of what they refer to as "due diligence." While it is not entirely clear how this review differs from what all donors have always done (reviewing financial disclosure documents, requiring the presentation of a strategic plan, and the submission to a site visit), the language change is designed to draw attention to the fact that great care needs to be devoted to the decision-making process leading to a commitment. In making the choice of which organizations will be supported, venture philanthropy groups, like New Profit Inc., view the ability of a nonprofit organization to achieve scale as a critical consideration. New Profit's long-term investments have focused on organizations like Jumpstart, a pre kindergarten program designed to help disadvantaged children get ready for school, which has plans to open sites in fifteen cities around the country.

One of the most visible efforts to apply business know-how to the reform of public schools is being undertaken by John Doerr, the Palo Alto venture capitalist. In 1998, Doerr founded the New Schools Venture Fund (NSVF) with the intention of providing seed capital for promising new for-profit and nonprofit organizations that had the potential to bring movement in the public education field. In choosing organizations to fund, Doerr applies a clear set of criteria. He seeks to support organizations that have strong leadership and that could have a direct impact on school achievement. What made his approach different was that he also insisted that the organizations that would receive support had to have a concept that could be brought to scale. Like any business investor, Doerr assembled a team of partners who invested in the fund. In all, some $20 million will be used to fund both nonprofit and for-profit initiatives. NSVF's early nonprofit investments included a comprehensive online guide to California public schools, both nonprofit and for-profit charter school management organizations, a school leadership training program, and a math curriculum development effort. On the for-profit side, NSVF invested in a network of charter schools operated by a business firm in New York. NSVF's approach to school reform continues to reflect a distinctive application of the venture philanthropy model. Drawing on the talents of a group of exceptionally successful entrepreneurs and CEOs, the Fund has developed its own idea about getting to scale: Beyond funding organizations that have real potential for growth and impact, NSVF also works to build a network of school reformers through which innovations and ideas can spread. Thus, NSVF both invests and convenes with the aim of maximizing the impact of its investees and moving them to scale quickly.

Because it draws on the business methods of venture capital, NSVF is willing to make a small number of large bets. After making these bets, the Fund stays with the organizations that are funded for an extended period of time, assuming the organizations can demonstrate progress and results. Investments made by NSVF range between $200,000 and $1 million. Sometimes, the efforts that are funded succeed, such as the ballot initiative backed by Roberts that pushed the California legislature to preemptively allocate billions of dollars for charter schools. Other times, big investments have not paid off so well: Advantage Schools, one of NSVF's for-profit portfolio organizations, has struggled to hold on to its public school contracts and was recently taken over by another firm. Nevertheless, NSVF's investments represent calculated gambles to achieve real impact and scale in a field like school reform, in which small projects hold little promise of changing the performance of large numbers of public schools.

Of venture philanthropy's three legs, the idea that nonprofits need larger and longer forms of support is certainly the strongest. Whether venture philanthropy has truly made good on its commitment to building strong organizations with the capacity to grow is another matter entirely. To date, many of the grants made by venture philanthropy funds have been relatively small owing to the fact that resources in these funds are very limited. In fact, all of the biggest gifts in recent years, including several hundred-million dollar gifts to universities, were all made independently of the venture philanthropy mantra. Thus, while providing major blocks of capital aimed at taking nonprofits to scale is a good idea, it is not an original one.

Consultative Engagement

In its effort to reengineer the mainstream model of philanthropy and reorient it toward achieving impact on a broad scale, venture philanthropy has also focused on changing the relationship between the funder and the recipient. Looking at the way many institutional and individual donors carry out their giving, the proponents of venture philanthropy observed that a tremendous amount of effort was being sunk into the process of selecting grant recipients, and very little effort was being devoted to helping nonprofit organizations succeed once the check was sent. Indeed, in many foundations, there is today very little follow-up or consultation between the two sides from the time the grant check is mailed to the time the final report on activities is due. One reason that most of the effort of philanthropy is directed at decision making about grants, not at effective implementation, is that there is real pressure on funders to be transparent, fair, and accountable for their actions. Given these demands, it is hardly surprising that many institutional funders have little time for anything other than careful review of applications, site visits before board meetings, and the writing of recommendations for the board. As grant cycles roll around and around, it can in fact be very hard for funders to break this cycle and engage with recipient organizations in a sustained relationship (Dowie 2001).

Venture philanthropy takes a different approach to donor-recipient or investor-investee relations, one that extends the time horizon and deepens the contact between all parties. Rather than cut a check and run, venture philanthropy believes that the work only begins once a financial commitment has been made. Given that the commitment is intended to be a long-term one, the new funders have set out to connect directly with the organizations in their portfolios. There are two perceived benefits to a high engagement strategy. First, nonprofits may learn something that they do not know already, especially if the consulting that is rendered involves specialized skills not usually found in nonprofits. At New Profit Inc., grant recipients receive hands-on assistance from the management consulting giant Monitor Group. Working with organizations that have received money from New Profit, Monitor's team of consultants assists with planning growth and tracking progress. For organizations such as Citizen Schools, an after-school program that uses adult volunteers to teach real-world teenagers skills through creative projects, this added service is intended to increase the likelihood that the organization will continue to flourish and grow. In lending the expertise of a management consulting firm to their investees, funders are both attempting to protect their investments and to increase the social benefits that are achieved. Beyond consulting advice, the investor can also provide nonprofits with useful connections: The New Schools Venture Fund explains that, "Our hands-on approach goes far beyond providing capital. It includes matching board members, recruiting management team members, consulting, and linking education entrepreneurs to a powerful network of peers and new economy resources."

The second perceived benefit of a consultative and engaged relationship has little to do with nonprofit performance, and has everything to do with the satisfaction of the donor. High engagement philanthropy is a social activity that satisfies the desire of many wealthy people to find meaning in their lives outside of business. Young entrepreneurs who are active in venture philanthropy enjoy taking a hands-on approach and view the process as one of learning and personal growth. At Social Venture Partners (SVP), one of the earliest venture philanthropy efforts, donors commit a minimum of $5,000 to the fund, and in exchange, they gain firsthand exposure to the nonprofits that SVP funds. Many of the investors in other venture funds get even more involved in the organizations they fund, either by helping with fundraising or by serving on the board.

There are several assumptions built into the engagement part of the venture philanthropy model: (1) that nonprofit organizations want outside help in strategizing and carrying out their work; (2) that those offering the consulting possess skills missing in the nonprofit world and that nonprofits will run better once they have been exposed to these tools and models; and (3) that engagement is ethical and appropriate in philanthropy. All three assumptions can reasonably be questioned.

First, several foundations that have surveyed their recipients discovered that nonprofit managers complain the process of working closely with a funder is draining and does not always add value to their work. As one might expect, the generally tense relationship between benefactor and supplicant is hard to transform into a balanced working relationship. Faced with the prospect of a relationship with the donor, many nonprofits view a no-strings attached check as the best form of support. Many nonprofit managers believe that they are in the best position to know how funds can most effectively be deployed, not a funder lacking field experience.

Second, when it comes to the skills of high engagement grantmakers, there is no clear evidence that the people who control capital in the business sector or those with expertise in business management have any special claim on knowledge about how to create a successful nonprofit organization. Nonprofit mission fulfillment does not always equate to satisfying the demands of clients or to responding quickly to market trends. Sometimes, nonprofits need to lead by offering services for which there is little immediate support, but that nevertheless speak to important, if overlooked, social needs. Creating and sustaining effective programs may be closer to an art than a science, and managerial lessons learned in the business world may not always be relevant and appropriate in fields in which complex social problems are being addressed.

Finally, in the matter of ethics, many religious teachings related to charity appear to run counter to the precepts of venture philanthropy. A recurring theme across many faiths is that the donor and the recipient need to be separated, preferably through anonymous giving, so that the recipient is not shamed by having to take money directly from someone else. Anonymous giving also promises to ensure that the donor's intent is pure and the gift is aimed to helping others, rather than gratifying oneself. By shielding the recipient from the donor, it is possible to create a transfer that is both practical and moral. Venture philanthropy's response to such objections is predictable: Venture philanthropy is making investments that are different from charity. Because they are given under different initial terms, the moral problems associated with charity do not apply. This is an argument that ultimately rests on semantic hairsplitting, however, and it skirts the reality of the asymmetric power in all forms of philanthropy. Still, venture philanthropy's secular, entrepreneurial turn is ultimately designed to satisfy the current generation of new entrepreneurial donors eager to express themselves through action in the social sphere.

Performance Measurement

Beyond a theory of achieving scale through new forms of financial and consulting support, venture philanthropists distinguish their work by the way they assess results. While all donors want to know whether their grants have an impact and lead to real changes in the world, venture philanthropy has elevated the importance of performance measurement and made it a centerpiece of their approach to giving. At the core of this desire to measure results is a dual commitment to both learn how to improve the programs of investees and how to make better investment decisions in the future. By focusing on assessment, venture philanthropy has hit a nerve in philanthropy. Many donors, particularly those who have made money in business, find the lack of standards and benchmarks in the world of philanthropy particularly troubling. Without good evaluation, giving seemed condemned to an emotive exercise that never asked tough questions about the social benefits produced through philanthropic intervention.

One of the earliest and most visible efforts to construct a performance measurement system for the new venture philanthropy was developed by the Roberts Enterprise Development Fund (REDF), a venture philanthropy fund founded by investor George Roberts of Kohlberg, Kravis, and Roberts fame. For years, REDF has experimented with the use of philanthropy to create social purpose enterprises within nonprofit organizations (REDF 1997a). These enterprises, ranging from a bakery to a janitorial service to a café, employ disadvantaged and untrained workers. The enterprises generate both financial flow for the nonprofits operating them and social benefits in the form of income for the employees who carry out the work. For REDF, there is the added benefit that this kind of philanthropy affords a unique opportunity to measure the impact these enterprises have on both a business and a social bottom line (Emerson 2000). REDF describes its effort at quantification as follows:

> REDF's efforts to calculate the social return on investment (SROI) of its portfolio of social purpose enterprises is one attempt to analyze and describe the impact of these enterprises on the lives of individuals and on the communities in which they live. REDF's approach to calculating SROI includes measuring the tax dollars saved by helping the people who work for REDF portfolio social purpose enterprises reduce their dependency on public assistance, homeless shelters, and other government-supported services (REDF 1997b).

Published in elaborate reports with high-end production values, REDF's publications provide an illuminating perspective on the problem of performance measurement in philanthropy. The "SROI Reports" (1997b) purport to measure the creation of blended value, consisting of enterprise value ("the financial return from the business") and social purpose value ("the monetized public cost savings and taxes generated by the enterprise employees"). Upon closer inspection of the actual data collected and analyzed by REDF, the calculation of SROI turns out to be nothing other than a very straightforward application of cost-benefit analysis, a tool for measuring program impact that has long been used by business managers and government policymakers. By christening cost-benefit analysis "the calculation of Social Return on Investment," REDF has succeeded in giving the venture philanthropy a new language that can appeal to younger donors, no matter that the underlying practices are evaluation techniques popularized in the 1960s.

One of the real problems now vexing venture philanthropy is the fact that the rhetoric of performance measurement has grossly outpaced the reality of performance measurement. While REDF's work on measuring the net benefits of employing disadvantaged persons in enterprises run by nonprofits is often held forth as the venture philanthropy model for quantifying results, it has little relevance for the vast universe of measurement challenges facing the field of philanthropy. For while the income streams of nonprofit business ventures and the employment and income gains of disadvantaged workers can be roughly estimated, there are large parts of the nonprofit programmatic landscape, including advocacy efforts, symphony orchestra performances, and faith-based counseling programs aimed at promoting family unity, to name just a few examples, for which no simple monetary measures are possible. Dreams of measuring SROI "at the push of a button" are rendered ever more distant by the reality that most social programs and initiatives do not operate in isolation from a multitude of other social and economic forces all affecting the ultimate client outcomes (REDF 1997b). Truly disentangling the programmatic effects and quantifying these effects requires an experimental approach to evaluation—built around researching the difference between control and treatment groups—that is time consuming and extremely expensive. While philanthropy could certainly benefit from more rigorous evaluations, it is not clear that the rhetoric of SROI introduced by venture philanthropy moves the assessment task forward in a productive way.

Beyond the problems of applying existing assessment tools, there is at least one huge assumption built into the performance measurement component of the venture philanthropy model, namely, that quantitative measures of social return on investment are worth trying to develop because they would advance and improve the field of philanthropy (Sievers 1997). To date, there is little evidence to support this assumption. Most of the efforts at building metrics for assessing the return of philanthropic investments have been primitive. The clearest evidence that the measurement of social return remains elusive is the continual rise of alternative assessment concepts and tools. In fact, much of the talk of performance measurement in venture philanthropy has now quietly slid into a conversation about "outcome measurements" that have little to do with measuring social return and everything to do with simply setting expectations and tracking programmatic progress. To carry out this modified objective, many venture philanthropists use tools such as the Balanced Scorecard (Kaplan and Norton 1996), a broad organizational assessment tool, and avoid too much detail when talking about the "return rate" of their funds.

Perhaps the clearest example of the loose connection between the use of the language of social return and the reality of true measurement can be found in the newly formed Chicago Public Education Fund (CPEF), which has set out to apply the venture philanthropy model to the problem of improving Chicago's public schools. Using business jargon to describe all of its activities, CPEF is seeking to raise some $10 million in local funding to support investments in programs aimed at recruiting a new cadre of school teachers and developing alternative routes to certification, creating a culture of professionalism in the school through programs that pay talented teachers to serve as mentors, and locating and training new talent to meet a shortage in school principals. The three main elements of CPEF are all directed at human resource problems within the school system and do not shy away from providing large blocks of capital to the Chicago Teacher's Union and to the Chicago Public Schools administration. Like some other venture philanthropy efforts, CPEF promises a new approach to philanthropy, one that emphasizes results and measurement. However, all the social returns that the Fund trumpets are described in terms of narrow, short-term outcomes, such as the training of two hundred teachers or the recruitment of thirty principals. These targets are no different from the goals and expectations that all the mainstream funders in Chicago have long established for their grantees. The only difference is the construction of an elaborate semantic superstructure.

On the larger issue of whether greater levels of performance measurement are really desirable, philanthropic taste enters the picture. To be sure, there are many donors who approach their giving with the intention of maximizing impact and the social value of nonprofit activity. There are, however, few clear ways to separate out subjective determinations of social value from objective ones. After all, the public's interpretation of public priorities has only gotten progressively more contentious in recent years and certainly not tended toward consensus. Lacking basic agreement about the meaning of socially valuable activities and a hierarchy for ranking them, it is hard to see how any project aimed at measuring ground level social return can be anything but a highly subjective and personal project, especially when philanthropy reaches into contentious areas of social problems. While many donors legitimately want some sort of evidence that their giving is making a difference, it is not clear that seeking to translate this difference into monetary terms will improve philanthropic practice in the long run.

Translating Venture Philanthropy

As more and more venture philanthropy funds come on line and as increasing numbers of donors reinvent themselves as social investors, it is important to pause and ask about the underlying coherence of this model. A chief driver behind this popular trend is the honest desire of donors, especially young entrepreneurs turned donors, to see social change happen as a result of their giving. Many of these young donors are very interested in public school reform and want to use their philanthropy to make a difference. The language and the metaphors used by venture philanthropy speak to deep-seated desires of these new donors to have an impact and measure the effects of their philanthropy. It is a language that can be obtuse at times, however. To help clarify the new terminology that venture philanthropy has spawned, table 7.1 provides a simple translation of many of the key terms.

Table 7.1
Venture Philanthropy Terminology

Venture Philanthropy Term	Translation
Investment	Grant
Investor	Donor
Social return	Impact
Performance measurement	Evaluation
Benchmarking	Standard setting
Due diligence	Grant review process
Consultative engagement	Technical assistance
Investment portfolio	Grant list

To date, venture philanthropy remains something of an unfulfilled promise. To truly make good on the new language created by venture philanthropy, important breakthroughs in practices are needed to create real distance between venture philanthropy and traditional giving. For now, it is very difficult to find authentic innovations that justify the new terms that have been introduced. Many of the investments made by venture philanthropists look just like the grants made by other donors. The best evidence of this fact is that many of the organizations supported by venture philanthropists regularly receive grant support from mainline philanthropic funders. In fact, only a few of the most high profile venture philanthropy investments represent substantial portions of the operating budgets of the nonprofit organizations on the receiving end. Similarly, the idea of "consultative engagement" that many describe as a trademark of venture philanthropy is hard to distinguish from the multiple forms of "technical assistance" that donors have provided to nonprofits for decades. Across many of the other terminological divides, the underlying practices do not appear significantly different from what has come before. The most egregious breaches of clear thinking have been in the area of evaluation, in which a rhetoric of measurement and return has far outpaced the practices that venture philanthropy has developed to date. Amidst all this confusion, there is at least one contribution that venture philanthropy has made to the field. It has created powerful discussion networks and social ties between new donors, and this is a positive development.

Conclusion

In the end, the excitement and energy created by the language of venture philanthropy have brought new people into the world of philanthropy who are being converted to the pleasures and challenges of trying to create public value. For those committed to public school reform, the desire of many venture philanthropists to do something about the performance of public education must be viewed as positive. At the core, venture philanthropy's search for new philanthropic tools has enlivened the field. After all, the problems of traditional philanthropy are clear and undeniable.

There is nevertheless something troubling about the frenzy of verbiage that has accompanied the movement. Although only a few critics have, to date, pointed to the holes in the venture philanthropy industry, time will tell how durable the business metaphor ultimately will prove to be. For now, one result is impossible to deny: By seeking to move concepts and language from the world of business to the world of nonprofit organizations, venture philanthropy must be viewed as a marketing triumph. As a set of practical philanthropic innovations, however, venture philanthropy's contribution to the field remains far harder to ascertain.

8

Charity and Philanthropy After September 11th

Peter Frumkin

The events of September 11th created tremendous human needs that called for an extraordinary response. While government agencies at the federal, state, and local levels moved quickly to respond, the first funds to reach those in need came from private sources. The philanthropic response on the part of private donors to the September 11th attacks was enormous and immediate. One survey reported that charities raising funds for September 11th relief and recovery efforts had collected at least $1.8 billion in cash and distributed $955 million by February 7, 2002, with the balance to follow. This massive outpouring of caring did more than demonstrate the speed with which private giving can react to public needs. It showed that simple, old-fashioned charity, governed by caring and compassion, still has a place within a landscape of giving dominated by modern philanthropy and geared toward complex interventions and social experiments.

The Foundation, Corporate, and Individual Response

Major private assistance following September 11th came from private philanthropic foundations, corporations, and individual donors. A total of 143 private foundations had, as of February, pledged or donated $185 million to relief and recovery efforts—for an average of just about $1.3 million per foundation. Most gifts were in the range of $10,000 to $200,000. The largest donations, all over $10 million, came from Atlantic Philanthropies, Carnegie Corporation of New York, Ford Foundation, Lilly Endowment, Andrew W. Mellon Foundation, and Starr Foundation. The September 11th Fund, one of the main charities created after the disaster to receive contributions, and the American Red Cross were the main beneficiaries of foundation grants, although a number of small specialized charities also received funding. Some foundations gave to specific types of organizations that fell within the purview of their respective missions. The Robert Wood Johnson Foundation, for example, gave $5.3 million to NYC-area health-care organizations that had been disrupted by the attack, and the Lumina Foundation for Education established a $3-million scholarship fund for children of attack victims.

Two things are notable about these foundation grants. The first is that they represent very large and open-ended commitments for institutions that all too often make smaller, targeted grants in support of clearly circumscribed projects. Clearly, the needs created by all the destruction changed the usual scale of foundation action and called forth very sizable and unrestricted grants, which in many cases were well outside the established grantmaking guidelines of many of the foundations. The second reason these foundation grants are significant relates to the way in which they were made. These donations broke down procedural conventions within foundations. Instead of going through proposal review and evaluation by staff, the standard operating procedures of foundations were largely abandoned so that funds could be delivered quickly. Many of the largest foundation grants were triggered by trustees, not professional staff. In this sense, the disaster funders broke through some long-standing procedural boundaries that vested grantmaking control in the hands of staff and left trustees with broader strategic duties, allowing foundations in this moment of need to act decisively.

Corporations stepped forward to offer their support following September 11th, making gifts both directly and through their corporate foundations. A total of 543 corporations had, as of February 7th, pledged or donated $621 million to relief and recovery efforts—for an average of $1.14 million per corporation. In some cases, both the corporate and foundation arms of companies gave money to relief and recovery efforts. Such was the case with Fannie Mae and the Fannie Mae Foundation. Most corporate gifts were in the range of $25,000 to $200,000, but there was a significant number of multimillion dollar gifts. The largest donations included those from Coca-Cola Company ($12 million), Deutsche Bank ($13 million), ExxonMobil ($15.25 million), Pfizer/Pfizer Foundation ($10.5 million), and Verizon Foundation ($13 million) (Renz 2002).

These corporate contributions were distinctive in that they broke with some of the standard operating procedures of corporate giving. While corporations traditionally view their giving as aligned with and supporting the core business functions, such as sales, marketing, and government relations, the gifts generated by the events of September 11th were made largely free of the usual "give and take" of corporate philanthropy, in which companies demand and get plenty of "return" for their giving. Because of the unique circumstances, few corporations sought to reap self-interested advantage from their citizenship work following the tragedy. In this sense, the disaster brought forth a purer and more disinterested form of corporate giving than is usually seen, one animated by a desire to offer support regardless of the bottom line.

Although foundations and corporations stepped forward to make significant contributions, individual donors played a central role in the mobilization of the philanthropic response. Individuals gave money, blood, material goods, and volunteer time in the wake of September 11th, with a total value of over $1 billion. According to a survey done two months after the disaster, 66 percent of Americans said they gave money to support attack victims and their families, with an average donation of $134, and a median donation of $50 (The Center on Philanthropy 2002). Another study conducted found that 70 percent of Americans reported some form of charitable involvement in response to September 11th, and that 58 percent gave a financial contribution (Independent Sector 2002).

Not all the philanthropy was in the form of cash contributions. Donations of blood surged in the wake of September 11th. Nationally, blood donations ran some three to five times higher than usual in the days immediately following the attacks, according to the New York Blood Center. The American Red Cross received close to 1.2 million units of blood between September 11th and October 30th, as compared to the 380,000 units the organization estimates it would have received during the same period of time. However, the organization learned within just twenty-four hours of the disaster that blood needs were minimal, because most of the victims were killed in the attacks. Donations of material goods also poured in following the attacks, though no government or other agency has formally tracked such donations. Among the items donated were canned goods, toiletries, teddy bears, and clothing. The usefulness of in-kind gifts left something to be desired, however: Donations coordinators at the Federal Emergency Management Agency reported that only a portion of the goods donated—somewhere between 30 percent and 50 percent—reached their intended recipients, namely, those directly affected by the attacks. The remainder of the donations were distributed to needy people not directly affected by the attacks (Barstow and Henriques 2002).

Beyond giving blood and material goods, individuals across the country also stepped forward and gave their time to the relief effort. One study found that 8.3 percent of those surveyed indicated they performed voluntary service to help the victims of the tragedy, at an average of seventeen hours of total volunteer time. While this number might seem small, it is actually significant given that many volunteers had to travel to areas where volunteers were needed, that the actual disaster sites were highly restricted in terms of access, and that volunteering was actually discouraged except in cases where people possessed specialized technical or medical skills. The outpouring of volunteerism has led some to predict that the social capital created by the disaster will translate into a more sustained culture of volunteerism in the future. Soon after the tragedy, President Bush proposed that a "USA Freedom Corps" program be created, which would expand Americorps, the National Senior Service Corps, and the Peace Corps, and establish a new citizen corps to support "homeland security" in the future. This effort and others at the local level have all sought to capture and channel the powerful impulse to help that was unleashed.

The Emergence of Relief Funds

The capacity to give and help must be joined with a capacity to receive. Relief funds needed to be created in the aftermath of the September 11th attacks to allow the philanthropic impulse to be translated into concrete action. These funds included a small group of large and visible charities that quickly provided a channel for foundation, corporate, and individual contributions. The three largest recipients of contributions—the Liberty Disaster Relief Fund, the September 11th Fund, and the Twin Towers Fund—all shared one thing in common. They were backed by old and respected organizations that had the public's confidence and trust. In a period of great uncertainty and trouble, it was necessary for the major recipients of relief funds to be above reproach and have the capacity to translate contributions quickly and efficiently into caring and assistance.

From the outset, the American Red Cross received enormous donations. It moved quickly to establish a separate fund, the Liberty Disaster Relief Fund, to benefit those directly affected by the attacks. The Fund soon raised over $500 million to be used for immediate disaster relief, the cash needs of families that lost at least one wage-earner in the attacks, and direct support costs. On September 25, 2001, the American Red Cross announced the first significant, mass transfer of donations to the families of those dead or missing at the World Trade Center and the Pentagon. These grants took the form of lump-sum grants of up to $30,000 each. These payments were intended to cover three months of living expenses, based on familial estimates of existing expenses.

The September 11th Fund was established by The New York Community Trust and by United Way of New York City "to meet the immediate and longer-term needs of victims, families and communities affected by the terrorist attacks of September 11th." A second related fund, the September 11th Telethon Fund, was established from proceeds from the television appeal, "America: A Tribute to Heroes," broadcast on the major television networks and dedicated to helping victims and their families. As of February, the two efforts had raised $456 million, and made grants totaling $204 million to families and local service organizations. Both funds operate as the September 11th Fund with a single board and staff. Of the total funds disbursed, 85 percent went to victims and families in the form of cash assistance and free health and counseling services for victims, 7 percent went to community organizations to help them provide services and assistance to the affected neighborhoods, and 1 percent was devoted to rescue and recovery expense reimbursements. In mid-January, the Fund publicly discouraged any more new gifts, and urged donors to send contributions to other organizations serving people not directly affected by the attacks (September 11th Fund 2002).

The Twin Towers Fund was established and is administered by the New York City Mayor's Office. It raised $148 million for the families of victims who were members of the New York City Fire Department and its Emergency Medical Services Command, the New York City Police Department, the Port Authority of New York and New Jersey, and other government workers who were injured or killed in the attacks on the World Trade Center. The Fund also agreed to pay benefits to twenty-eight civilian rescue workers, including six emergency workers for private ambulance companies, thirteen Port Authority employees, a Secret Service agent, and an FBI agent, who all died assisting the rescue effort during the attack.

Many other organizations channeled funds and services to relief and recovery efforts. The International Association of Fire Fighters (IAFF) created the New York Fire Fighters 9-11 Disaster Relief Fund to support the families of firefighters killed in the attacks. The Fund raised $132 million. The New York Times 9/11 Neediest Fund, established to help the poorest of those directly affected by the attacks, received $52 million in donations. The American Society for the Prevention of Cruelty to Animals (ASPCA) Disaster Relief Fund secured $1.7 million in gifts to provide rescue assistance, medical treatment, and homes for pets whose owners were killed or were missing as a result of the attacks. Catholic Charities USA established the Terrorist Attack Relief Fund, for which it has raised $27 million to help victims and their families, recovery workers, and others affected by the attacks, through financial assistance and social services. The Salvation Army raised $77 million for the National Disaster Fund, Operation Noble Eagle, and Operation Compassion Under Fire to help victims and their families pay for basic needs, such as housing, utilities, food, and transportation. The Robin Hood Relief Fund, a fund of the Robin Hood Foundation in New York City, garnered $53 million in contributions in support of low-income victims of the September 11th attacks and their families. Other funds were established to provide scholarships for the children of victims and for a range of additional purposes.

While pooled funds of various kinds were the main vehicle of choice of donors, the acts of terrorism brought forth at least one major philanthropic surprise: Internet-based fundraising was unusually successful, particularly in the first few weeks following September 11th. Roughly 10 percent of all the early giving came in through the Internet. Large and small organizations realized major successes. The American Red Cross reported that it had received $60 million in online donations within two weeks of the attacks, or nearly 30 percent of the total $211 million it raised during that period. The organization's director of online giving estimated that traffic on the organization's Web site on the day of September 11th increased fifty-fold over its normal levels. The September 11th Fund had raised $8 million online out of a total $120 million raised by the end of September. Catholic Charities USA raised $300,000 online by the end of September, out of a total $1 million by the same date. The organization's total online fundraising for all of 2000 was $75,000. The Salvation Army raised more than $1.6 million online, out of a total of $21 million raised by October 4th.

Prior to September 11th, many viewed Internet fundraising as an underachiever that had only produced modest results while imposing substantial technical costs. The most money any charitable organization had raised online in the past was $2.7 million, a record set by the Red Cross during 1999, and fueled by donations for relief efforts in Kosovo. After the attacks, Americans turned to the Internet to channel their compassion and giving at a surprising rate. One possible explanation for this lies in the nature of a crisis and the desire for immediate action that it brings with it. Donors used the Internet to give in record numbers because it represented a fast and efficient way to give, once the decision to give had already been reached. Many donors gave online not because they saw a banner advertisement or a call for money, but because they were looking for a simple way to fulfill a charitable decision that had already been made. Donors used the Internet to give because they knew which organizations they wanted to help and where to reach them quickly. Despite the overwhelming success of online giving immediately following the attacks, Internet donations dropped off considerably in the following months. While the Red Cross had raised $60 million via online donations in September, the organization took in just $2 million online during the first two weeks of October. Thus, while the Internet was a potent source for channeling the first wave of compassion, its relevance diminished with time as the vast majority of donors eventually sought out more traditional means to give such as by mailing a check or calling a telethon or an organization.

Emerging Tensions

For all the success of the relief efforts in mobilizing support for victims, difficult questions emerged about what role private philanthropy should play in disaster and, more importantly, how private efforts should be organized. Given the size and range of the private philanthropic response to September 11th, it was inevitable that a number of issues, controversies, and criticisms would arise in regard to the collection, administration, and disbursement of funds. The main issues broke down into three main categories involving: (1) the efficiency of the process; (2) the effectiveness of the charitable strategy; and (3) the equity of the results. Concerns about efficiency were connected to questions about the cost and pace at which funds were released, which appeared slow and cumbersome to many. Concerns about effectiveness turned on the question of whether relief funds could be used more usefully for longer-term preparedness and the needs of the communities around the disaster sites. Finally, equity concerns after the attacks were broader and more multifaceted. They included worries about the perceived overcompensation of surviving families of uniformed personnel killed in the attacks, the use of offsets for charity in federal compensation grants, and the potential diminution of support for nondisaster charities.

Efficiency Concerns

In judging the quality of a charitable response, it is important to consider the efficiency with which funds are distributed. Efficiency has at least two main dimensions in the case of disaster relief: speed and cost. On the one hand, donors legitimately want disaster funds to be pushed out the door just as fast as possible so that help quickly gets to those in need. At the same time, the process of disbursing funds needs to be done at a reasonable cost so that most of the charitable resources are directed at the needs of victims, rather than to administrative overhead. Yet, in the case of the response to September 11th, speed was compromised at times, and administrative costs became an awkward issue for several of the relief charities.

Although all the charities strove to respond to needs quickly, the issue of disbursement rate was posed in a pointed way when families began to complain about the pace at which the Twin Towers Fund was assisting families of killed or injured uniformed rescue personnel. This early criticism was addressed by Mayor Rudolph Giuliani, who defended the fund's disbursement pace as necessary for equitable and wise administration. However, at one point, the fund did suspend payments while it awaited a decision from the New York State Attorney General on whether control of the fund might be transferred from the Mayor's Office to a nonprofit organization that would be headed by Giuliani. According to the Mayor, many donors said from the start that they wanted Giuliani to remain involved in the Fund's administration, even after his term as Mayor ended. Still, this proposal to create a new nonprofit entity was nevertheless criticized by families of attack victims as being too bureaucratic and slow.

The Twin Towers Fund also was criticized for spending too much on administrative overhead. To support this charge, the families of victims pointed to the minimal administrative costs of the comparatively large fund established by the International Association of Fire Fighters, which managed to keep administrative expenses low. However, the Mayor's Office countered that administrative expenses would be donated, and that salaries would constitute only about 1 percent of the total budget. Other relief funds soon had to contend with calls for low overhead rates, and several of the major relief organizations were led to promise that no donations would be used for administration and that overhead expenses would be raised separately. While all donors want their funds to reach the needy, the public debate over appropriate overhead costs never fully came to terms with the fact that almost all charity involves at least a small amount of overhead, especially when intermediary organizations are working to connect donors to recipients. Instead of an honest and realistic discussion of what these costs should be, the public debate degenerated into a series of promises and claims that proved difficult to fulfill.

With so many relief efforts and funds operating, a different kind of efficiency concern surfaced, one connected to the overall coordination of efforts. To improve the efficiency of the disbursement process overall, some in government believed that it was essential to coordinate and track cash awards and services, so as to avoid duplication of effort, wastefulness, and even potentially fraud. The discussion over coordination started soon after September 11th. Within two weeks of the attacks, the New York State Attorney General proposed that all names of relief aid recipients and amounts received be listed in a central database (Bjorklund 2002; House 2002). The proposal was criticized by several relief organizations, including the American Red Cross, which contended that such a list would make victims hesitant to come forward for assistance, and violate the privacy of those who did. This proposal was met with support by other charities, including the Salvation Army and the Robin Hood Foundation, which saw it as a tool to improve the operational efficiency of the relief efforts. Other organizations argued that, while coordination was warranted, centralization could—far from simplifying the task at hand—render it more bureaucratic, inefficient, and slow.

Under pressure from many directions, a coalition of about a dozen charities announced in December the creation of the 9/11 United Services Group. The coalition was created to coordinate relief efforts and oversee a database of records on some 30,000 people affected by the attacks. The group plans included the creation of a case management program to assist applicants for relief aid, a toll-free hotline for affected persons, and an informational Web site. In response to concerns over privacy, the 9/11 United Services Group took security precautions, and allowed only a small handful of people access to the database. With the creation of this centralized database, relief efforts were ultimately able to achieve some level of coordination.

Effectiveness Concerns

Speed, cost, and level of coordination are all surely critical dimensions on which to judge the efficiency of charitable efforts following a disaster. But efficiency is not the only dimension that counts. Effectiveness is important, too. Charities that receive donations must use these funds to fulfill a charitable mission, and in the process they must at times make difficult choices regarding how best to allocate available funds. In the case of this disaster, the vast majority of grantmaking involved cash assistance to the families of victims. Throughout the relief effort, some voices, particularly within the world of large foundations, urged that a broader grantmaking agenda be considered, one that addressed the needs of displaced workers, threats to civil rights at a time of heightened suspicion, and neighborhood and community needs around the sites of the attacks (Fazlollah and Nicholas 2002).

After September 11th generated a huge outpouring of contributions, the idea of using relief funds to support efforts aimed at a broad range of public needs was appealing because it appeared to fulfill the duty of charities to use charitable funds responsibly. However, in the pursuit of greater levels of effectiveness, charities had to be careful to adhere to the wishes of the donors and to fulfill their charitable intentions. Conflicts can arise between the most effective use of funds and the use that donors intend. For charities, this can and often does pose significant challenges. In the confusion and chaos that followed the attacks, some donors did in fact focus on the issue of the sanctity of their charitable intent, particularly as it related to the American Red Cross's use of funds. As hundreds of millions of dollars poured into the Red Cross, the organization faced a clear dilemma. It could exclusively write checks to victims, or it could attempt to use some of these to advance its broader organizational mission of helping those in need during disasters in the future. In the name of using the funds the most effectively, the Red Cross's initial plan was to set aside some September 11th donations for a general emergency fund and strategic blood reserve. The Red Cross believed that a strategic use of funds for both immediate and long-term needs was the responsible and most effective course of action (Berresford 2002).

The American Red Cross's plan to use as much as half of the more than $500 million raised for the creation of an emergency fund and the strengthening of blood reserves in anticipation of future terrorist threats turned out to be a disastrous decision, at least from a public relations perspective. Members of a Congressional subcommittee assailed the organization's president, Dr. Bernadine Healy, when she appeared at a committee hearing on relief efforts. Healy defended the plan in the face of sharp criticism, saying that Red Cross solicitations and television ads had repeatedly said that donations would be used to cover "emerging needs" beyond just those directly related to September 11th. However, in the face of mounting criticism, the Red Cross announced on November 14th that it would restrict the scope of its Liberty Fund to immediate disaster relief, financial assistance to families affected by the attacks, and direct support costs. It further announced that programs that had been folded into the Liberty Fund (the Strategic Blood Reserve, Community Outreach, and the Armed Forces Services) would be separated entirely from the Fund. The Red Cross's desire to use the fund effectively ultimately led the organization to suffer a major public relations disaster at a time when the organization should have been cementing its image as the leading private charity in the United States concerned with helping people in distress. Its mistake was simply to underestimate the significance donors attached to their charitable intent and to overestimate the importance of effectiveness at a time of national crisis.

The Red Cross was not alone in seeking to think through alternatives to simple cash transfers to families of victims in the name of greater effectiveness. Representatives of the philanthropic establishment in New York attempted at times to make the argument that cash assistance alone would not be the most effective use of the resources raised and the needs of the affected communities were in fact broader. However, these suggestions never gained much traction. While the need to help displaced low-wage workers, to combat possible racial profiling, to help neighborhoods reorganize, and to carry out other indirect services may have been real, donors were focused on something simpler and more concrete: the needs of the victims' families. While public funds were eventually made available to compensate families on a scale that dwarfed the private philanthropic response, few donors seemed to care about the effectiveness of their gifts. For many individual contributors, a crucial part of giving turned out to be the expression of compassion and caring. Thus, questions about whether private funds might have been used more productively to help groups of people not covered by government's eventual compensation program were ultimately only aired, and aired relatively quietly, within the tight-knit networks of institutional philanthropy.

Equity Concerns

Beyond efficiency and effectiveness, the relief charities were subject to considerable second-guessing about the equity of their decisions. Equity concerns focused both on the amount of funds that various groups of victims received from private sources, as well as the effect this new disaster giving would have on existing nonprofits in the two affected cities. If funders were the chief source of effectiveness concerns, the families of victims took on the role of publicly articulating equity concerns, starting soon after the attacks.

New York City's fire and police departments suffered great casualties in the collapse of the World Trade Center: A total of 389 New York City uniformed personnel perished (this figure includes twenty-three police officers, 343 firefighters, as well as emergency medical service workers and other city rescue personnel). Several funds were established specifically for families of uniformed personnel killed in the attacks, including the New York Fire Fighters 9-11 Disaster Relief Fund. This fund was established by the International Association of Fire Fighters (IAFF), which raised $132 million and disbursed $323,703 to each of the 343 families suffering a firefighter death in the attacks. Other private sources provided additional benefits, including the law firm of Wachtell, Lipton, Rosen & Katz, which established a $5-million scholarship fund for children of uniformed personnel. Moreover, all spouses of deceased firefighters were eligible for $275,000 in city and federal death benefits, in addition to the deceased's salary for life. The Heroes Fund of the New York City Police Foundation set aside $8.5 million to help meet the financial, physical, and psychological needs of police personnel and their families, and the emergency needs of the NYPD.

The preponderance of funds for families of uniformed service personnel, especially firefighters, created the appearance that some families might end up being overcompensated for their loss compared to others. Assuming that some differences in levels of private assistance to victims' families exists by virtue of the existence of uniformed personnel funds, the large and unanswerable question is whether there should in fact be any differentiation made between victims based on the circumstances of their death, or whether all families should be treated exactly the same. Donors to the various funds expressed through their giving a clear sense that those who died trying to help others were indeed a special class and deserving of special consideration. As donations flowed into the private funds, public opinion polls showed that a majority of Americans believe that all the families of victims will be better off economically than they would otherwise have been.

In seeking to compensate victims, private efforts were forced to deal with the issue of fairness and equity, and to develop a plan that provides assistance without delivering unreasonable amounts of money. This task was made harder when government decided to enter the field and offer its own compensation packages, a decision that created new, and even more complex, equity concerns. Two weeks after the attacks, the federal government established the September 11th Victims Compensation Fund to provide financial support to families of those killed or injured in the attacks. In offering awards to families for lost wages and pain and suffering, the Fund broke new ground, in that the federal government made a commitment to assist victims of terrorism. Still, from the start, there were questions about whether and how much awards should be reduced by the amount of charity a family accepted from other sources. Normally, federal compensation is reduced by "collateral sources" of compensation, including life insurance, death benefits, and pension plans. However, the law made no mention of charity as a collateral source. Those arguing in favor of the reduction (such as watchdog groups and some congressional leaders) say that the point of the federal fund is to adequately compensate victims' families, not to make them rich. Those arguing against any offsets (including victims' rights groups and other congressional leaders) say that to reduce federal awards would in effect only subsidize government and hence violate donors' intent to help victims' families. The debate left victims' families wondering whether and how closely they should account for any charitable money they received, while charitable organizations were left to ponder whether they should instead give financial support to people who would not otherwise receive the federal aid (Gallagher 2002).

The U.S. Department of Justice was charged with writing the rules that would govern the Fund, and for appointing a special master to oversee the Fund. The Attorney General of the United States consulted with numerous congressional leaders and others on the question of offsets for charitable contributions, and in early November, a consensus developed inside the Department of Justice that charitable donations should not be considered a collateral source that could reduce government awards. Kenneth Feinberg, a former chief of staff to Senator Edward M. Kennedy and a former court-appointed mediator in disputes including claims over Agent Orange, was appointed to the post of special master in late November 2001. In announcing the Fund's rules, Feinberg estimated that the Fund could cost taxpayers as much as $6 billion, and would make tax-free awards averaging $1.65 million to the families of people who died in the attacks. Because the Fund's awards must be reduced by collateral sources—other than charity—such as life insurance, death benefits, and pension plans, the families of uniformed rescue personnel killed in the attacks worried that they would receive less than other families because they were slated to receive generous benefits as part of their union contracts. All of which helped raise once again a set of issues related to the equity of the disbursements. This time it was the families of uniformed personnel who felt the rules were inequitable (Barstow and Henriques 2001; Kolbert 2002).

In addition to sorting out equity issues between families, relief funders also had to contend with fairness issues raised by the large universe of nonprofit organizations not involved in the disaster relief effort. These nonprofits worried about being squeezed as funds flowed freely to relief organizations active after September 11th. With Americans giving en masse to relief charities amidst a deepening economic slowdown, many nonprofit leaders worried that Americans' charitable impulse would run dry. The concern was at least partly justified, as some organizations did experience a short-term drop-off in fundraising. Data on whether and to what extent September 11th affected the financial condition of the broader nonprofit community in each of the affected cities is difficult to interpret definitively, given the number of factors that affect giving levels. Still, a study released on February 7, 2002, found that 44 percent of nonprofit organizations raised less money since September 11th, 2001, as compared to their fundraising efforts during the same period of the previous year. More than 20 percent of respondents reported a 20 percent or greater drop in funds raised after September 11th. Another indicator of trouble was a decline of 8.2 percent in the Philanthropic Giving Index between the summer and December of 2001. The index measures the charitable giving climate, and the 8.2 percent drop is the largest since the inception of the measure in 1998. The index is based on surveys of 145 consultants and fundraisers nationwide (America Gives 2002; Cohen 2002).

As a luxury during a time of urgent need, the plight of arts organizations received attention because they appeared particularly vulnerable. Many theaters and museums nationwide did in fact report sharp declines in the number of visitors in the months following the attacks, in what would normally be a busy season for the arts. One report based on surveys with 150 New York arts organizations showed that 90 percent had raised fewer funds than expected, and that 50 percent reported that at least one major gift or donation had been postponed or cancelled. While some may view the arts as nonessential, the arts do play an integral role in the economic vitality of New York City and other major cities, and their decline has caused concern for the local economy. New York City's 2,000 arts and cultural organizations contribute $13 billion annually to the city's economy. Even with these pressures, many arts groups felt some apprehension about complaining about the fairness of donors, especially when the basic needs of thousands of families seemed overwhelming. Because many nonprofit leaders at established organizations viewed the equity issues raised by the sudden demands placed on donors for a new cause as temporary, very few nonprofits dramatically changed their appeals or criticized the massive flow of relief funds to families. Thus, even though charitable dollars are limited and may be part of a zero-sum game in which some nonprofits win while others lose, the short-term inequities between organizations appeared to be manageable enough so that time alone would take care of them (Kleiman and Duitch 2001).

Taken together, the efficiency, effectiveness, and equity concerns raised after the attacks should give charities in other cities cause to ponder how they would have handled a crisis of such large proportions. In reality, few cities are prepared philanthropically to organize and operate large relief efforts. Of course, national charities with the greatest visibility and name recognition, such as the American Red Cross and the United Way, will likely play a central role in future cases should terrorism resurface in America. But local charity officials need to organize themselves now so that they have a response mechanism in place more coordinated and creative than the one that took hold in New York after September 11th. This will require planning and collaboration. The end result of such a process, however, will be the emergence of local charitable communities that are better able to mobilize and disburse private charitable resources efficiently, effectively, and equitably in times of great need.

Lessons for Philanthropy

Although several controversies arose related to the administration and expenditure of billions of dollars of relief funds, the real implications of this chapter in the history of American philanthropy are potentially more profound, yet harder to see immediately. In making choices about the kind of help that would be offered, donors defined a vision of giving in times of need that was distinctly closer to old-fashioned charity aimed at offering direct help without preconditions, than to modern, ambitious philanthropy aimed at the root causes of social problems. The return of charity was remarkable in that the moral authority and claims of organized philanthropy have loomed large in recent decades. Still, when needs were great and when the stakes were high, donors turned back to a centuries-old style of giving.

Philanthropy's challenge to charity can be traced back about a century. Seeing flaws in charity's model of almsgiving to the poor, Andrew Carnegie and John D. Rockefeller, the early progenitors of the new "scientific philanthropy" in the United States, sought to change the principles of giving. At the center of these two men's earliest ideas about philanthropy were two powerful notions. The first idea was that giving could be a positive force when it helped people find ways to help themselves. Both men believed that if philanthropic resources were to be used well, they would have to serve as tools or implements that recipients could use to create lasting opportunities for themselves. The second idea was that giving had to aim at root causes of problems if it were to make good on its claim of being an improvement over never-ending almsgiving. Absent such an approach, philanthropy would be condemned to a continuous cycle of temporary symptom alleviation, never leading to a direct cure. Both the ideas of targeting giving at creating opportunities for self-help and of attacking underlying causes of social problems have had a profound influence on the development of philanthropy—particularly institutional philanthropy—over the past century.

Today, most large foundations do not see themselves as doing charity work. Instead, they understand their work as bringing about the resolution of difficult social problems through the use of sophisticated "theories of change" and "logic models." Social problems and public needs are often taken to be technical challenges that require the application of expert knowledge and cutting-edge philanthropic techniques aimed at addressing problems at their core, leading to lasting solutions. One consequence of this move toward more sophisticated and complex models for giving has been the steady professionalization of the field of philanthropy. Grantmaking expertise has come to be recognized as a critical preparation for work in the field of philanthropy and long-term careers in foundations have become commonplace, a departure from the old approach which tapped well-rounded generalists for short stints in foundations. As philanthropy has evolved toward the status of a profession, the tools of the trade have gotten progressively more complex. Many foundations rely on requests for proposals, make program-related investments, offer strategy coaching to grant recipients, commission detailed independent evaluations, and engage in a host of non-check writing activities.

By professionalizing their workforce and by ramping up the technical complexity of their grantmaking work, the large foundations have had a profound influence on the broader philanthropic world. New donors who come to philanthropy often aspire to the same levels of technical sophistication that large foundations display in their work. In this sense, when foundations abandoned the backwoods of charity in favor of scientific philanthropy, they brought the broader field of giving with them. Aspirations of donors for greater effectiveness have increased, and some have even attempted to push philanthropy one step further by introducing business tools and techniques into giving. The rise of venture philanthropy, and with it the claim of turning grants into investments through rigorous performance measurement and oversight, is but one sign that philanthropy has openly and aggressively embraced an increasingly ambitious, technocratic, and hard-nosed approach.

The aftermath of September 11th has thrown many of these assumptions and ambitions into doubt. At a moment of national crisis and doubt, one might have expected that donors would have gone to ever-greater lengths to ensure that their funds were used for the most effective purposes imaginable and for the most highly leveraged solutions to the crisis that arose after the attacks. One might also have expected that charities would compete to attract donations by designing innovative strategies, programs, and interventions. But almost nothing of the kind happened. To be sure, a few foundations tried to make the case that the needs of displaced low wage workers and community members near the sites needed attention, and that the rights of immigrants required safeguarding at a time of great anger. These messages were drowned out by a much louder chorus for something far more simple, namely, aid to the families of victims. The claims of organized philanthropy fell largely on deaf ears and the most basic forms of charity and victim assistance—the giving of cash grants to those in need—took center stage. It was not long before even the largest and most institutionalized donors fell in line in terms of abandoning decades of rhetoric and practice related to grantmaking. And when the American Red Cross began to talk about long-term capacity building and strategic blood reserves, it encountered a firestorm of resistance and contempt. Similarly, when the Twin Towers Fund sought to employ staff to help carry out its work, it, too, was castigated for wasting charitable money on something other than cash for needy families. So hungry were donors for simple cash transfers to victims, many of the charities were led to make pledges that no overhead would be assessed for their work, pledges that proved very hard to fulfill and that required additional targeted funds be located to support their operational costs.

Of course, all of this raises the interesting question of why old-fashioned charity rose up from the ashes after the disaster, and what this tells us about the claims of scientific philanthropy today. The simplest way to interpret the turn away from "high impact," "high engagement," or "high leverage" giving is to point to the need for certainty that relief funds would meet the needs of victims. Large administrative overhead, complex programs, long-term planning—all may have appeared too uncertain to those who were moved to give. By contrast, cash transfers seemed concrete and they guaranteed that contributions would be of some value to those in need. In this sense, charity's relationship to philanthropy may well be like banking's relationship to venture capitalism. In times of trouble, donors may well seek out a safer, but lower rate of return. The risk profile of modern philanthropy may simply have been too great for donors feeling the need to do something concrete. But this is not a complete explanation. The turn toward intermediaries that simply provide cash to victims tells us something about the confidence large numbers of Americans have in the expertise of grantmakers to really add much of value. For years, opinion poll after opinion poll have tracked a declining trust in government. The public reaction to the claims of philanthropic leaders was a similar vote of no confidence and lack of trust in "scientific philanthropy," though many within the world of institutional giving have sought to call it a failure in communication.

Conclusion

Does this mean that philanthropy is on the way out and that old-fashioned charity and almsgiving will continue to make a comeback? Probably not, because the number of situations donors will encounter, such as the one after September 11th, is likely to be very limited. What is clear is that in a world in which the hubris and pretensions of philanthropy have increased with every passing decade, a small chink in the armor is now present. When everything was at stake and when the whole country was watching, high-concept philanthropy beat a hasty retreat and gave way to primitive charity. It was a retreat that was barely noticeable to some, but whose consequences are likely to only become more obvious over time, as we continue to reflect on what was learned about the nature of private assistance in times of great national need.

9

National Service in Theory and Practice

Peter Frumkin

National service is a very broad concept that takes many different forms. At its core lies the idea that citizens should serve their country through an extended period of community work. Over time, multiple initiatives promoting service have been implemented with very different programmatic goals, including delivering services to poor communities, inspiring and mentoring students, involving older adults in community volunteering, and increasing the global perspective of people of all ages through service overseas. Starting a decade ago, AmeriCorps became the most visible of all these efforts and focused on placing young adults in community organizations for a year of service. Today, the profile of AmeriCorps is on the rise as both sides of the political spectrum see national service as potentially an important element of building patriotism and creating a sense of national purpose. AmeriCorps is scheduled to increase substantially in size, though the government body charged with managing national service has been nagged by management problems recently that have slowed this expansion. Still, interest in national service continues to be high, even though evidence of the ultimate effectiveness of AmeriCorps remains elusive. Billions of implementation dollars later, after the idea of national service became a reality, we still lack a very clear theory of what these efforts are really supposed to accomplish, which has made it hard to conduct useful evaluations and come to a meaningful conclusion about the overall effectiveness of national service initiatives.

One of the distinctive features of national service programs is that they represent the principal point of direct contact—and occasional friction—between government and volunteer efforts. As government has sought to encourage volunteer service through programs such as AmeriCorps, it has made a significant assumption that there is a role for government in kindling the volunteer spirit, rather than simply allowing it to emerge spontaneously in communities. This assumption, which anchors the national service idea, has been debated extensively over the years and remains highly contested. Some see a role for government in promoting service, while others see a dangerous meddling of government with the private voluntary impulse. While it may not be possible to resolve this deep philosophical question definitively, significant progress can be made by simply clarifying the assumptions of national service programs and by setting forward a plausible and comprehensive explanation of this effort to join government and volunteerism together.

Policies and Controversies

The idea of national service is based on the notion that citizenship is not a passive concept, but rather demands enactment and commitment (Putnam 1993, 1999; Chrislip and Larson 1994; Perry and Thompson 1997). One of the best ways to transform citizenship into action is through the organization of national service programs that sends people into communities to work on projects that will enhance the lives of others. While the American penchant for individualism and autonomy has not always seemed well aligned with the idea of nonmilitary forms of national service, in recent decades Americans have embraced a host of government programs designed to cultivate community commitment and the ethos of service (Rothenberg 1984; Democratic Leadership Conference 1988; Eberly 1988).

AmeriCorps, the largest program of the Corporation for National and Community Service (CNCS), was and still is seen by many as one of President Bill Clinton's signature domestic policy achievements (Waldman 1995). While it is tempting to trace the CNCS back to the early days of the Clinton Administration, the roots of the organization actually go back much further (Citizen and National Service Act—The Nunn-McCurdy Bill—1989). Not only were agencies such as VISTA and ACTION long active in the effort to mobilize public resources to support service, but the first President Bush had also created the Office of National Service in the White House and the Points of Light Foundation to foster volunteering. During the 1980s, an assortment of entrepreneurial service programs came into being, leading to an adjustment in the relationship between federal and state agencies, and nonprofit organizations. Colleges around the country were also beginning to develop service programs that placed students in community organizations in which they could get hands-on experience (The Federal Domestic Volunteer Agency 1990; Saidel 1991; Waldman 1995). In 1990, Congress passed and President Bush signed the National and Community Service Act, authorizing grants to schools to support service learning (now Learn and Serve America), and demonstration grants for national service programs to youth corps, nonprofits, and colleges and universities.

In early 1994, President Clinton delivered to Congress a legislative proposal that would become The National and Community Service Trust Act. The bill proposed a unique federal agency that would take the form of a corporation, having a flexible personnel system, a decentralized program network, and strong ties to the business and nonprofit sectors. It set forward a plan to engage youth in useful tasks that were "real work." The plan was to develop a new agency that would help remedy national trends towards balkanization and political separatism, while building job skills, instilling civic spirit, improving communities, and building bridges between classes and races (MDC, Inc. 1988; Waldman 1995). Since its creation, the Corporation for National and Community Service has been plagued by criticism and attacks, and the idea of national service has divided the political landscape in strange and unpredictable ways.

Unfortunately, political disagreements about the wisdom of subsidizing volunteer activity for any purpose have largely displaced reasoned analysis based on real information or data. The politics surrounding the issue are strident and complex, often driven more by theory than data, and differentiated by political ideology (Evers 1990). One reason why national service has elicited such strong political reactions is that it calls into question the legitimate role of government and its relationship with the private impulse to help.

For liberals, the appeal of national service is considerable. Programs like AmeriCorps hold out the potential to breed a new kind of idealism and public spiritedness that can only empower individuals and strengthen democracy (Munter 1988; Nakatani 1998). By injecting people into community organizations and giving them the ability to engage in community projects, liberals see national service as potentially leading to the kind of open-mindedness, compassion, and perspective that programs such as the Peace Corps generated earlier (Newmann and Rutter 1983; Cohen 1997; Rhoads 1997). Moreover, the chance to serve one's country and community might also be a potentially important way to ensure that youth are given employment and educational opportunities that can lead to more productive lives (Markus, Howard and King 1993; Intili, Kissam and Wrigley 1998). Efforts such as VISTA were a central component of the "War on Poverty." They generate memories of a time when we had a more activist government and new programs were an expression of the public sector's desire to be an agent of social change (Landrum 1992). But liberals, too, have their issues with national service. The higher education establishment has always objected to a requirement of service in exchange for federal student aid eligibility, arguing that the system requires only poor people to serve in order to attend college. Unions and labor proponents worry about the displacement of low paid social services workers by subsidized "volunteers" (Moskos 1990).

Conservatives are deeply split by the issue. On the one hand, national service might be a useful tool for building citizenship, strengthening patriotism, and expressing gratitude (Buckley 1990; Constitutional Rights Foundation). But some conservatives also view national service as a dangerous threat to individual freedoms by conscription, or incursion of government into the world of volunteerism. They fear that the authority of the nonprofit organizations hosting government subsidized workers would be undermined, that volunteer activity would be reduced to low grade employment, and that a new and costly government bureaucracy would be created (Friedman 1989; Evers 1990; Moskos 1990). Conservatives have often ridiculed the idea of paying people to volunteer, seeing this as a gross perversion of de Tocqueville's early observation that voluntary action among citizens was a critical training ground for democratic politics (De Tocqueville 1956; Schmeigelow 1993). True service is voluntary service. Service for pay, or in exchange for certain social benefits, is regarded by some as "coercive utopianism" only slightly disguised (Chapman 1990). Conservatives have also sometimes worried that a civil national service program might be deleterious to the military's morale, discipline, and enlistment efforts (Government Printing Office 1980), and that labor markets will be distorted by the introduction of large numbers of government-subsidized workers, potentially leading to job losses among full-time workers.

Among communitarians, national service has a distinct attraction if it can be used to build trust, create greater levels of solidarity within communities, and combat trends of civic disengagement (Fukuyama 1995; National Commission on Civic Renewal 1998). Programs such as AmeriCorps fit the communitarian vision because they represent tools for the construction or reconstruction of social capital, in areas too long suffering from isolation and anomie. By bringing people together to carry out work as varied as planting public gardens to tutoring children, service programs may well build new networks of collaboration and understanding that will have value and use long after the service work is completed. Not just communities, but civil society itself might be revived through civil service (Kemmis 1990; Dionne 1999).

Amidst this confusion and turmoil, national service programs have slowly grown and been refined. At the center of the process of implementing a national service program has been a new government entity charged with bringing under its umbrella the many disparate manifestations of the idea of service, the Corporation for National and Community Service (CNCS). The mission statement of CNCS has changed little between 1995, when it was reported to Congress, and today. In an early incarnation it stated: "The Corporation will engage great numbers of Americans in a wide range of service activities designed to address America's most fundamental societal issues, and create results that can be seen. In so doing, the Corporation seeks to inspire good citizenship, strengthen community, and provide educational opportunity in exchange for substantial work." While the main elements of its mission remained stable, there have been subtle changes and modifications over time to the Corporation's mission that have tempered the early ambition of the Corporation. Specifically, the 1995 mission statement pledged that the Corporation will engage Americans of all ages and backgrounds in community-based service, and that this service will target "the nation's education, human, public safety and environmental needs" to achieve direct and demonstrable results. By contrast, a more recent version of the mission statement hedges a bit. The differences are minor but do reflect a bit more caution. The current mission statement no longer promises to engage Americans of all ages and backgrounds in service. Instead, it promises to provide them with opportunities to engage. Similarly, the current mission statement contains no promise that community service will address the nation's human needs, as well as needs in education, public safety, and the environment. Instead, it more realistically states that some human needs other than education, public safety, and environmental will be addressed. Finally, the current mission statement articulates an original principle previously not specified: to encourage all Americans to engage in service.

Significantly, the slogan of the Corporation, which has survived for more than a decade, is "Getting things done." This phrase was designed from the start to speak to the political environment and the general public. In claiming to be about getting things done, the Corporation sought to reinforce the fact that national service was not just about youth development, self-actualization, and idealism, but that it could also lead to concrete results in communities. The precise nature of the "things" that would be done was very broad, spanning planting trees, painting houses, tutoring children, and assisting the elderly. More important politically than the precise nature of the work carried out by volunteers was the fact that things would indeed be done and that the program would be practical.

While the Corporation has many commitments and programs, AmeriCorps remains the core program of CNCS. It engages Americans age seventeen and older in community service and provides educational awards in exchange for service. AmeriCorps programs are run through local, state, and national organizations with which AmeriCorps forms partnerships. Habitat for Humanity, Boys and Girls Clubs, Big Brothers/Big Sisters, YMCAs, and faith-based organizations are examples. In FY 2000, individual education awards for one year of full-time service were $4,725, paid in the form of vouchers through the Corporation's National Service Trust. AmeriCorps articulates five goals, which parallel the mission goals of the Corporation.

1. *Getting Things Done*: AmeriCorps helps communities find solutions to their problems and have an impact.
2. *Strengthening Communities*: AmeriCorps helps unite a diverse group of individuals and institutions in a common effort to improve communities

through service. It aspires to act as a catalyst helping to build community capacity, leveraging local resources, and linking volunteers to existing service efforts.

3. *Expanding Opportunity*: With their participation, members broaden their own individual perspectives and receive scholarships to help pay for college, vocational training or student loans.

4. *Encouraging Responsibility*: Through service experiences and civic education, corps members learn to take responsibility for solving community problems.

5. *Supporting Service Infrastructure*: Through its interaction with local service agencies, Americorps seeks to help existing programs and organizations become more efficient and effective.

All of these are laudable goals, but they are not easily achieved. As it has moved to translate these goals into reality, CNCS has been burdened by its funding and administrative arrangements.

Federal funding for the Corporation is a very complex matter, to say the least. The Corporation's programs are authorized under two acts: the Domestic Volunteer Service Act (DVSA) of 1973 and the National and Community Service Act (NCSA) of 1990. The House and Senate Appropriations Committees have jurisdiction over the Corporation's funding, but two different appropriations subcommittees provide funding: The NCSA programs (including AmeriCorps State/National, Learn and Serve America, and AmeriCorps NCCC) are funded through the House and Senate Subcommittees for the Departments of Veterans Affairs, HUD, and Independent Agencies (VA-HUD). The DVSA programs (AmeriCorps, VISTA, and Senior Corps) are funded through the House and Senate Subcommittees for the Departments of Labor, Health and Human Services, and Education (Labor-HHS).

From the start, the Corporation included the newly created AmeriCorps and subsumed the previously established programs such as VISTA, Learn and Serve, and Senior Corps. Not starting with a clean slate has ultimately proved problematic for CNCS. Today, because it supports a wide array of preexisting programs under one organizational umbrella, CNCS's financial and administrative processes are cumbersome. The Corporation actually administers its programs through two sets of state offices, through which funds are disbursed and decisions are carried out. One set of service commissions is operated by state governments and works with CNCS, while the other—made up of federal offices for VISTA and Senior Corps—somehow persists across the country, even after these programs were folded into CNCS. This overlapping system of state administration has survived because the Corporation never was able to merge the preexisting state commissions, which were seen as a symbol of local control, with its own state-based governance system.

The Corporation's very structure has been a sore point as well. It was created as a wholly owned government corporation. When it was founded in

1993, it was the only noncommercial government corporation covered by the Government Corporation Control Act. Initially, it retained the same board as its predecessor organization, the Commission on National and Community Service, established by the National and Community Service Act of 1990. Even though it was designed to be an efficient agency that would be part of the move to reinvent government, CNCS was thus burdened from the start by major bureaucratic obstacles. Rather than operate like a lean and aggressive business corporation, CNCS's financial and management systems make it hard for CNCS to avoid many of the classic pitfalls that public sector organizations face. For many years, its books were in disorder and it failed to pass its audits.

The goals and intentions of national service programs such as AmeriCorps have not been integrated into a clear and compelling theory of change for national service, a model that lays out how these objectives are to be achieved. I believe the absence of a clear model has been a major stumbling block for the national service movement over the past decade. By offering such a model (figure 9.1) and by reviewing the most important research relating to the elements of this model, my goal is to begin to clarify what we know about how service works, and how this knowledge might be used to improve the quality and impact of service programs in the future.

Research on National Service

Today, CNCS occupies several floors of a modern office complex a few blocks from the White House, has offices and commissions in states across the country, and operates with an annual federal appropriation approaching $750 million. Despite all these trappings and its appearance as a solid piece of the federal bureaucracy, CNCS continues to struggle for respect and legitimacy. At the core of many of its troubles remains a poorly articulated theory of change or underlying logic model, which explains how national service works, who benefits from it, and what the end results are of the effort by government to promote volunteerism.

Looking at existing research, I suggest that national service programs need to be conceived as working at three different levels. First, at an individual level, national service attempts to contribute to the growth and development of the people who give the time and effort to service. Second, at an organizational level, national service initiatives attempt to infuse community groups, schools, and nonprofits with labor resources that will build capacity and sustainability. Third, at a community level, national service is deeply concerned with building new networks of collaboration, trust, and cooperation by bringing communities together to complete significant community projects. Within each level, there are many distinctions that can be made. For instance, the individuals involved in service might be people who are AmeriCorps members—typically high school or college-age youth, though there are certainly "volunteers" in other programs who are older and far more experienced. The organizations hosting volunteers are typically nonprofits, though some are public sector organizations such as schools. Some are very large and established organizations. Others are struggling organizations that are just getting started. Most are secular, but some are faith-based in their orientation. Communities can be construed as neighborhoods, towns, cities, or other places, or they can be defined as groups of people somehow bound together and connected together by geography. Although it leaves plenty of room for interpretation, by using this tripartite framework for thinking about the effects of national service, much of the existing work on the effects of service comes into focus.

Individual-Level Impacts of National Service

A substantial body of research exists on the individual-level effects of national service. There are abundant theories and studies that address the impacts of service on individual participants on youth development (Oi 1990). The effects of service as a pedagogical tool—where it is actually integrated into the curriculum—and, more generally, as an inspiration for better learning, have been reviewed by education theorists (Markus, Howard and King 1993; Astin 2001). Integrating service experience with classroom instruction is thought by some sociologists and psychologists to provide a balance of instructional and reflective components to a curriculum, assisting adolescent students in the critical task of establishing a "social-historically coherent identity" from which to grow (Youniss and Yates 1997). The theory is based on Piaget's premise that reality is not given, but constructed by individuals reflecting on their actions in order to make sense of past experience and anticipate their own future actions. Attitudinal effects of national service are the subject of several studies on race, class, ethnicity, and gender in national service programs. Some theorize that service learning changes lives forever, while others are more circumspect in measuring attitudes change and personal development in the long and short term (Munter 1988; Bloomquist 1992 including Cook Ethnic Interaction Scale, Conrad and Hedin Social and Personal Responsibility Scale, Gorlow and Noll Measure of Attitudes and Personal Development Outcomes; Macro International 1997; Tschirhart 1997).

Some studies test the impact of national service on civic responsibility, political engagement, and effective citizenship, addressing generally the success of national service programs in strengthening democracy by inspiring youth and creating future leaders (Constitutional Rights Foundation; Bellah et al. 1985; Youniss and Yates 1997; Barber 1998; Furco, Muller, and Ammon 1998; Peter D. Hart Research Associates 1998; Galston 2001; Zaff and

Michelsen 2002). One worry is that an unclear distinction exists in service programs between shaping and manipulating young minds. National service has been called a youth policy that rejects the free choices made by young persons, each possessing unique abilities and interests, and who often resist attempts to control their behavior and actions. Service has even been condemned as "homogenization by social planners" (Oi 1990). Other difficult-to-measure concepts, such as social trust, institutional confidence, and personal values, have been the subject of more positive studies focused on service learning (Simon and Wang 1999, 2000).

There are many general studies on the impacts of national service on individuals, including some that are ongoing. One of the most extensive is a 1999 report, submitted to CNCS by Aguirre International, entitled Making a Difference: Impact of AmeriCorps*State/National Direct on Members and Communities 1994–1995 and 1995–1996. Findings pertain to research results following the first two years of AmeriCorps. They are divided into three categories: Life Skills, Civic Involvement, and Educational Attainment/Opportunity. In the area of life skills, the study found that most members who considered their own life skills to be deficient achieved substantial or dramatic gains in every area except use of information technology. Benefits occur for all AmeriCorps members, especially those with the least developed skills upon program entry. And all ethnic groups share in the reported gain in skills. Significant effects were also found in the areas of civic involvement and educational attainment, with volunteers reporting greater interest in public service and improved leadership skills, as well as heightened educational goals upon completion of service.

More recently, Abt Associates published the results of the first of a series of reports designed to measure, over time, the effects of a national service experience on individual members. The report contains baseline data, collected in the Fall/Winter of 1999/2000, identifying a set of individual characteristics determined by Abt to be indicators of AmeriCorps success in achieving its goal of developing its members. These outcome characteristics include civic engagement, education and employment goals, life skills, and attitudes. Characteristics are divided into potential outcomes, to be measured upon commencement of AmeriCorps service (baseline), one year after baseline (for most, the end of the service period), and three years after baseline. The study will track a group of individuals who are members of AmeriCorps programs, and a comparison group of similarly situated individuals who are not. This large, experimental data will be the most comprehensive collected to date and will certainly advance our understanding of the effects of service on participants.

Other researchers have taken a more focused approach to tracking the individual-level effects of service. Youniss and Yates (1997) take a close look at the educational and attitudinal impacts of community service on a class of

1993–1994 high school juniors in a typical, mostly African-American, urban school in Washington, D.C. They contend that by integrating a community service experience into the learning process, thereby creating a "complementarity of instructional and reflective components in a service curricula," schools can advance learning far beyond what occurs in just reading about or hearing lectures on the subject. Significantly, alumni surveys by Youniss and Yates demonstrate clear linkages between the social justice experience in high school and civic engagement and social justice attitudes later in life. In a survey of the alumni of three high school classes, they found that of the sixty-eight alumni who had not done community service while in high school, 29 percent had volunteered after high school graduation, while of the fifty-one alumni who had volunteered during high school, 68 percent had volunteered after graduation.

Another school of research has considered the benefits to individuals who integrate community service into their educational experiences in terms of "otherness"—the experience of crossing over into unfamiliar zones of cultural territory as a means of defining self in relationship to society. Service programs woven into the college experience offer an important pedagogical opportunity for educating the whole self and fostering participatory democracy (Rhoads 1997). Put another way, when one observes human realities that are shockingly different from one's own experience and contrary to prior presuppositions, one is challenged to grow by confronting new questions involving personal relationship to varieties of human existence (Jahoda 1992). These more qualitative contributions to the discussion of the individual impacts of national service are extremely valuable, for what they tell us—and what they encourage future research to focus on. Much of the "data" consists of compelling stories, and each individual anecdote is likely representative of countless others, pointing to the conclusion that students exposed to community service in combination with a thoughtful curriculum are profoundly and positively affected by their experiences.

A lingering question is whether, and to what degree, community service fosters positive moral development in young people. Moral development involves the formation of social values, appreciation for difference, tolerance, respect, compassion, and agency. Agency is a person's perceived capacity to act, and make a difference. Generally, it has been found that high school students engaged in community service, and given concurrent opportunities for structured individual and group reflection, manifest increased moral sensitivities at the life-stage when moral identities are being formed. Students often claim a moral awakening, and profess intentions to make service a part of their lives. However, once again, long-term program success, described in terms of deeply instilled individual values and lifetime social commitment, is still largely unknown (Erikson 1968; Youniss and Yates 1997).

In a recent article, Simon (2002) tested the hypothesis that AmeriCorps is biased toward liberal participants, and that such participants become more politically liberal by the time of completion of their program participation. Based upon research involving the participants in 56 major AmeriCorps projects in four Pacific Northwestern states, Simon concluded that participants do not change their political ideology as a result of their service experience, and that both self-identified liberals and self-identified conservatives emerged from their AmeriCorps service experiences significantly more likely to become engaged in whatever their agenda might be in their own communities (Simon 2002).

Across these and many other studies, the effects of service on volunteers has thus been explored and analyzed in many different ways. This heterogeneity demonstrates that a consensus has yet to emerge about what national service is trying to accomplish when it shapes the lives of those called to service.

Organizational-Level Impacts of National Service

Nonprofit agencies of various types are affected by the introduction of government-sponsored workers—and all the technical assistance that comes with them—into their organizations. Compared to the literature on individual-level effects of national service, relatively little has been written on this subject. While it is recognized that a major shift in the relationship between government and the voluntary sector has occurred as public funds have entered these organizations, our knowledge of what these new partnerships mean for the organizations involved is incomplete (Smith and Lipsky 1993). Much research has been directed towards program assessment, organizational achievements (Abt Associates) and the Center for Human Resources, Brandeis University 1994; Aguirre International 1997; American Youth Policy Forum 1999), and cost benefit measured in terms of government expenditures and societal results (Neumann 1995; Wang and Owens 1995; Dawkins, Corrie and Kielsmeier). These issues are important, but not as relevant to our understanding of organizational impact as others, such as the effects of these new partnerships on mission focus, capacity, governance, independence, management strength, sustainability, and community relations.

One early study did address the impact of AmeriCorps on organizations (Aguirre International 1999). The report was the culmination of a four-year, $3.2 million evaluation project commissioned by CNCS. The key findings apply to organizations of all kinds, but the study does distinguish among different types of organizations, depending on the nature of their relationship to AmeriCorps. Thus, "sponsoring organizations" are defined as those that received and administered AmeriCorps grants. Some sponsoring organizations were direct service providers, and some were not. "Partner" organizations do provide direct services, but do not receive AmeriCorps grants directly. They receive them through sponsors. "Involved organizations" include "partner organizations" and any organization that participated in the program, or provided resources or technical services other than money. The study involved sixty sponsoring agencies. About one-fourth were national nonprofits and federal departments. The remaining three-fourths were state-funded programs. Over 90 percent of the programs studied were new recipients of Corporation funding. The study tracked the capacity of the organization, the standards of service delivery, the level of community connectedness, and other factors. On the specific question of AmeriCorps', impacts on organizations, five key findings did emerge:

1. AmeriCorps expanded the number and type of institutions involved in direct community service.
2. AmeriCorps increased the service capacity at existing institutions.
3. AmeriCorps caused new community institutions and partnerships to develop.
4. Participation in AmeriCorps helped most programs raise their professional operating standards.
5. Partnerships of community organizations created by AmeriCorps streamlined the delivery of community services.

One theory is that organizational efficiency will actually decline with the sudden availability of a large force of untrained and temporarily motivated workers: The more manpower there is, particularly the more manpower there is that is paid for by somebody else, the less effectively it will be utilized (Eberly 1968; Bernstein 1991; Tabori, Rogard, Gordon, and Martinez 1997; Mesch, Tschirhart, Perry, and Lee 1998). But these concerns have not been fully tested. One way to collect information about the impact of the introduction of national service volunteers on organizational capacity and performance is to treat the vast number of technical assistance interventions carried out on behalf of CNCS as data. Each year, large contracts are given to outside vendors to provide training and technical assistance to the organizations that receive substantial support from CNCS. The reports of these service providers could be a potent and to date untapped source of data and information on the organizational effects of service.

Perhaps the best data on the organizational effects of national service will come from a study that is now being undertaken at City Year, in which a broad analysis of 270 partnerships in four cities is being carried out, along with twenty-two more in-depth case studies looking at how organizations hosting volunteers were changed through contact with national service. This study will illuminate how national service programs contribute to the capacity, sustainability, and viability of the organizations that decide to work with AmeriCorps volunteers.

Community-Level Impacts of National Service

Useful outcome data on community-level effects of national service is sparse. Theories abound, but few are buttressed by facts. Arguably, with community-level impacts more so than with individual-level or organizational-level impacts, it is difficult to establish causality between AmeriCorps program activity and improved community indicators. Whereas an AmeriCorps member can demonstrate personal growth and attribute it to the AmeriCorps experience, or an organization can show increased capacity that was created with AmeriCorps resources, it is difficult for a community to link a specific good outcome directly to AmeriCorps. How can it be proved that reduced rates of poverty in a neighborhood, or higher rates of literacy in a city are the result of AmeriCorps work? This may be one reason that hard data on community-level impacts of AmeriCorps is so lacking, and that the major studies on community impacts tend to measure the opinions of community leaders about AmeriCorps effectiveness, rather than data showing quantified improvement (Aguirre International 1999). Still, it is critical that we develop and interpret well the data on community-level impacts of national service.

Theories of community disintegration and individual withdrawal are familiar to many through the work of Robert Putnam whose basic premise is that social connectedness is diminishing, and with it goes "social capital"— the value added by trust and reciprocity among individuals, organizations, and communities (McCurdy 1990; Putnam 1993, 1999). However, not all authorities are as pessimistic as Putnam, and some feel he has overstated his case. Among most observers, there is general agreement on the importance of a strong civil society, either as a curb on growth of big government (conservatives and libertarians), or as a basis for building a government that is responsive and energetic (liberals and progressives). Some argue that civil society is the bedrock of good government, and that it provides a democratic culture that authorizes democratic government. Many agree that civil society must coexist with government and business, as a sort of stakeholder and partner (Dionne 1998).

Strong communities are essential ingredients in vibrant civil societies. The role of national service in strengthening communities was affirmed at the Presidents' Summit for America's Future in 1997, and incorporated into CNCS's 1997 strategic plan in Goal Two: "Communities will be made stronger through service" (Strategic Plan Corporation for National Service Fiscal Years 1997 to 2002). But experience has shown that it is possible for untrained workers and disorganized programs to damage communities. Distinctions must be drawn between engaging in a harmful activity, and engaging in a beneficial activity in an unhelpful way (Evers 1990). Recent studies commissioned by CNCS do address the effects of national service on community. One study began with the question: "Do AmeriCorps programs build strong communities?" and sought to measure community effects by looking for the following impacts: strengthened sponsors and involved institutions; involved community members and organizations in service; improved community infrastructure; improved linkages between community organizations; and mobilized community members and improved community morale (Aguirre International 1999). The study went on to identify a list of fifteen measures of project performance deemed relevant to the achievement of community strength. Researchers asked community leaders to rate the project accomplishments of AmeriCorps on measures such as overall project impact, impact on community, strengthening of community ties, working across organizational boundaries, community mobilization, cultivation of community leadership, and other measures of community building.

Still, on the fundamental issue of mission-related community impacts—the community outcomes sought on a short and long-term basis—researchers face their greatest challenge. The Aguirre study (and a five-year follow-up in the same format) indicates that community representatives overwhelmingly agree that AmeriCorps programs do good things in specifically described ways, but we do not know how communities have changed as a result of AmeriCorps work. There has been, however, no real effort to measure community-level impacts and to relate these effects to those produced at the individual and organizational levels. This represents the key frontier for both future research on national service and the eventual use of research findings to improve national service initiatives.

Across all the existing research at the individual, organizational, and community levels, several concrete questions emerge that this future research will need to address. What are the ways in which service changes communities? What kinds of civic resources are generated as a result of service? Can we track the network of ties that constitute the critical bonds of trust and reciprocity that constitute social capital?

Toward a Unified Model

While there is certainly room to argue about the precise meaning and scope of these three levels, it is still useful to think of national service as a nested system that works at all three levels simultaneously. To clarify how these levels operate and how they differ substantially from one another, it may be useful to sketch the theory of change as a model with three levels and multiple stages leading toward the fulfillment of the many goals of service. The "General Theory of Change for National Service" (see figure 9.1) illustrates how at each level of analysis it is possible to sketch out a series of causal linkages leading from the inputs that are needed, to the activities or processes that take place, to the outputs or units of service that are produced in the short run, all the way to the outcomes that the efforts ultimately generate.

Figure 9.1
General Theory of Change for National Service

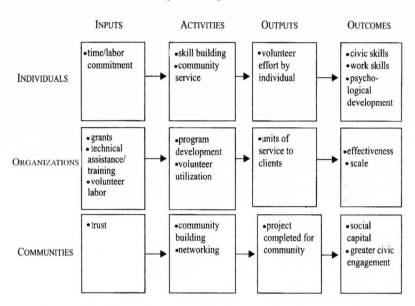

The most complex element of the model is still missing, of course: linkages between levels. What is needed is an argument about how individual, organizational, and community-level effects interact with one another, and which level represents the best starting point for leverage impact across the full range of goals embedded in national service programs. Individual effects do aggregate into organizational effects and organizational effects do combine to create community effects. Specifying the exact processes by which these levels are linked, however, represents a conceptual and research challenge of substantial proportions. Most of the research conducted on national service has focused on one or another of the three levels in isolation. This research has also been quite narrow and has focused on only one part of the causal chain. Thus, a key intellectual work in the field in the future should involve theory building and synthesizing existing knowledge.

New Directions for National Service

How did CNCS get to where they are today? Over time, political opposition to national service led to increased scrutiny and criticism of the Corporation's work, put CNCS on the defensive, and amplified—rather than solved—the problems experienced during the Corporation's first years. Few of these problems were as acute as the one of evaluation and performance measurement. Because CNCS never really settled on a single clear logic model or theory of change for national service, meaningful evaluation was very hard to carry out. It was not clear how the programs delivered by the Corporation were causally connected to the multiple outcomes that were being pursued. The result was research within the Corporation did little to guide policy development and program design. Evaluation was first and foremost a tool for managing the political environment, designed to buy time for CNCS, and demonstrate that things were in fact "getting done." Instead of building knowledge to guide policy development, research was commissioned with the aim of building public support for national service and responding to demands for greater accountability.

In 1997, Congressional testimony of CNCS CEO Harris Wofford was an early sign that CNCS lacked a clear understanding of its work. When asked to speak on the issue of Corporation accomplishments in order to justify a significant budget increase, Wofford responded with a long statement which did not focus on outcomes and how they related to mission. Instead, he said of national service that outsiders simply had to see it to believe it. He claimed that the real test of AmeriCorps and the Corporation's other programs "is what you find is really happening in the districts." Wofford encouraged members of this committee, and all members of Congress, to visit projects in their districts to understand what was happening, and noted: "It's hard to get a real sense of what AmeriCorps is because it's doing so many things, but it has a thrust and a focus that you can only see when you meet the members, see what they are doing, and talk to the nonprofit organizations that find this people power a tremendous new contribution to their own work." This was an enthusiastic expression of support, but hardly a clear statement of Americorps core achievements. The Corporation's inability to articulate the actual effects of its work and relate these to a set of clearly specified goals would nag CNCS for many years to come.

Even with nebulous understanding of what exactly Americorps was achieving, a series of evaluations of CNCS's programs were produced over the years. By one estimate, as much as $40 million has been spent evaluating Corporation programs since 1993. Records show that the Corporation commissioned no less than 136 assessment and impact studies from universities and outside consulting firms in the same period. In November 2000, the Corporation reported that it had conducted over 100 studies since 1994, and that every year the Corporation commissions fifteen to twenty competitively awarded large-scale evaluation studies from independent research firms. The same report gives insight into the nature of some of the studies and what the Corporation took to be significant results of one of the major studies. The report contains a list of key findings of a 1999 study by Aguirre International into the impacts of a random sample of programs receiving AmeriCorps*State/National grants. The list includes the following "key" findings:

- All AmeriCorps programs studied had meaningful service accomplishments
- The majority of institutions that received AmeriCorps grants reported that association with AmeriCorps improved their organization's quality or quantity of services and increased their overall professionalism
- 82 percent of community representatives interviewed reported that AmeriCorps' impact on their community had been "very good" or "outstanding"

This sort of reporting and tracking raises a host of questions: What is a "meaningful service accomplishment," and meaningful for whom? How does a meaningful accomplishment show that AmeriCorps is achieving anything real with respect to education, the environment, public safety, or other human needs? What is the result of having "improved organizational quality or quantity of services"? How are these impressionistic measures connected to real social outcomes? How can this kind of information be used to redesign and improve the quality of programs? The answers are not clear to any of these questions.

More often than not, the Corporation simply commissioned studies of the activities, or outputs, or contented itself to collect ratings of its programs, particularly AmeriCorps. This might mean going to sites around the country and tracking how many students were tutored, how many trees were planted, how many lots were cleaned, or, in the alternative, how various stakeholders felt about the activities that they had witnessed, or participated in. Ironically, despite the huge expenditures of time and money, evaluation efforts never really took center stage within the Corporation. In the same meeting that he introduced the Corporation's newly created Department of Evaluation and Effective Practices in 1997, the Board Chair identified the four focal points for Corporation improvement: staff development, Congressional reauthorization, the Presidents' Summit on America's Future, and management and internal controls. Program evaluation was not even on the list. Finding ways to create usable knowledge and then ways to use data to drive program design was simply not a priority.

Instead, for years, CNCS used evaluation as a tool of political legitimation and as a device for managing Congressional relations. CNCS's flawed measurement agenda was heavily driven by two factors: First, AmeriCorps promised to "get things done," so measuring what got done became a central focus, no matter that it did not explore the deeper and more complex effects of service on youth, service providers, or communities. Second, the Corporation was for years operating under heavy criticism from Republicans who resented the AmeriCorps' association with Clinton, and who more than once tried to cut and even close down the program. As a consequence, the evaluation unit of the Corporation, which should have been providing critical information on how well the programs were performing against the broad mission of the Corporation, was led to adopt a very defensive posture leading to a series of performance reports more intended for the external environment than for the senior managers of the Corporation.

The tendency to view evaluation as an instrument of political management, rather than as a tool of operations management, was particularly problematic given that the Corporation was struggling to define the purposes of national service and could have benefited from data that tested some of the core assumptions about national service's impact. Instead, for many of the early years, the Corporation simply published volume after volume of tracking studies showing that things were in fact getting done, but not saying much about the quality of the work, or the long-term effectiveness of national service as a tool for building social capital and idealism among young people. Fearful of what they might find, or more likely struggle to be able to measure simply, the evaluations of the Corporation shied away from the most difficult but important questions related to the value of national service programs.

The 1997–2002 Strategic Plan that was presented by the Planning and Evaluation Committee in January 1997 did strongly endorse program evaluation, and not all of it in the form of bean counting. The Plan provided an extensive list of proposed evaluation projects for the Corporation as a whole, and each of its three major programs. Some were in response to requirements of the Government Performance Review Act (GPRA) and most were output-oriented. Others, however, were independent initiatives designed to determine program impact through outcome measurement. The description of one such project, called a Program of Longitudinal Research on National Service Participants, states among its primary tasks: defining what outcomes should be used to assess the impact of service on participants; determining how to operationalize those outcomes in data collection; and assessing what existing data sources could be used as baselines for longitudinal tracking. This represented a positive change in the area of measurement. Still, institutional and cultural patterns are hard to break. The Corporation has a very long history of counting things, instead of evaluating them. It has been very slow to fully accept that outputs are only valuable if they produce good outcomes.

The events of September 11th affected all aspects of government, including national service. The Bush administration's interest in faith and community responses to public problems was pushed almost completely off the radar screen. Homeland security and international affairs took center stage as the country sought to understand what had happened and how to prevent future attacks. The tragedy raised major questions about the purpose of national service and the kind of work that volunteers should carry out in communities around the country. As the Corporation wrestled with these issues, the past loomed large. Not only was CNCS adrift for much of its brief history, but the new Republican administration did not have much time before September 11th to develop and enact a new vision of national service. President Bush planned a major expansion of service during his State of the Union address, though many of the goals articulated, including a 50 percent increase in the number of Americorps volunteers, were not achieved quickly.

In the end, the evolution of CNCS is the story of a government agency that began its early development under political pressure, and that was led to operate in a defensive mode for most of its existence. The Peace Corps was able to flourish for years because it basked in the glow of John F. Kennedy's legacy. AmeriCorps had Bill Clinton as its face and this proved to be a major political liability. Unclear about what the real effects of national service might be and how to measure them, CNCS ended up focusing heavily on producing data that tracked levels of programmatic activity, rather than the effectiveness of programs and the individual, organizational, and community-level outcomes produced by service. Propelled forward by the urgent need to show that "things were getting done," the Corporation never really settled on a clear "logic model" or theory of change that renders explicit how programmatic activity produces results that represent meaningful progress toward fulfilling CNCS's mission.

Conclusion

To date, however, the transformation of CNCS from an idea about the importance of service to a functioning tool of government action remains incomplete. After nearly a decade of growth and change, CNCS still searches for political acceptance and legitimacy. As the new leadership of the Corporation attempts to meld the traditional goals of national service with the desire to contribute to homeland defense in the aftermath of September 11th, CNCS will surely continue to evolve. It will seek to find an argument and a rationale for national service to resolve some of the partisan criticism that national service continues to stir. One of the most important steps CNCS could take in the near future is defining for itself a clear model of what it is trying to accomplish. The theory of change presented here is one possible interpretation of the goals of national service, and other interpretations are certainly possible. Being clear about how AmeriCorps and other programs operate and what they attempt to accomplish would make national service programs more effective. It would also begin to ease some of the partisan politics that still surround the idea of national service.

Part 4

Nonprofits, Religion, and Government: Opportunities and Challenges

10

Understanding Religious Organizations: Implications and Concerns for Public Policy and Social Welfare Services

Thomas H. Jeavons

Over the past several years, there has been a sometimes contentious and often confusing debate in the United States about the character, functions, efficacy, and significance of (so-called) "faith-based organizations." Unfortunately, many involved in this debate seem remarkably ignorant of the characteristics and operations of these organizations, and of what such organizations actually do now—or can do—for society at large. Many scholars, including some who study public policy and the nonprofit sector, also appear not to understand what religious organizations are, or where they fit into that sector or the political economy of the United States. Finally, a relatively new term being employed in this dialogue—"faith-based"—obscures vital differences between various kinds of entities that operate in the service of religious convictions.

This chapter explores prevalent assumptions about what religious organizations are and do, how they fit into the realm of the independent sector and networks of social service provision, and what is then reasonable to expect of them or for them. It reviews some basic facts about the nature, scope, operations, and support of religious organizations. It concludes by commenting on some of the policy implications of what is revealed.

Definitions and Types of Religious Organizations

It is important to recognize at the beginning of this discussion that there is much confusion surrounding the definition of a "religious" or "faith-based" organization. It is by no means clear which organizations belong inside or outside these sets of entities, or how these sets may or may not overlap. This is a topic I have explored in depth elsewhere (Jeavons 1993). Other scholars have made significant contributions to this discussion as well (e.g., Monsma 1996, 2002b; Smith and Kosin 2001; Sider and Unruh forthcoming).

In this paper, the term "religious organization" will be used as the overarching category. Then, for purposes of constructing an accurate and useful analysis, a distinction is drawn between congregations, on the one hand, and religious services entities of various types, on the other. Only this latter group is referred to (sometimes) as "faith-based organizations."

Why is this important? Because, if understanding is our goal, then the now typical use of the new term "faith-based organization" as an inclusive category for all religious organizations is problematic in at least two ways.

This is a problem, first, because it glosses over the substantive and serious—even fundamental—differences between congregations and other religious organizations. These are differences that cannot be ignored if one wants to make valid generalizations about the character and functions of religious organizations in our society. It is simply misleading to speak of congregations as faith-based organizations. Few, if any, pastors, rabbis, or imams understand themselves to be leading faith-based organizations. They lead churches, temples, synagogues, or mosques—that is, some kind of congregation. These are organizations whose core function is worship, whose essential nature is sacerdotal. In bringing together communities of worship and mutual care, congregations undoubtedly generate other important social goods. Research shows most engage in a range of social service activities intended to benefit both their members and others in the community (Cnaan 1999; Chaves and Tsitsos 2001; Dudley and Roozen 2001). This last feature does not, however, make them "service agencies." Being a worshipping community is the central purpose of virtually all congregations. Then, for most congregations and their members, service is an expression of that faith or religion which is taught, nurtured, and celebrated in worship.

Moreover, individuals are "members" of congregations in a more profound and multifaceted sense than is true of almost any other kind of organization. The dynamic of affiliation here is much more powerful than in almost any other membership. Robert Wuthnow, a leading sociologist of religion, has argued that other special purpose religious groups—often described before now as "parachurch organizations"—have come to have a much more important role in American religious life in recent decades (Wuthnow 1988, 1994). That is surely true. Yet is it still the case that for most religious people the congregation is where they "belong" in the most vital sense, where they expect a wide range of personal, practical, and spiritual needs to be met? For most of these people, no affiliation with any other religious organization has the same primary, all-encompassing character.

The second reason the use of the new term faith-based organization is a problem is because it suggests there is a new type of organization on the American landscape. Faith-based may be a good adjective to describe some organizations whose primary functions are some kind of service activity for the benefit of the wider community, motivated and shaped by religious experiences and principles. It is clear, however, that this is not a new phenomenon. These kinds of organizations—groups whose members share a set of religious convictions, and are doing work that is of service to others because of those convictions, perhaps in a distinctive manner shaped by those convictions— have existed and done this kind of work since the origins of the nation (Bremner 1988; Hall 1990; Jeavons 1994).

It is also important to understand that many organizations of this kind have received government funding in different ways and at different times throughout our history as a nation. Government money has flowed through these organizations to support service activities in the past, and it still does today. Conditions attached to that funding have changed over time, yet often not as much as many people think. (See, for example, Winston 1999.)

It is helpful to look more closely, then, at religious organizations, where they fit and what they do, in the American political economy and the independent sector. In this examination, congregations and religious service entities (or faith-based or faith-related organizations) will be treated separately for the purpose of getting a clearer picture.

Congregations: What They Are and Do

Congregations are the basic units of organized religious life in almost every spiritual tradition visible on the American landscape. Membership in a particular congregation is often the most important element of individuals' religious lives.

For purposes of public identification people typically describe themselves in terms of a larger tradition—such as a Catholic, Lutheran, Mormon, Jew, or Muslim. Yet, increasingly, people choose to be part of a particular congregation because that specific community of believers best meets their spiritual and practical needs, or best gives expression to their own understanding of their faith, or both. This is reflected in the growing tendency in recent years for persons to "church shop" and change denominations (Wuthnow 1988, 1998; Roof 1994, 1999). It is also demonstrated by the fact it is far more common now for Catholics to choose to attend a church outside their geographical parish than used to be the case, even though that is still contrary to traditional expectations and official rules.

Counts of the number of congregations in the United States vary according to the methods used to get them, and membership statistics are even less reliable. In the first instance, a key problem is that new congregations, like new businesses, start and die off with some frequency. As for membership numbers, churches are notoriously bad about responding to questionnaires, even those sent them by their own denominations.

Such cautions about data noted, one can still be sure that there were more than 350,000 religious congregations in the United States as the new millennium began. The *Yearbook of American and Canadian Churches* reports 349,506 in a count that only includes those affiliated with Christian traditions (Lindner 2000). There certainly have to be thousands of additional synagogues, temples, mosques, and other congregations dotting the American landscape.

This means that congregations represented more than a quarter of all "public benefit" nonprofit organizations in 1996 (Salamon 1999). This makes congregations, as a particular type of organization, by far the single largest component of the independent sector.

Additionally, findings of the biennial surveys on giving and volunteering in the United States show us that over the last two decades, between 67 percent and 75 percent of Americans said they were members of some congregation or another at any given point in time (Hodgkinson and Weitzman 1993, 1996; Kirsch, Hume, and Jalandoni 1999). (These surveys, *Giving & Volunteering USA*, were conducted and published every two years from 1986 through 1996, but are now being done every third year.) That means roughly 200 million people in the United States are members of some congregation. The *Yearbook* (Lindner 2000) reports an inclusive membership of almost 160 million people in just those congregations that are part of the Christian denominations they have figures for, which does not include many unaffiliated Christian congregations, nor non-Christian congregations. Certainly, there is no other type of nonprofit organization that can claim to have nearly as many members as congregations have, and this in a context where membership generally has more significance in terms of actual participation, than is the case for most other organizations.

Within seminaries and among church historians there is a tradition of "congregational studies." These are case studies and histories of various congregations which make efforts to illuminate common themes and trends in the characteristics and dynamics of congregations (see Wind and Lewis 1994). Sociologists and other social scientists have also done analytical and comparative studies of congregations in a broader organizational and cultural context to identify how they are changing, thriving, or failing within their communities (e.g., Ammerman 1999). This literature gives a more detailed narrative perspective on how congregations operate than can be fully summarized here. Furthermore, it would be difficult to make reliable generalizations on the basis of case studies of a (necessarily) very small sample of the total population of congregations.

Fortunately, additional survey-based research on large sets of congregations has been done as well. This includes *From Belief to Commitment* (Hodgkinson and Weitzman 1993), the annual reports of National Council of Churches called *The Yearbook of American and Canadian Churches* (Lindner 2000), and a recent massive study conducted by Hartford Seminary, *Faith Communities Today* (Dudley and Roozen 2001), which examines factors that lead to or predict congregational vitality and growth, or distress and decline. This literature and data provides a base on which to construct a reliable overview of what congregations do, how they are supported, and how they use the resources they have. What follows are the key features of that "big picture."

Some of the Basic Characteristics of Congregations

One of the most important things to know about congregations is that they tend to be small. The average congregation probably has between 100 and 200 members. Many, perhaps most, have fewer than 100. Hodgkinson and Weitzman (1993, 7) found at least 20 percent reporting fewer than 100 members, and only 28 percent reporting more than 400 members. Dividing the National Council of Churches USA (NCCUSA) figures for total number of members by the total number of congregations, the average per congregation is still smaller, around seventy-five members (Lindner 2000, 351). The Hartford study shows half of congregations have fewer than 100 regularly participating adults (Dudley and Roozen 2001, 71).

In addition, it is very important to see that these matters vary considerably by theological tradition or denomination. The membership numbers of Roman Catholic parishes typically range from 1,500 to 3,000. Yet Protestant churches that large are rare, with most having fewer than 150 members. Finally, it is worth noting than in most cases the number of members on the rolls is significantly larger than the numbers that are active. (There are a few exceptions to this rule.)

What all this means is that congregations are, for the most part, very small organizations in terms of the number of active participants in each—with a few notable exceptions. All the press given to "mega-churches" in the last decade tends to give a different, but false, impression.

It is also useful to discuss the age of congregations. Hodgkinson and Weitzman (1993, 6) found that among congregations active in 1992, almost a third had been founded before 1900, and 80 percent were at least twenty-five years old. The median age for an existing congregation was fifty-five years old, and the mean age was sixty-nine years old. Dudley and Roozen's data (2001, 7) shows more than half of existing congregations were founded before 1945. Thus, it is important to see that congregations tend to be among the most enduring institutions in their communities.

Last, the location of congregations is significant. According to Hodgkinson and Weitzman, 40 percent were located in large or small cities, with another 46 percent located in suburban areas and towns. The rest were rural. Dudley and Roozen found only 25 percent located in urban settings. Despite some disparities in this data, it is still clear that congregations are likely to be common, visible, and significant institutions in the urban environment, much more so than many kinds of commercial institutions, and perhaps more so than most other nonprofits.

The Activities and Priorities of Congregations

As previously noted, the core activity of virtually every congregation is worship, typically followed in importance by religious education. It is certainly true that many congregations are intensely involved in and care deeply about providing practical and social services to their members and their surrounding communities. The Hartford study shows 85 percent of congregations offer some social service program (Dudley and Roozen 2001, 43, 48), with most offering a number of programs ranging from tutoring to substance abuse to cash assistance. In most religions, however, it is understood that the commitment to and practice of ministry and service to others is born of and sustained by the practice of worship, deriving from both the inspiration and the teaching that occurs in worship.

The Hartford study confirms that the vitality of the worship experience is the most important predictor of congregational health and growth (Dudley and Roozen 2001, 31), although being active in service in the community is a significant secondary factor. A practical measure of the relative importance of these matters to members of congregations is what predicts changes in leadership. Ask those who work regularly with congregations, and they will tell you: Changes in clergy leadership initiated by congregations are far more likely to be caused by dissatisfaction with the worship, ministry, or pastoral care than with service programs. Nonetheless, community service and outreach ministries are not unimportant.

Another reliable indicator of the relative importance of any activity in an organization's life is its place in the budget. As some organizational scholars have noted, budgets are political as well as fiscal documents, reflecting the importance of priorities and the relative power of various stakeholders in an organization (Pfeffer and Salancik 1974; Morgan 1986). So examining how congregations spend their resources can provide important insights, too.

Looking at how congregations spend both time and money confirms the observations just made. In congregational budgets typically 75 percent of expenses are for religious program activities (including worship and religious education) within the congregation. Still, 25 percent typically is expended in donations or direct services to others (Hodgkinson and Weitzman 1993, 80). The way clergy report dividing their time interestingly reflects a very similar allocation, with 73 percent going to "ministry and religious education" and 27 percent to other kinds of service foci (Hodgkinson and Weitzman, 66).

Looking at the way other church employees and volunteers (members) spend their time, further confirmation of the relationship between worship and ministry as a core activity, and service as an outgrowth, is evident. Lay people typically spend about 55 percent of their time on ministry and religious education, and 45 percent on other service activities (Hodgkinson and Weitzman 1993, 66). So it would appear that while members contribute their energy to worship and religious education, work is more the responsibility of the clergy. Then, inspired and directed by those experiences, members give more of their time to other kinds of service and outreach.

Another important thing to note in these data is they contradict those scholars and critics who want to classify congregations as "member serving," rather than "public benefit" nonprofits. If congregations and denominations are the recipients of 43 percent to 60 percent of the charitable giving in this country (Kirsch, Hume and Jalandoni 1999; Kaplan 2000), and they turn around and expend more than 20 percent of their income on services to their communities, then they are among the most significant philanthropic agencies in our communities. In addition, Hodgkinson and Weitzman's findings (1993, 62) show that the clergy, other employees, and volunteers from congregations provided more than 125 million volunteer hours for services (other than worship and religious education) to their communities in 1992. That is a lot of community service.

Finally, the role of congregations as originators and sustainers of social service activities is augmented by their role as providers of the physical facilities for such services. And they play these roles in many communities in which those services are most needed. The recent studies of Partners for Sacred Places have documented how, particularly in depressed urban settings, houses of worship are among the most important—often the only—providers of the space for essential community services, and how frequently those services are created, staffed, and financially supported by those congregations (Cohen and Jaeger 1998).

Other studies show that congregations housed in older buildings are key providers of social services on the kind of small scale and emergency basis large agencies rarely provide. In inner-city Philadelphia, for instance, a survey of 24 congregations in historic properties showed almost half (or more) offering food pantries, clothing closets, and recreational and tutoring programs for children and teens (Cnaan 1999, 232–3).

How Congregations Are Supported

How is all this paid for? The ministry and service of congregations is supported almost entirely by gifts of individuals to those congregations, almost entirely by the generosity of their members. Only a very small number of congregations, then usually only the largest, get any foundation or government funding.

The *Yearbook of American and Canadian Churches* reports that in 1998, members of the denominations reporting to them gave $26 billion to their churches, for an average of $528 per member. Of those contributions, roughly 15 percent were for "benevolences," that is, gifts that were designated to go to, or pay for services rendered to, persons beyond the congregations. Benevolences as a percentage of total contributions have varied from 21 to 15 percent over the last eight years (Lindner 2000, 11). These figures suggest that many Americans give generously to their congregations to support activities both within and beyond the congregations themselves.

According to Hodgkinson and Weitzman (1993, 73), 86 percent of the revenues of congregations come from contributions, on average, and only 14 percent from other kinds of fees or payments. That mix varies slightly (and predictably) depending on the size of the congregations—typically 88 percent for small congregations to 84 percent for large ones. Of the 86 percent of revenues that come as contributions, more than 83 percent of this comes as gifts from individuals.

In the 14 percent of income that congregations report as "program revenues," the three largest categories by far—ranging from 20 to 25 percent for each of these categories—are fees for services, school tuitions, and investment income. Again, these vary according to the size of the congregation, with the smallest congregations having significantly less fee for services or investment income. Income from government sources is nonexistent for smaller or medium size congregations, and represents only 9 percent of the program revenues of larger congregations.

A First Partial Summary

What does all this data tell us? Congregations are among the most important of nonprofit, public benefit organizations. This claim can be supported on the basis of the number of congregations, the number of members, the support they receive, and the support they give to others. This claim is reinforced when one sees their significance in communities in which enduring, trustworthy, caring institutions are least evident and most needed.

Furthermore, they are among the most independent of all nonprofits, if the test is, "Are they beholden to others for support?" Organizational theorists describe "resource dependency" in terms of organizations being unable to chart their own course, adhere to their missions, or hold to their values because they cannot afford to alienate outsiders whom they count on for support (Pffefer and Salancik 1978; Scott 1987). A key question is, "Can nonprofit (or religious) organizations be innovative, experimental vehicles through which citizens gain a voice, and agencies that can be advocates for those they serve—even prophetic advocates—if they depend on funding from government or businesses" (Douglas 1987; Wallis 2001)? The case study literature on nonprofits is full of examples of agencies that experienced goal displacement or mission drift because they had to chase external funding to survive (see Zald and Denton 1963).

For congregations this is rarely a problem. More than 80 percent—often all—of their support comes from inside. Further, those inside are persons who likely became members because they felt an affinity with the organization's values and goals. Only in the very rare instances that large numbers of members want to see a radical change in a congregation's direction are they likely to withhold (or attach conditions to) their gifts to effect that change. Even then, as these are the members asking for this, the independence of these congregations would be intact.

However, the description of financial independence just offered for congregations would rarely fit religious service agencies. Those entities, often called faith-based organizations, tend to be very dependent on outside funds for survival. Their situation is examined next.

Religious Service Entities or Faith-Based Organizations

William Penn once said, "True godliness does not turn men out of the world, but enables them to live better in it, and excites their endeavors to mend it" (Penn 1971). Some evidence that he was right is found in the enormous number of organizations created and operated by religious people for the purposes of trying to "mend the world." While such entities are not new on the American scene, they are getting more attention in the last five years than perhaps at any time in our history as a nation.

So what is known about these religious or faith-based organizations that are not congregations? What do they look like? What do they do? How are they supported?

Most are nonprofit organizations, and the vast majority is engaged in some form of social service, education, health care, advocacy, or evangelism. While the existence of an identifiable "nonprofit" or "independent sector" may be new (Hall, 1992), the involvement of religious people and groups in these kinds of activities long predates the founding of this country.

Years ago, before most academics interested in the nonprofit sector recognized how many organizations were religious, James Douglas observed, "The fields of activity we most readily associate with nonprofit organizations include health care, education, religion, the arts, and a vast array of social welfare services. In medieval times these activities would have come primarily within the jurisdiction of the church rather than the state" (Douglas 1987). Historians of philanthropy and the nonprofit sector often highlight the key role religion played in laying the foundation for voluntary organizations, the impetus for charitable behavior of many types, and the rationale for and development of an "independent sector" as it is now sometimes called (Hall 1984; Adams 1986; Bremner 1988; Hammack 1998).

Nor has this changed much. In 1996, there were 1.2 million public-serving nonprofits in the United States. Besides the 350,000 congregations, an additional 655,000 were service providing agencies of some type, and 140,000 were action agencies (Salamon 1999, 22). There is good reason to believe that the descriptors of "religious, faith-based, or faith-related" (in some sense) fit a large number of these organizations.

Their names offer a clue. First there are the many, many "St. Whoever" hospitals, schools, and shelters. Then there are Gospel Missions and service agencies with all kinds of biblical names. Then there are the many that bear denominational monikers—such as Presbyterian Homes, the Mennonite Central Committee, and so on.

There are also large numbers of self-evidently religious public benefit nonprofits. These range from parochial schools to evangelical international relief and development agencies, from camps for the young to retirement centers and nursing homes for the elderly sponsored by particular denominations and churches, and from groups focusing on one-to-one evangelism to groups promoting the views of various religions in public policy. Many are community development corporations that were started by, are housed next door to, work in the neighborhoods of, and are entirely controlled by the members of one congregation or another, or some ecumenical body.

Finally, there are large numbers of service agencies that do not have direct ties to religious groups, or explicitly religious missions, but which were started by, and may still be, governed by boards made up entirely of religious people. There are many agencies that were in their origins (literally) "church basement nonprofits," that grew up and moved out, but in which there is still a strong sense of the work representing the religious values of those who run and serve in the organization. The evolution of such agencies is an interesting study in and of itself (Jeavons and Cnaan 1997).

As indicated before, the existence and character of this last set of agencies raises all kinds of hard questions about what defines an organization as religious (Jeavons 1993). Still, the presence of so many examples shows how many faith-based organizations—other than congregations—there are out there. Recognizing their presence in the nonprofit sector, one can ask the same kinds of questions about them as about congregations.

Basic Characteristics of Faith-Based Agencies

The difficulty with asking these same questions about faith-based agencies, however, is that they really do not provide (as a group) a unified set of entities for study, with some clear and widely shared characteristics, in the way congregations do. In fact, nowhere is there a collection of data on such agencies per se, because for purposes of professional affiliation, regulation, or study, they are identified more by the industry in which they operate than by the characteristic of being religious. (This is no surprise as we cannot define, and they would probably not agree themselves, what it means for them to be religious.) One can only surmise, then, what is very likely to be the case for these religious nonprofits, based on what one can observe directly and know about other nonprofits that are very similar in terms of their organizational profiles and fields of services:

- *In terms of size,* they range from very large, like Catholic Charities, to very small, like the numerous storefront and church basement programs with no staff, with many agencies of varying sizes in between. If these faith-based agencies or institutions parallel the characteristics of other nonprofits— and there is every reason to expect they do—the vast majority are very small, with no staff and revenues of less than $25,000 per year. Just a few are very large. Note that the very small organizations constitute up to 70 percent of all the public benefit nonprofits (Salamon 1999), and so this is very likely the case with faith-based organizations.
- *In terms of age,* there is (again) every reason to expect they are distributed in ways that parallel other public benefit or advocacy organizations. Because of the nature of their purposes and support, these organizations are more susceptible to the effects of market mechanisms, changes in social and economic conditions, and political pressures than congregations. The survival of those who are heavily dependent on fees for service may be threatened by an economic depression. So, too, changes in priorities of government (or other external) funders regarding which social problems most need attention, or what approaches to remedies they most favor, may cause the demise or a total shift in mission for some of these organizations.

    This means faith-based social service agencies are not likely to have the same durability or constancy as congregations. Many simply run out of money and go out of business. Recent waves of mergers among nonprofit social service and health agencies seeking to attain economies of scale in the face of market pressures, as well as the disappearance of many agencies, indicate that they are not as durable as congregations seem to be.
- *In terms of location,* faith-based organizations do not seem to offer the same presence in many of the communities in which their services may be most needed as do congregations. It may be the case that many social service agencies have continued to locate, or stay, where the people they serve are located. But examining many depressed urban neighborhoods suggests not.

What is clear is that many faith-based health and educational institutions that once served those areas are gone. Religious hospitals that provided charity care, and many of the religious schools that offered better educational opportunities, have all but vanished from most of these neighborhoods. Some new initiatives in health and education are being founded by newer congregations—this seems particularly evident around new Muslim congregations—but again, congregations are the ones providing a base for services.

Activities and Missions of Faith-Based Agencies

When considering faith-based agencies independent of congregations, that is religious nonprofits more broadly, there is some evidence that their mission and service activities are distributed by industry in ways that parallel other public benefit or advocacy organizations. So there are many religious hospitals, colleges, schools, social service agencies, nursing homes, day care centers, and the like.

Obviously, there are some missions and activities, such as evangelism, secular nonprofits would never pursue. There are also some causes or concerns which seem to particularly attract religious people, such as working with young people, the elderly, or the poor, in which religious agencies may be overrepresented in comparison with secular agencies. (These commitments align with priorities suggested in Scripture. The Jewish and Christian communities are constantly reminded that they will be judged by how they care for "the poor, the widow, the orphan, and the stranger.") Finally, there are some issues or concerns that have been less traditionally a focus for religious activity, such as the arts or environmental work, in which faith-based organizations are probably underrepresented.

How Faith-Based Agencies Are Supported

Since faith-based agencies look much more like secular nonprofits than congregations, one would expect their sources of income to be, on the whole, much more like those of other nonprofits, than congregations. An examination of the budgets of a sample indicates this is true. Additionally, the most important predictor of revenue mix appears to be the industry or field of service.

For instance, in the field of social services, the Salvation Army, Catholic Charities, and Lutheran Social Services depend heavily on government funding. For these agencies, the three biggest faith-based groups in social services, private support accounted for only 51 percent, 17 percent, and 10 percent (respectively) of their income last year (Chronicle of Philanthropy 2001, 37). In 1996, on average nonprofit social services agencies drew only 20 percent of their revenues from private giving, while 37 percent came from government grants, and the rest from fees for services (Salamon 1999, 37). In the cases of the three large faith-based agencies just cited, some were getting more private support than the average and some less, but what is important to observe is that all are heavily dependent on government support to survive.

Private giving typically provides an even smaller percentage of the support for health and educational institutions than for social services agencies (Salamon 1999, 80, 99). Even among community development corporations that are closely allied with particular congregations, as is sometimes the case with those founded by large African-American churches, the vast majority of funding comes not from private contributions or congregational budgets, but rather from earned income and government grants or contracts. What is clear is that faith-based service agencies cannot—apart from a few rare exceptions—count on the gifts of individuals who are insiders to their work to free them from needing large amounts of support from external sources.

A Second Partial Summary

So what do these data on and observations of religious service agencies—or faith-based organizations, in this limited sense—reveal? First, that they demonstrate remarkable diversity in character and mission, operating in very different industries, so much so that they really do not represent a "coherent set" of organizations in any way. Even what defines them, or what they understand to be true about themselves, in terms of being religious may differ radically from one to the next. In this they are very different creatures from congregations.

Second, they vary considerably in terms of size, like congregations but even more so. The largest of these faith-based organizations dwarfs even the biggest congregations. Moreover, the difference in size between the largest and smallest faith-based organizations is much greater than between the largest and smallest congregations.

Third, they do not appear to have the same durability or constancy that congregations do, especially in particular communities. Many faith-based agencies have been around a long time. However, it seems the average age of faith-based agencies is significantly lower than the average age of a congregation (sixty-nine years old). And it seems there have been many more agencies started in the last twenty or thirty years than has been the case for congregations.

Finally, it is clear that these agencies are heavily dependent on external funding, and quite frequently very dependent on government funding. Very few survive now on individuals' contributions, nor can they count on private giving to sustain them.

Implications for Current Policy Debates

What, finally, should one learn from all this? First, that more and better information is needed on the actual, rather than the presumed, character, goals, operations, and effects of faith-based service agencies. There is almost no hard data comparing the effectiveness or efficiency of faith-based versus secular service agencies (Johnson 2002). Some researchers appear to be making progress in some studies that may generate a modicum of this kind of data in limited contexts (e. g. Monsma 2002a). Still, it will continue to be exceedingly difficult to gather the data for a broader overview, because agencies have not been categorized, nor do they tend to define themselves, in these terms. The question of what defines religious work will not go away, and will continue to complicate this research and discussion.

Second, since congregations are very different from even obviously religious service agencies, one should be concerned as there are many questions not now being posed that must be asked about any policy proposals for faith-based organizations that gloss over these differences. It is critical to know that providing social services is not typically the primary purpose or goal of congregations and their members. It is presumptuous to expect that congregations want to or should change in this respect, but some of these proposals seem to assume that they will.

Congregations are, in fact, often exemplars of what it means to be community-based. But they are also a different kind of organization from social services agencies. To change in the ways that would be needed to make them successful as social services agencies—becoming more task-centered, more professional, more accountable to an external public as regards their priorities and behavior, and (possibly) just generally larger—might destroy many of the features that make them so successful as community-based organizations. Being relationship-centered, voluntary, driven by values and priorities in which they are accountable primarily to one another and God, and (perhaps) even being generally small, may be key to their being able to reach people and change lives in the ways they do now.

Third, given what is known about the typical size and character of faith-based service agencies (small, with a simple structure), more questions need to be asked about what these same policy proposals expect of and for them. Is it the primary intention that these faith-based agencies increase their service capacities? If the tool for that is government funding, which must come with new requirements for accountability, how will that change these organizations? Will increases in size, with additional staffing and more clients, cause changes in the organization that work against its ability to serve those clients in the ways originally anticipated?

Researchers have documented how complex and trying the relationships are between nonprofits and the government agencies supporting them (see Gronberg 1993; Smith and Lipsky 1993). These relationships inevitably stress and alter the nonprofits involved. It increases the bureaucratization of these agencies, typically requires them to divert energy to administration and away from program services, and limits their flexibility in delivering those services. Scholars argue that this is a response to increased size and complexity in all organizations, even if their funding sources are not government (Perrow 1986; Scott 1987).

Finally, someone should ask, "What is the primary intention of the policies proposed for 'faith-based and community organizations'?" (The present administration gives multiple and variable answers to this question in pushing these proposals.)

Is the goal here simply to move funding for, and decisions about, approaches to social services closer to the grassroots? Or is the intent to involve more religious people in the work of social services? Or is it just to give religious organizations, that want access to government funds to do social services work, the same chance to receive those funds as secular agencies?

The goal here seems to be to fix something. Yet it is not clear what precisely is broken, or even what those proposing these policies think is broken. And until there is greater clarity about what is actually broken, it is hard to judge what remedies make sense. Before new policies are put in place it is critical that someone look long and hard at the potential side effects of any proposed remedies, lest they end up doing more harm than good to these religious organizations.

For instance, if the problem these policies are supposed to fix is simply that community-based organizations, most of which are small and many of which are religious, have difficulty successfully negotiating the government granting or contracting processes, then it would seem to make sense to simplify those processes as much as possible to make that easier. However, since these are still public funds, there has to be real accountability for the uses of and results gained from these monies, which means there will inevitably be some limits on how simple these processes can be. Then it is worth noting that the obstacles here seem to be primarily ones of organizational capacities and competencies, not whether they are religious or not.

Furthermore, it is possible to seriously harm community-based (and faith-based) agencies by providing too much funding if they are not prepared to use and account for it well. Such funding could create unwanted dependencies on government, end up distancing these organizations from their communities as they "professionalize," or cause mission drift as they learn how to "chase the grants."

If the problem is that some faith-based agencies who do good works as effectively as some secular agencies—and without actively proselytizing for their own particular faith—are often denied access to government funds that would allow them to do more of that work (to the benefit of us all) just because they are religious, it might be desirable to fix that. If ways can be found to "level that playing field" without having government pay for efforts to proselytize, that would seem good, especially if this allows us as a society to be more effective in addressing particularly difficult social needs and problems. Again, however, it is worth noting that little or no evidence of systemic, widespread discrimination against faith-based agencies has been presented. There is considerable evidence that religious service agencies are among the most frequent and largest contractors at the state, county, and local level (Roundtable on Religion and Social Policy 2002).

Finally, questions need to be asked about what kinds of religious organizations should be funded this way. This analysis has shown how different congregations and service agencies are, but there is some evidence that a number of congregations have an interest in having government money to do these things (Sherman 2002). Is it wise for government to fund them for this work? What are the risks? And what will be lost if we do not?

Five years after the passage of the original "Charitable Choice" legislation, the total number of agencies who have pursued this funding is small, and the number of congregations that have done so is a minuscule fraction of all congregations—130 out of 350,000 (Sherman, 2002). Some evidence shows the number of congregations interested is growing, but other studies suggest most congregations do not want to pursue government funding for this. In the end, there may be very few who want to be involved in this.

Moreover, given the very limited administrative capacities, and the intermingling of worship and service typical of congregations, having any government funding go directly to congregations seems unwise at best. The availability of funds, the ways they are provided, and the demands for accountability that must come with them, certainly have the potential to cause goal displacement and mission drift, a loss of independence and vitality, and an erosion of the separation of church and state, for both congregations and religious services agencies, as government seeks to use these organizations to pursue public policy agendas. Unless great care is taken, real damage can be done.

A policy suggested in some proposals for funding faith-based activities would require them to set up separate 501(c)(3) entities to provide a needed and valuable safeguard against the use of these funds to support worship and to proselytize (see Working Group 2002). This would limit the number of congregations involved, because the vast majority are simply too small to handle that kind of administrative task. However, if one is concerned about preserving the integrity of both religious organizations and public funding, then again it is important to recognize that encouraging organizations to take on tasks they are not prepared to handle, and providing them more funds than they can manage, can do them serious harm.

A Summary Caution

It may be most useful to remember that many clearly religious organizations, generally larger ones, are already taking government money to provide social services. Frankly, many are doing this while including explicitly religious elements in their programs, and feel little if any pressure to compromise their religious character or witness. In talking about the Bush administration's faith-based initiative, a senior officer in the national headquarters of the Salvation Army told me, "I don't see what all the hubbub is about. We've been doing what they are talking about doing, with government money, for one hundred years." (Again, see Winston 1999.)

The truth is, many religious agencies could say the same. Even some small, church basement or storefront service ministries have had the same experience. They have done good works, in part as a way of promoting their faith, sometimes with government funding, for many years. Ultimately, what this examination of religious organizations reveals is that congregations are among the most independent of all the organizations in the independent sector. They are also active in serving public needs in many ways, in addition to meeting the spiritual and practical needs of their members. They have been doing this for a very long time, and appear to be generally as healthy now as they were one hundred years ago.

As for religious service agencies, they, too, have a long and storied history in the United States. Despite their differences in size and focus, theological and denominational outlook, and other variations in character and operation, the vast majority of them seem also to serve the public good in many valuable ways. They have long been, and continue to be, among the most important organizations in the nonprofit sector, and in our society more broadly. They look much more like other nonprofits, often struggling with issues of resource dependency and market pressures that make it hard for them to pursue their missions in the ways they would most like. But they, too, seem to be another kind of religious organization that is thriving.

So it appears that religious organizations—both congregations and religious service agencies—are now, for the most part, doing good and doing well. Moreover, this seems to have been true for a long time.

Despite this, a wide range of proposals have been put forward for changes in government policies designed, depending on who is talking, to "help them," "promote them," or "use them." These policies also seem to be intended to fix a problem, but the proponents of these policies offer no clear picture of, nor strong evidence for, something really being broken. Much closer scrutiny needs to be given to the possibilities that the proposed remedies could do more harm than good. If we are not very careful, these new policies could end up causing some serious damage to a crucial and vital set of organizations in American society.

11

Nonprofit and Faith-Based Welfare-to-Work Programs: Government's Partners or Government's Captives?

Stephen V. Monsma

As part of a four-city study of welfare-to-work programs, I interviewed the executive director and education director of a nonprofit program that emphasizes literacy training. The previous year they had had two hundred students, and in the first two months of the current year, they were down to only fourteen students. Why? It was explained to me that they receive 90 percent of their funding from government sources, and the government had adopted new rules that resulted in the precipitous drop in the students they were serving. They stated that they had not been consulted before the new rules were adopted. When asked if they were frustrated by the new rules, they replied, "Yes, more than a little! What is the background of the people making these decisions? . . . How do they come up with their rules? . . . But they are not willing to listen to us."

Earlier the organization had been a community-based group that had been privately funded. When I asked the executive director—in light of her frustration with the new rules that had been imposed on them—if she thought it would be better if they had stayed community-based with no government money, she replied:

No, I don't think it would be better. You can't replace the level of government money with private money. There is no way we would be able to serve the number of people that we serve unless we had our government funding. . . . I would never go back and be a small nonprofit with a budget of a couple hundred thousand dollars a year, which is what we could raise from private sources. . . . We would be doing a disservice to do that. The need is so great that turning down public money would fly in the face of our trying to serve.

171

This interview illustrates a basic dilemma with which I seek to deal in this essay. Most of the secular nonprofit welfare-to-work programs in the four cities my study covered receive large amounts of government money, make a significant contribution in providing welfare-to-work services to many in desperate need, but have also lost most of their independence. Most faith-based welfare-to-work programs do not receive large amounts of government money, and maintain their independence, but are so small that they make only a very limited contribution in providing needed welfare-to-work services. In this essay, I explore this dilemma in the welfare-to-work field. First, I demonstrate that secular nonprofits are able to offer major welfare-to-work services due to their receiving government funding, but at the cost of losing their independence. Next, I show that faith-based programs, with only modest amounts of government funding, have maintained their independence, but at the cost of being able to serve very limited numbers of the needy. In the third section of the paper, I suggest a way out of this dilemma.

The data that I will be using in this paper were gathered as part of a study of welfare-to-work programs in Los Angeles, Chicago, Dallas, and Philadelphia. I used a mailed questionnaire to obtain responses from five hundred welfare-to-work programs in the four cities, and either my associate researcher or I conducted follow-up, on-site visits to forty-seven programs in order to obtain a more in-depth understanding of the programs.

The Secular Nonprofit Programs

Of the five hundred welfare-to-work programs that responded to the questionnaire, 229, or 46 percent, reported that they were nonprofit organizations with "no religious base or history," or that they at one time had "a religious orientation," but today are "largely secular in nature." These secular nonprofit programs reported employing 27 percent of all the full-time staff the five hundred programs employed. The medium number of clients they served was three hundred and their median budget was $434,000 (see table 11.1). All of these are sizeable numbers, indicating that the 229 secular nonprofit welfare-to-work programs are significant players in the welfare-to-work field in the four cities.

The data also show that 87 percent of the secular nonprofit programs reported receiving government funding for their services, and that 87 percent received an average of 73 percent of their budgets from government sources. Clearly, they are heavily dependent on the government for their funding. But does this mean they have lost their independence? This is a hard question to answer by way of a written questionnaire. But in the forty-seven on-site visits, my associate researcher and I both came away with the distinct impression that the nonprofit organizations had lost much of their independence. They receive so much funding from government, and had so few other sources

Table 11.1
Comparative Size of Secular Nonprofit and Faith-Based
Welfare-to-Work Programs

	Percent of Full-time Employees*	Median Budget	Median Number of Clients Served
Nonprofit/secular	27.1% (N=221)	$434,000 (N=198)	300 (N=221)
Faith-based/segmented	3.7% (N=67)	$90,000 (N=53)	200 (N=69)
Faith-based/integrated	1.7% (N=48)	$114,082 (N=40)	110 (N=47)

*Based on the percentage of the full-time, paid employees working for the 500 of the welfare-to-work programs studied (governmental, for-profit, secular nonprofit, and faith-based).

of funds, that their fundraising strategy seems largely to consist of figuring out for which government grants or contracts they could qualify. As a result, they are bound by the rules and terms laid down by the government. This was the case with the executive director I cited in the opening paragraphs of this essay. She complained bitterly about a decision government officials had made without consultation, but felt her agency could not get along without government money without cutting services way back, thereby leaving many in need.

To take another example, when visiting a secular nonprofit agency that receives 100 percent of its welfare-to-work funding from government contracts, I interviewed several staff members who work directly with welfare recipients. They told me that basic life skills are very much needed by their clients. When asked if they favor more spending on life-skill classes, they responded: "Yes! On budgeting, saving, and buying what they need before luxuries, on nutrition, on cooking instead of snack foods. Self-esteem training is needed... . Many have no knowledge of nutrition—their kids get too much sugar, and therefore they are hyper at school and the teacher wants to medicate them. One thing leads to another." Then when asked why such classes are not offered, their response was simply there are no government monies available for such classes. As far as they were concerned, that was the end of the story—there was nothing to be done. My associate researcher and I ran into this situation and attitude in heavily government-financed programs time and again. Other researchers have reported similar findings. As Peter Frumkin (2000, 201) has summarized, "This new wave of research on public-nonprofit relations has located time and time again substantial tension and loss of autonomy within nonprofit organizations as a result of a dependence on government contracts."

Not that the government contracts, the programs they funded, or the rules accompanying government funds were universally seen as bad or constricting. Quite the opposite. When asked whether or not they were satisfied with their contacts with government officials, 74 percent of the secular nonprofits indicated they were either very satisfied or usually satisfied. When presented with a laundry list of ten possible results of their receiving government funding (five of which were positive results and five of which were negative results), 75 percent of the secular nonprofits cited more positive than negative results, with 36 percent citing three to five more positive than negative results. In short, the strong majority of the secular nonprofits seemed to be highly satisfied with their relationship with government. But this does not alter the fact that they had lost their independence. When they are told a certain program is ending, it ends. When told a program is changing, it changes. When told there is no money to meet a perceived need, that need is not met. Most of the time, the secular nonprofits felt the government programs and conditions were appropriate, but this does not change the fact of who is in charge.

The Faith-Based Programs

A total of 120 faith-based programs—or 24 percent of the total—responded to the questionnaire. Since faith-based programs can vary from those that are nominally religious to those that are deeply and pervasively religious, the questionnaire presented all of the faith-based programs with a laundry list of ten religiously based practices, and asked in which of them they engage. Based on the number and type of practices they reported engaging in, I divided the faith-based programs into faith-based/segmented and faith-based/ integrated programs. The latter are programs that seek to integrate religious elements into the welfare-to-work services they provide, and the former largely keep any religious practices either implicit or separate and distinct from the social services they provide. Seventy-two of the faith-based programs fell into the faith-based/segmented category, and forty-eight into the faith-based/ integrated category. This means that of the total of 500 programs responding to the questionnaire, 14 percent were faith-based/segmented and 10 percent were faith-based/integrated.

Of the seventy-two faith-based/segmented programs, forty, or 56 percent, reported receiving government funding. Of the forty-eight faith-based/inte-grated programs, twenty, or 42 percent, reported receiving government funding (see table 11.2). Equally important was the percentages of their budgets they reported receiving from government. The faith-based/segmented pro-grams receiving government funding reported receiving an average of 50 percent of their budgets from the government, and the faith-based/integrated programs receiving government funding reported receiving an average of 30 percent of their budgets from government. These numbers stand in sharp contrast with those of the nonprofit/secular programs, in which almost 90 percent of the programs receive an average of 73 percent of their budgets from government.

Table 11.2
Government Funding

	Percent Receiving Govt. Funding	Mean Percent of Budgets from Govt.
Nonprofit/secular	87% (N=229)	73% (N=177)
Faith-based/segmented	56% (N=72)	50% (N=36)
Faith-based/integrated	42% (N=48)	30% (N=18)

Do these figures mean that the faith-based welfare-to-work programs possessed more independence than their secular counterparts? Again, the questionnaire data do not answer this question directly, but our on-site visits tended to answer this question with a strong yes. In our interviews with the directors and other administrators of faith-based programs, we often were told stories of government funds turned down and initiatives taken in the absence of government funding. A clear sense of freedom or independence came through in countless ways, both subtle and direct, even though they are hard to quantify. For instance, one assistant director of a faith-based/integrated program that does not receive any government funds related this story: "One day we got a check for $10,000 from the government and along with it a big box filled with the paperwork that needed to be filled out. Ben [the director] packed it all up and sent it back! There seems to be so much red tape involved with government. We probably could take some money for some programs, but then we would have to be so careful about when we talk about Christ. Ben's philosophy is that if we do not have to have it, it is better to get along without it."

A faith-based inner-city ministry, that receives 40 percent of its funding from government sources and 60 percent from private donations, illustrates the ability of providers with independent sources of money to move into new fields and to meet new needs as they recognize and define them. The assistant executive director told us that there are now fewer single mothers on welfare in their area, "but former welfare recipients who are single moms are now working one or two jobs trying to make it. Their kids are left to wander the neighborhood, so now we have shifted our programming to provide a safety net for unsupervised children." In a similar vein, the head of a faith-based inner-city program that has received government funding, expressed strong opinions about what she saw as the harshness of the government regulations and her program's use of private funds to overcome them: "They [the government] make it difficult for us to do what you know people need because they tell people they have to leave [the program after a period of time]. . . . So, in the interest of continuity, we have programs set up for continuity."

But this independence comes with a price: one of small size and limited impact. Although 24 percent of the five hundred welfare-to-work programs included in the study were faith-based, table 11.1 shows that only 5.4 percent of the full-time workers employed by the five hundred programs worked for faith-based agencies. It also shows the median budget of each type of the faith-based programs was about $100,000, compared to over $400,000 for the secular nonprofit programs. They also served fewer clients, although this is a less reliable guide to program size since it does not take into account the length or depth of involvement with clients.

The dilemma seems complete: Does one choose government funding and an ability to make a significant impact on the welfare-to-work needs in one's community, but at the cost of losing one's independence? Or does one reject government funding and maintain one's independence, but at the cost of being so small that one's impact on the welfare-to-work needs in the community is very limited? This, of course, assumes that faith-based providers have a choice when it comes to government funding, and that if they would only apply for government funding they would receive it just as their secular counterparts do. There is room to doubt the accuracy of this assumption, but that is an issue I do not attempt to deal with in this essay.

One final observation from my data is needed to complete the picture of the independence of the secular nonprofit and faith-based welfare-to-work programs. Table 11.3 shows the types of contacts the nonprofit/secular and the two types of faith-based programs reported they have with government officials. In light of the much lower level of government funding of faith-based programs as compared to secular nonprofit programs, the most surprising aspect of this table is the almost total absence of any difference among the three different types of programs in government contacts. Even the faith-based/integrated programs—which had the lowest level of government funding—reported as many contacts with government officials as did the other two types of programs. Even when it came to informal consultations with government officials, the faith-based programs—including the faith-based/ integrated programs—were as likely to be sought out by government officials as were the secular nonprofit programs. This shows that the independence of the faith-based programs was not bought at the cost of being isolated from and ignored by the governmental welfare structure, nor that an added advantage of the secular nonprofit programs that helped counterbalance their loss of independence was achieving access to the governmental welfare structure. Government funding seems to be largely independent from being included in the network of welfare-to-work agencies and services.

Table 11.3
Types of Organizations and Contacts with Government
(Percentage reporting various types of contacts)

	No Govt. Contacts	Referrals from Govt.	Referrals to Govt.	Licensed by Govt.	Safety, Health Inspec- tions	Clients in Govt. Jobs	Informal Consulta- tion Contacts	Other Contacts	N
Government	5.7%	72.9%	38.6%	11.4%	11.4%	31.4%	54.3%	18.6%	70
For-Profit	4.2%	79.2%	41.7%	29.2%	29.2%	16.7%	54.2%	20.8%	24
Non-Profit/Secular	6.0%	75.1%	43.8%	17.5%	26.7%	22.6%	58.1%	15.7%	217
Faith-Based/Segmented	13.4%	52.2%	41.8%	14.9%	32.8%	6.0%	56.7%	9.0%	67
Faith-Based/Integrated	6.3%	60.4%	47.9%	8.3%	37.5%	10.4%	56.3%	22.9%	48

A Proposed Way out of the Dilemma

There is no easy, complete way out of this dilemma. But there are three key steps that I submit to offer at least a partial resolution of it. These steps are rooted in the belief that some independence from government on the part of organizations that make up the "independent sector" is good for society. Otherwise, why have an independent, nonprofit sector at all?

Limit the Amount of Government Funding for Any One Nonprofit Program

The first principle is that the amount of government funds for any one program should be limited to something less than 100 percent. It is foolish to think that programs run by nonprofit agencies that receive 100 percent of their funding from government—whether secular or faith-based— can retain any real sense of autonomy. This may also be the case with a program that receives something like 75 percent of its funding from the government, and becomes even more likely as the percentage moves upward. This is true for three reasons. First, there are the inevitable pressures on program administrators to adhere to any and every directive coming from the supervising government officials. When a faith-based housing program in Washington, D.C., funded by HUD ran into charges of some improper activities, the president of the program said, "We will adjust and make any necessary adjustment that HUD suggests" (Leonnig 2002, A01). This is where administrators of programs 100 percent funded by government all too often end up. The programs are totally dependent on government, and without the continued blessing of the government, workers will be laid off and persons in need sent away empty. In such a situation, he who pays the piper indeed calls the tune.

As I have written elsewhere, a second and less obvious factor also comes into play (Monsma 2000, 177–178). As the percentage of a program's budget from government sources goes up, government officials will feel more justified in making demands on the program administrators—and program administrators will often feel a greater obligation to accede to those demands. This is a subtle, psychological factor, but that does not make it any less real or powerful. The reason the payer calls the piper's tune is rooted in economic realities, but it is also rooted in the felt right of the payer to call the tune. As the proportion of a program's budget that comes from government sources goes up, it is almost inevitable that the agency-government relationship will shift from one of partnership to one of supervisor-subordinate.

A third factor at play is that once a program has become totally or largely dependent on government funds, it loses any ability it might have had, or could have developed, to raise its own independent funds. Contacts with corporate or foundation grant officers are lost, potential major donors are no longer cultivated, and mailing lists of supporters become outdated. This means alternatives to government funding wither away, adding to the dependence on government funding and a greater loss of independence.

This limiting of the percentage of a program's budget that originates with government can be achieved in two ways: Agencies can impose some self-limitations and government can require nonprofit organizations to put up some matching funds. Taking the self-limitation first, any agency—whether secular or faith-based—that wishes to remain a part of the independent sector in fact as well as in name, should establish an internal policy that it will not allow government funding for any one of its programs to exceed a certain set percentage. There is, of course, no one magic percentage, but ideally the percentage of government funding would be kept at or below 50 percent. That may not be a realistic goal for many organizations and programs, and for some programs and organizations government funding in the 50 to 75 percent range may be compatible with maintaining a strong measure of independence. But as the percentage of government funding moves above 75 percent, the danger of losing one's independence goes up exponentially. These percentages are not rooted in any empirical data, but represent my best sense, based on interviews with many program directors in secular and faith-based nonprofit organizations in three countries over the past ten years. Further research to confirm or modify these estimates is badly needed.

On the assumption that government itself has an interest in keeping the independent sector independent—for purposes of the stronger public policies that flow from the flexibility and innovativeness of the independent sector—government should require a certain level of matching funds from nonprofit and faith-based agencies seeking its funds to support their social services. Government should supplement—even heavily supplement—privately raised funds. It should not totally supplant them. When government offers 100 percent funding to independent sector agencies, it creates a temptation that is almost impossible for a financially weak organization, desperately seeking to meet overwhelming needs in its community, to ignore. But what may appear to be the most beneficent action to take in the short run may be the most destructive action in the long run. If that agency, due to the availability of 100 percent government funding, loses or never establishes strong roots in its community, its effectiveness is likely to remain limited, to the ultimate detriment of the very community it is seeking to serve.

Tax Benefits for Charitable Giving

A second key step that I believe should be carried out to protect the independence of faith-based and other nonprofit organizations is to broaden the tax benefits that both individuals and corporations receive for making contributions to nonprofit organizations and their programs.

This can be accomplished by several proposals that have been circulating in Washington for the past several years. Currently, they are embodied in the CARE (Charity Aid, Recovery, and Empowerment) legislation jointly introduced by Senators Joe Lieberman and Rick Santorum (S. 272, 108th Congress). This legislation would create a new charitable income tax deduction of up to $500 for individual taxpayers and $1,000 for couples who do not itemize their tax returns. This provision would be especially helpful in encouraging low- and middle-income families—the ones most likely not to itemize their tax returns—to make additional contributions to nonprofit organizations. This bill also allows persons to make charitable contributions to nonprofit organizations from their IRA accounts, and has provisions to encourage more foundation and corporate giving.

Other incentives to increase private giving to nonprofit organizations' social service activities could be explored. Former Senator Dan Coats, for example, while in the Senate proposed an outright tax credit of up to $500 for individuals and $1,000 for joint filers for contributions to nonprofit agencies whose primarily purpose is the alleviation of poverty (S. 1216, 104th Congress). Other, even more creative, options could be developed.

The first two steps towards maintaining both government funding and nonprofits' independence work together. One emphasizes the importance of faith-based and other nonprofits maintaining a funding base outside of government sources. The other seeks to make it easier for them to develop their own independent funding base.

Protecting the Autonomy of Faith-Based Organizations

A third step I believe is vital to solving the dilemma described earlier is to protect the autonomy of faith-based organizations by applying the principles of what has come to be termed "charitable choice," whenever government helps fund faith-based social services programs. Charitable choice was first adopted as a part of the 1996 restructuring of the welfare system, and since then similar language has been included in the Welfare-to-Work Act (1997), the Community and Services Block Grant Program (1998), and the Substance Abuse and Mental Health Service Administration drug treatment program (2000) (Center for Public Justice 1997; Sherman and Green 2002, 6–7). It has three main goals: (1) to assure faith-based groups are able to compete equally with secular groups for contracts and grants to provide social services; (2) to protect certain religious autonomy rights of the faith-based groups receiving government funds; and (3) to protect the rights of those receiving services from faith-based providers.

It is important to apply these principles of charitable choice whenever government funds faith-based social services programs. To understand why this is the case, it is necessary, first, to note the uncertain nature of church-state law. Sorting out what is and is not constitutional in regard to government helping to fund social services rendered by faith-based groups has been rarely litigated up to the Supreme Court. In fact, there have been only two such cases, and one of these was from the nineteenth century. This means there are almost no Supreme Court precedents that deal directly with the constitutionality of governmental funding of welfare-to-work and similar social services programs of faith-based organizations. This would not be so bad if church-state law were clear, since then one could draw a clear line from other areas to the governmental funding of the social services of faith-based groups. But, as two legal scholars have written, establishment clause decisions of the Supreme Court "are riven by contradiction and bogged down in slogans and metaphors" (McConnell and Posner 1989, 1). In 1987, Justice Antonin Scalia referred to "our embarrassing Establishment Clause jurisprudence," and to the Supreme Court as having created "such a maze of the Establishment Clause that even the most conscientious governmental officials can only guess what motives will be held unconstitutional" in *Edwards v. Aguillard*, 482 U.S. 578 (1987, 636 and 639). Church-state law is anything but clear. There are precedents that can be cited to support almost any kind of government funding of faith-based social services. Others can be cited to oppose the very same funding. The end result is massive uncertainty.

My own research has shown that many faith-based organizations—even those that integrate religious elements into the services they provide—often receive government funds for their social services programs, and do so with few complaints about government officials interfering with their faith-based practices (Monsma 1996). In the welfare-to-work study I have used in this essay, 42 percent of even the faith-based/integrated welfare-to-work programs reported receiving government funds. Not one reported that they have had to curtail any of their religious practices!

But that is not the whole story. Frequently, in discussing this issue with directors of faith-based welfare-to-work programs receiving government funds, it became clear that something such as a "don't ask, don't tell" policy was in place. As the associate director of an inner-city ministry told me: "My theory is that in the inner city nobody really cares what you do. One can evangelize, etc., without persons asking questions. This is different in the suburbs—there the ACLU would be all over you. . . . The political alliances are different here in the inner city. The ACLU and we are on the same side on many issues, not at odds. This helps." Similarly, when the executive director of a faith-based agency that receives limited government funding discussed the ambiguity surrounding government money, and what they may and may not do of a spiritual nature, I suggested that perhaps it was a don't ask, don't tell policy. She responded: "Exactly!" and then went on to compare the situation to that of the city building code, which is workable only because it is usually not enforced in all its particulars. Similarly, she suggested that as long as they welcome persons of all faiths and do not require participation in religious exercises, and as long as she maintains a good working relationship with the government officials, questions are not raised about their faith-based practices.

But this is shaky ground for partnerships between government and faith-based organizations to be based. As a result, many faith-based groups do not accept government funds out of fear that doing so would compromise their religious mission. Of the sixty-two faith-based welfare-to-work programs included in my study that do not receive government money, 24, or 39 percent, said they have a self-conscious policy of not accepting government funds (compared to 19 percent of the 31 secular nonprofit programs that do not receive government funding).

The on-site interviews with the leaders of faith-based welfare-to-work programs have convinced me that the fear of having to limit their religiously inspired practices is one key factor leading many of these programs to avoid government funds (although other concerns are also a factor). For instance, the senior pastor of a church heavily involved in inner-city ministries that does not receive government funds told me his church "would be very cautious in regard to any arrangement with the government that would in any way compromise the autonomy of our ministry, and especially our message. . . . To us the message is everything—word and deed are both important—the word message is essential to the action. We do not want to compromise that." The head of a Los Angeles faith-based program that has applied for, but not received government funding, insisted that, "we don't want to compromise parts of our program for governmental sources of funding."

One should also sympathize with the government officials charged with administering government contracts or grants with little legal guidance as to what is and is not proper in a potential partnership with faith-based providers. In the absence of clear legal precedents from the courts and of clear legal language from Congress, it is not surprising that they sometimes decide the safest course of action is to err on the side of putting stringent restrictions on the funding provided faith-based providers, or to even avoid partnerships with faith-based groups altogether.

In short, uncertainty breeds fear, and fear leads to an avoidance of seeking government funds on the part of many faith-based providers, and a hesitation to partner with faith-based groups on the part of some public officials. And that is the problem. Faith-based groups—many of whom have strong track records of offering effective help to the needy of our society—usually remain small and limited. This is primarily unfortunate, not due to a concern for the faith-based providers themselves, but due to a concern for the most needy in our society who would be helped by the services of these providers, if only they could expand their programs and services. They—and not the faith-based providers themselves—are the losers when legal uncertainties drive either government program administrators or faith-based providers to avoid government-faith-based partnerships.

Given these constricting uncertainties and fears, it is incumbent on Congress to legislate what the rules of the game should be when it comes to funding faith-based social services programs. Without greater legal clarity, faith-based social services programs are likely never to realize their full potential in contributing to the most needy among us.

But does charitable choice represent the sort of rules of the game that Congress should enact? I believe there are solid theoretical, constitutional reasons to answer with a clear yes. There is a growing group of constitutional scholars who are arguing that what the First Amendment's religion clauses require above all else is that the government be neutral on matters of religion. Douglas Laycock has formulated what he terms substantive neutrality, and what I have elsewhere termed positive neutrality, in these words: "the religion clauses require government to minimize the extent to which it either encourages or discourages religious belief or disbelief, practice or nonpractice, observance or nonobservance. . . . [R]eligion is to be left as wholly to private choice as anything can be. It should proceed as unaffected by government as possible" (Laycock 1990, 1001–1002; Monsma 1993). Increasingly, the Supreme Court is moving away from the old strict separationist standard and in the direction of adopting this conception of neutrality (Rosen 2000).

If this is the standard that one seeks to apply, it is clear, first, that beneficiaries of the social services programs at least partly funded by government should (1) be open to persons of all faiths and of none, and (2) a variety of faith-based and secular services should ideally be available from which beneficiaries can freely choose, and if only a limited number of programs can be made available, at least one should be secular in nature. The government ought never to fund faith-based programs and not provide a secular alternative. To do so is for government to tilt in favor of religious over secular social services programs.

But it is equally clear that to offer funds only to secular programs, and not to faith-based ones, is a violation of governmental religious neutrality. To do so would be to favor secular programs over religious ones, and would be no more neutral than favoring religious programs over secular ones. Similarly, to provide money to faith-based social services programs only on the condition that they secularize the services they are offering is also to violate the norm of neutrality. Then government would be saying to a faith-based welfare-to-work program, for example, that it will help support the services they are offering, but only on the condition that they give up certain of their religious beliefs or practices. The governmental pressures to alter the religious practices or mission of the organization are clear. This is anything but neutrality or evenhandedness.

It is important to see charitable choice as an attempt to give legislative voice to the principle of governmental religious neutrality. Under charitable choice, government may not favor either faith-based or secular providers over the other, nor may it favor providers of one faith over another. There is to be, as it is often put, a level playing field. This is neutrality.

This is where the all-important right of faith-based organizations to make hiring decisions on the basis of religious criteria comes in. It is crucial to understand what is at issue here. If a faith-based group can no longer define its membership on the basis of beliefs and practices vital to that faith's tradition, it will virtually cease to exist as a faith-based organization. A Muslim or Jewish organization, most of whose staff are Christians, ceases to be Muslim or Jewish in the full sense of the word. This has long been recognized by legislation and the courts. Section 702 of the Civil Rights Act of 1964 specifically provides that religious groups may hire on the basis of religious criteria, even though nonreligious groups may not do so. In 1987, a unanimous Supreme Court ruled that such provisions are fully constitutional in *Corporation of Presiding Bishop v. Amos*, 483 U.S. 327 (1987). Maintaining certain religious criteria in hiring is, in Justice William Brennan's words, "a means by which a religious community defines itself, " in *Corporation of Presiding Bishop v. Amos*, 342. Here the law is clear. This means that charitable choice merely says that due to their accepting some government funding for their social services programs, religious organizations will not lose a right they already possess, and one that many feel is vital to their continued existence as an autonomous entity.

It is also important to protect the rights of the beneficiaries of social services programs that receive government funding. They, too, are now sometimes left in an uncertain, untenable position because their rights have not been clearly delineated by the courts. I was appalled when I visited one California county and was told several of the judges there will give first time drug offenders a choice between going to prison or to a pervasively religious drug treatment program. Charitable choice clearly requires that recipients of services must be given a choice: If they object to receiving services from a faith-based provider, there must be an equivalent secular program they can attend. Unless they are in a program already covered by charitable choice, this is a protection they may not now have.

It is by allowing faith-based providers to compete for government funds without either being given special advantages or special handicaps, by protecting the right of faith-based groups receiving government funds to be true to their faith tradition, and by assuring that recipients of services are not forced into faith-based programs they do not wish to be in, that government is truly neutral on matters of religion. It is by following these principles that government does not favor religion over secularism, or secularism over religion, or one religion over another. That is living out a positive, substantive neutrality that does not favor a person or group of any particular faith, or of none. And that, after all, is what the First Amendment is all about.

Conclusion

This essay has argued that presently our polity faces a dilemma when it comes to nonprofit and faith-based social services providers: The unfortunate choice now seems to be between small size and not meeting many pressing needs, or large size made possible by government funding but with a loss of flexibility and independence. In this situation, the secular nonprofits and faith-based providers lose, the needy among us lose, and the government— whose public policies are seeking to meet societal needs—also loses. By limiting the percentage of the independent sector providers' budgets that comes from government sources, by making it easier for providers to develop private and independent funding sources, and by establishing legal rules of the game for the government-faith-based provider partnership, I am convinced the independent sector would regain much of its independence, receive an infusion of new strength from revitalized faith-based providers, and recipients of faith-based services would find new protections. Most important of all, new resources would be unleashed for meeting social needs that now all too often appear intractable.

12

Faith in Communities: A Solid Investment

Amy L. Sherman

Faith-based organizations—FBOs—are hot. Politicians, religious leaders, and media talking heads have all weighed in on President George W. Bush's ambitious "faith-based initiative." This public discussion is useful, for the faith community has long been a major contributor in the national effort to fight poverty and rejuvenate distressed communities, but its role has frequently been neglected.

The issue of the faith community's proper place in the public square is not only hot, but controversial. Supporters of the Bush initiative assert that FBOs can do a better job than government agencies in curing some of the nation's social ills, such as drug abuse or teen pregnancy. Citing evidence indicating that FBOs are discriminated against or otherwise hindered by government policies, supporters are demanding reforms (Esbeck 1996; The White House 2001). They assert that FBOs often provide a disproportionate amount of social services, compared to the amount of government funding they garner. John DiIulio, former director of the White House Office of Faith-Based and Community Initiatives, notes that, for example, in Philadelphia, 25 percent of the housing rehabilitation work being done in many neighborhoods is by grassroots faith-based organizations, and yet only one congregation, Cookman United Methodist, has received a government contract under charitable choice (DiIluio 2001). New public investment strategies should, in his view, be advanced to address this disparity.

Many supporters applaud the "charitable choice" guidelines, new rules attached to four federal social welfare programs since 1996, that seek to protect the religious character of FBOs doing business with government. In brief, charitable choice is aimed at facilitating fruitful collaboration between government and the faith community that protects the religious integrity and character of FBOs accepting government dollars. Under charitable choice,

FBOs contracting with government retain authority over their mission, governing board, and prophetic voice. They have the right to maintain a religious atmosphere in their facilities. They retain the right to use religious criteria in employment decisions. Simultaneously, charitable choice seeks to protect the civil liberties of individuals who receive services from FBOs collaborating with government. Religious groups must offer their services to all eligible participants, regardless of their religious affiliation (or lack of affiliation). In addition, if a client objects to receiving services from an FBO, the government must ensure that he or she obtains assistance from another organization. Moreover, FBOs must not use government funds for purposes of "sectarian worship, instruction, or proselytization," and they must not require service recipients to participate in religious practices. Supporters of the faith-based initiative desire to see these "faith friendly" guidelines attached to other federal programs that underwrite such activities as housing for the low-income elderly and education for at-risk youth.

Other supporters worry about direct government funding of FBOs through contracts, but in general do favor strategies aimed at directing greater public and private resources to faith-based "outposts of health and healing" (such as through changes in the tax code). Some, such as Marvin Olasky, Michael Horowitz, and Robert Woodson, favor charity tax credits (Horowitz 2000).

Critics charge that the faith-based initiative is misguided. Some worry that charitable choice breaches the separation of church and state (U.S. House of Representatives 2001). Others believe publicly funded FBOs should not be allowed—as charitable choice permits—to discriminate in their hiring on the basis of religion. The ACLU, Americans United for Separation of Church and State, and the Jewish Council for Public Affairs have all raised this objection. Supporters of charitable choice argue that its provisions are nothing new: Title VII of the 1964 Civil Rights Act provides an exemption for religious organizations that effectively permits them to take religion into consideration in employment decisions (Esbeck 2000). Still others contend that congregations and faith-based nonprofits will suffer from excessive government entanglement under charitable choice. Some fear a secularization of FBOs' work on the frontlines if FBOs take government money (Loconte 1997).

Supporters and critics both make valid points. But much of their discussion has been "Beltway-centric": too focused on the legislative fortunes of the Bush administration's faith-based initiative on Capitol Hill, and neglectful of what is actually happening, "on the streets," across America. A look outside of Washington, away from the political discussions, sheds much-needed light on the issue of faith-based social action. It offers a compelling case for greater investment in "faith in communities," as well as important insights about how to construct government-faith collaboration in ways protective of FBOs and fruitful for the disadvantaged citizens they serve.

Scope and Scale of Faith-Based Social Action

The first observation "from the ground up" that can move the discussion to a more productive level is simply this: Faith communities are making an enormous contribution in assisting needy families and bettering distressed neighborhoods.

The best current data we have concerning the community outreach activities of religious congregations come from the Hartford Seminary Faith Communities Today survey (http://www.fact.hartsem.edu). A massive undertaking, the survey examined 14,000 congregations of diverse faith groups (Christian, Jewish, Muslim, Buddhist, and others). The survey revealed that 85 percent of these congregations provide at least one community service. Most common are relief-benevolence activities: providing food, money, clothing, or emergency shelter. But many congregations are involved in much more extensive social services efforts. Over half of the congregations are engaged in providing health care services, and one-third are involved in tutoring children, ministering in prisons, offering substance-abuse programs, or providing housing for the elderly.

The Hartford study's findings more or less accord with those from University of Pennsylvania professor Ram Cnaan's ambitious and in-depth survey work (Cnaan 1999). Cnaan's data suggest even more congregations are active in community outreach. His study estimates that 92 percent offer at least one social service. He also estimates that one-third of all day-care programs in America are housed in religious buildings, and that congregations spend some $36 billion annually on social services. Andrew Billingsley's investigation of the social impact of African-American congregations shows them vigorously engaged in community serving programs. In various regional samples of hundreds of such churches, Billingsley regularly found that nearly 70 percent of African-American congregations are involved in outreach (Billingsley 1999, 199). My own recent investigations of the outreach conducted by Hispanic congregations came to similar conclusions: 69.5 percent of the 427 congregations surveyed offered social services for community residents (Sherman 2003).

While we know much about religious congregations' efforts in investing in community social services, there have been fewer studies on the contributions made by faith-based nonprofit organizations. In 1985, the Council on Foundations published a study indicating that faith-based nonprofits spent between $7.5 and $8 billion annually on social services—not including religious hospitals, orphanages, or adoption agencies (Cnaan 1999, 180–181). A 1998 study by researchers at the Aspen Institute sheds a little more light, though the data combines both congregations and nonprofits. This one estimated that, "religious congregations, national networks, and freestanding organizations spend between $15 billion and $20 billion of privately contributed funds a year on social services" (McCarthy and Castelli 1998, 6). These scholars noted that in 1994, "private contributions to six major religion-sponsored social service providers alone totaled $1.7 billion" (1998, 19). (The six organizations were: Salvation Army, Catholic Charities USA, Jewish Federations, YMCA, International Union of Gospel Missions, and Christian Social Services Agencies.)

Also available is anecdotal evidence that the sheer number of faith-based nonprofits committed to serving broken families and broken places has been increasing over the last decade. The National Congress of Community Economic Development Corporations (NCCED), for example, has seen steady growth in membership of faith-based community development corporations. Twelve years ago, the Christian Community Development Association began with 35 member organizations. Today, it boasts over four hundred.

Moreover, based on about five years of poking around in distressed urban communities throughout America, I have discovered that there are many small but active faith-based organizations completely "under the radar screen" that do not register in formal counts of religious social services agencies. I'm not alone in this experience. Professor Michael Mata of the Urban Leadership Institute at Claremont reports two recent experiences with professional agencies hired to do community asset-mapping in low-income Los Angeles neighborhoods. In the first instance, the agency failed to identify twenty-one FBOs that existed in the community. In the second, the firm "totally missed the churches," Mata says. His organization identified nearly one hundred congregations and FBOs in that community. "The professionals contracting to do [asset] mapping are not seeing churches as a vital part of the community," Mata laments (telephone interview by author with Michael Mata, director, Urban Leadership Institute at the Claremont School of Theology, February 27, 2002).

Clearly, between the programs and resources offered by congregations and religious nonprofits, hundreds of thousands of disadvantaged citizens are being served every year. These services are being conducted both by large, well-known groups, such as Catholic Charities and the Salvation Army, and by tiny and mid-sized faith-based groups. Any constructive public engagement with the faith sector should be premised on an appreciation of the role FBOs and congregations are already playing, as well as clarity about the diversity of groups active on the front lines.

Does It Work?

The second observation helpful to the debate about the role of FBOs is that there is considerable anecdotal evidence, as well as a small, but growing, body of empirical research, as to their effectiveness. The anecdotal evidence has been sketched out by a wide number of observers and scholars. A literature review of much of this work is available in my book *Reinvigorating Faith in Communities* (Sherman 2002). This data includes book-length studies of individual congregations, such as in Freedman (1993) and Edington (1996). A number of more recent books—Sherman (1997); Woodson (1998); Carle and DeCaro (1999); Harper (1999); Sider, Olson and Unruh (2002)—provide detailed portraits of the community outreach efforts of many diverse congregations. Articles published in various religious periodicals (*Christianity Today*, the *Christian Century*, and *Prism*), secular magazines (*Newsweek*, the *American Enterprise*, *Philanthropy*, *Reason*, and *Policy Review*), and a host of newspapers, have highlighted the successful work of faith-based nonprofits engaged in everything from rehabilitating prisoners and wooing kids out of gangs to mentoring welfare recipients and fixing broken inner-city schools.

One faith-based program highlighted in a number of media accounts is the National Jobs Partnership. This organization operates job training and mentoring programs in over twenty U.S. cities and boasts an 83 percent job retention rate among its 1,100 graduates. Many of the graduates are former welfare recipients and most faced multiple barriers to employment, such as homelessness, a criminal record, or substance abuse issues (Sherman 2001). This compares very favorably with job retention rates achieved by government programs. The best comparative statistic I located was from a study of job retention rates of 1,836 welfare recipients in job training programs in four cities (Chicago, IL; Portland, OR; Riverside, CA; and San Antonio, TX). Just over 39 percent retained their jobs one year following the training program (Rangarajan and Novak 1999). Another reasonable comparison of the Jobs Partnership's achievements is with the job retention rates reported among individuals that have exited the welfare rolls under various state welfare reform programs. In state-sponsored "leaver" studies examining how welfare-to-work clients are faring, New York reported a 50 percent job retention rate for its clients, Arizona 53 percent, and Wisconsin 68 percent (National Campaign for Jobs and Income Support 2000). The Urban Institute's estimates are more optimistic. Nationwide, they estimate employment among welfare "leavers" at 64 percent. Clearly, none of these comes close to the Jobs Partnership's 83 percent job retention rate (Loprest 2001, 3).

As to empirical studies, the Center for Research on Religion and Urban Civil Society (CRRUCS), directed by John DiIulio, is the leading organization. Associate Director Byron Johnson's report *Objective Hope: Assessing the Effectiveness of Faith-Based Organizations* provides the most comprehensive literature review of studies examining the efficacy of FBOs available (Johnson, Tompkins and Webb 2002). In addition, CRRUCS has published several important studies of its own on the topic in the past two years.

One examines the role played by African-American churches in reducing deviance among inner-city youth, and concludes that, "involvement of African-American youth in religious institutions significantly buffers or interacts with the effects of neighborhood disorder on crime, particularly serious crime" (Johnson 2001–2002). In layman's language, African-American kids who live in dysfunctional neighborhoods are less likely to get involved in crime if they go to church. A second CRRUCS study demonstrated that African-American inner-city kids who are involved in religious activities are less likely to take illicit drugs. Importantly, the study also found that these "churched" inner-city kids were less likely than nonreligious, better-off suburban kids to be using drugs (Johnson 2000–2001). Both studies cite a few other scholarly inquiries on related questions, but lament the general dearth of attention to the "faith factor" in academic research. A third CRRUCS study examined the influence of religious engagement on inner-city youth's school performance, and found that religious involvement aids the resiliency of such teens. That is, involvement by inner-city adolescents in churches is much more likely to contribute positively to their academic progress than is involvement in religious activities by wealthier suburban kids. Attending church, the researcher found, helps inner-city teens to stay on track in school and assists them in improving their educational status (Regnerus 2001–2003).

Several empirical studies have evaluated the work of Prison Fellowship, a national faith-based ministry launched by former Nixon White House official, Chuck Colson. Prison Fellowship was founded twenty-five years ago to "exhort, equip, and assist the Church in its ministry to prisoners, ex-prisoners, victims, and their families, and in its promotion of biblical standards of justice in the criminal justice system." (See www.prisonfellowship.org for the organization's vision and mission statements.) A 1996 study by the Center for Social Research considered the impact of prisoners' participation in Prison Fellowship activities on their likelihood of incurring prison infractions. At the Lieber Prison in South Carolina, 19 percent of the inmates had participated in Prison Fellowship activities. Less than 10 percent of these inmates incurred prison infractions, compared to over 23 percent of inmates who had not participated (O'Connor, Ryan and Parikh 1997).

Perhaps more important are the recidivism studies that have been conducted. A 1997 National Institutes of Health study found that former inmates in New York state that had participated in Prison Fellowship Bible Studies were nearly three times less likely to be re-arrested during the twelve months following their release than were a comparable group of inmates who had not attended Prison Fellowship programs (Johnson et al. 1997). The so-called "Loyola Study" of Prison Fellowship tracked recidivism data over an eight-to-fourteen-year follow-up period for 180 graduates of the Prison Fellowship Washington Discipleship Seminar, matched against a comparison group of 185 inmates who did not attend the seminar. Seminar graduates had lower rates of recidivism than did the control group. Among women, the findings were particularly impressive: 19 percent of the Prison Fellowship attendees recidivated, compared to 47 percent of the control group women. For men, the comparison was 45 percent for Prison Fellowship graduates versus 52 percent for the control group (Young et al. 1995).

A handful of studies have also been conducted on the effectiveness of Teen Challenge, a faith-based drug rehabilitation program. An early study (1976) by the National Institute on Drug Abuse found that an astonishing 86 percent of Teen Challenge graduates remained drug-free seven years after their graduation from the program. This compared to a success rate in the single digits for government-run, secular programs. A follow-up study in 1994 surveyed alumni of Teen Challenge over a thirteen-year period, and documented again very high numbers of graduates who had remained drug-free. Even though 72 percent of the participants in the study had failed in other drug rehabilitation programs before entering Teen Challenge, 67 percent of those who graduated were continuing to abstain from drug and alcohol use. The most recent assessment of the ministry was conducted by a Northwestern University Ph.D. candidate. Her dissertation showed that 86 percent of those who complete the Teen Challenge program have remained drug-free and that nearly all had escaped the "revolving door phenomenon" of substance abuse treatment (Elliott 2000).

The anecdotal and limited empirical evidence gives plausibility to the idea that some faith-based approaches do indeed work well, though additional rigorous empirical studies are needed before any broad-ranging claims about the superiority of faith-based approaches over others can be justified. After all, in DiIlulio's witticism, the plural of anecdote does not equal data. Nonetheless, a body of evidence suggesting the power of FBOs appears to be gradually accumulating.

Why Does It Work?

To the extent we have some reason to believe that faith-based approaches are effective, the next logical question is, Why? The easy sound bite here, of course, is: "They work because of the faith." That is, they get people "right with God" and this aids in producing positive social outcomes. This is a very important and often fully accurate statement. Indeed, it is frequently the main point made by clients of faith-based programs who have achieved some measure of success (e.g., gotten clean from drugs, stayed out of prison, remained chaste, started working). Many clients report that they used to "drift," and the faith-based program gave them a moral anchor—some signposts and objective standards of right and wrong to live by. Or they say that they had failed in other programs because they felt unloved and hopeless, but that their participation in the faith-based ministry connected them to a real and loving God, and they began drawing great hope from their newfound spiritual relationship. Or they report that they found power to change through prayer. Or they point to a decisive, supernatural intervention that brought change (such as clients of Victory Fellowship's drug rehabilitation program who, through the power of prayer, came clean from drugs "cold turkey" with no withdrawal symptoms).

All these may be statements that make social science researchers a bit uncomfortable, but these are the very things reported by many successful clients themselves. I have heard such statements often in the course of on-site research at FBOs in a variety of distressed urban communities over the past six years (see Sherman 1997, 1999). Clearly, for many participants in religiously affiliated initiatives, the program worked because it brought them into a faith that decisively changed their lifestyle for the better.

But this answer—faith-based programs work because of the faith—while true and important, is also incomplete. This is because some clients of faith-based programs are already people of faith. They do not experience a religious conversion through their participation in the program, because they already are religious believers. Thus, they cannot say that conversion led to lifestyle changes that produced new health. According to many of these clients, two other important characteristics of faith-based programs contributed to their success. For some, the FBO trained them in the practical application of their faith, influencing their development of new strategies for overcoming their obstacles. For others, participation in the FBO connected them with a supportive community of faith from which they drew emotional and practical support and which legitimized their striving for a better life.

Client interviews reveal a number of other important key characteristics of the faith-based organizations that helped them to achieve success. *Accessibility* is one—the program was located in their neighborhood and was operated by people who were available "24/7/365." This made their participation easier, and they found that they could get help when they needed it—even if it was "after business hours." *Trust* is another factor mentioned. These clients engaged more thoroughly with the helpers they found at the FBO, because they trusted those helpers more than they did staff at government agencies. *Individuality* is still another—that is, clients testified that the FBO, unlike other agencies, did not treat them like a number. They experienced a "personal touch" at the FBO that they appreciated, and that often motivated them to remain engaged in the program, whereas they had dropped out of other programs run by different agencies that felt less friendly and more bureaucratic. On a related matter, clients said the faith-based programs were *flexible*—they felt that their individual problems had been examined and that a personalized action plan had been constructed. They succeeded because they were not forced into a one-size-fits-all program.

Outside observers of faith-based programs—Marvin Olasky, Robert Woodson, Barbara Elliott, Ron Sider, Carl Dudley, and others—have offered additional insights as to why faith-based programs work. One is that faith-based programs work because they rely on volunteers. Program participants feel more loved, supported, and inspired, because they know those who are helping them are not getting paid to do it. This motivates them to stick with the program, whereas in other situations, they quit. Another is that such programs work because they hold participants accountable for giving back— they make demands on program participants, and these demands enhance the dignity of those being served (Woodson 1998, 92–94). This approach causes program clients to look at themselves in a new, more positive way, since others are telling them that they really do have a contribution to make. They really do have gifts to offer.

A third is the "being there" thesis: Faith-based organizations succeed because they are present. The physical, constant presence of the FBO and its staff and/or volunteers in the community enables a level of engagement with local kids and families that can effectively compete with the constant negative presence of the drug dealers and the gang-bangers. (Ronald Sider comments on "incarnational servanthood" in *Churches That Make a Difference*, Sider, Olson, and Unruh 2002, 137–138.) Being there is an irreducible part of winning the battle for safer streets in urban America. An article in *Newsweek* about Rev. Eugene Rivers, leader of a Christian community development ministry in Boston that targets urban at-risk youth and gang members, related the following story about when Rivers first moved into the neighborhood:

> Rivers sought out a local drug dealer and gangbanger named Selvin Brown—"a sassy, smartass, tough-talking, gunslinging mother shut your mouth," he says, not without some appreciation. Brown took the Reverend into crackhouses, introduced him to the neighborhood. And he gave Rivers, a Pentecostal, a lesson in why God was losing to gangs in the battle for the souls of inner-city kids. "Selvin explained to us, 'I'm there when Johnny goes out for a loaf of bread for Mama. I'm there, you're not. I win, you lose. It's all about being there'" (quoted in John Leland, "Savior of the Streets," *Newsweek*, June 1, 1999).

Finally, other observers and I assert that faith-based programs work because they are holistic—they seek to find ways to meet clients' wide-ranging needs, including those that might not initially seem to be relevant to the particular program at hand. For instance, an FBO might help a woman in its job-training program to kick out an abusive boyfriend, or deal with a crack-addicted sibling who constantly expects the woman to baby-sit for her. Unless these problems at home are addressed, the woman may not be able to secure and retain a job. Or, the FBO offers its services to "problem people" connected to the strivers in their program. A participating client may be on a good path towards better employment and rising wages. But if there is a leeching, unemployed boyfriend in the house who is wasting the income, the woman is unlikely to move out of poverty. Suppose the boyfriend is unemployed because he cannot get into a decent training program—because the eligibility guidelines of many government programs may prohibit his enrollment. FBOs usually lack such stringent eligibility requirements. And if they are able to serve the boyfriend and help him into constructive employment or training, the impact on the woman, who has been striving hard to climb out of poverty, is substantial.

Creative, Fruitful Government-Faith Collaboration

If all or many of these propositions as to why faith-based programs work are accurate, then the implication is that public officials should avoid implementing policies that rob FBOs of the very elements that lend them success. What should government's relationship to the faith-based social action community be?

Theoretically, a number of options are possible. One is benevolent neglect. Government would simply stay out of the way and let these groups flourish. A slightly modified version of this would be public officials simply using the bully pulpit to commend FBOs, cheer them on, and encourage private support for their efforts. A third version would be the "first do no harm" approach, assisting FBOs by identifying where government is hindering their work (perhaps through intrusive or unnecessary regulatory policy) and reforming harmful policies. A more engaged strategy would be the "help indirectly" position—that is, provide public support for FBOs through vouchers, charity tax credits, or tax reforms permitting more Americans to deduct charitable contributions to poverty-fighting FBOs. More aggressively, government could attempt to help FBOs directly, by expanding government funding of faith-based social service programs through grants or contracts.

Federal policy under George W. Bush has exemplified a combination approach. The president is spotlighting and cheering FBOs from the bully pulpit regularly. His White House Office of Faith-Based and Community Initiatives has conducted an audit of five major cabinet departments (Education, Labor, HUD, Health and Human Services, and Justice) to identify policies and rules that discriminate against or otherwise harm faith-based efforts (The White House 2001). Initially, House Republicans pressed forward the faith-based initiative's legislative goals in H.R. 7, the Community Solutions Act. It sought to: (1) expand the charitable choice guidelines to additional federal social welfare programs, thus opening up the possibility of increased government contracting with FBOs; (2) empower Cabinet Secretaries to "voucherize" millions of dollars worth of social services; and (3) implement a charitable tax deduction for Americans who do not itemize their deductions. H.R. 7 stalled on Capital Hill over concerns about charitable choice. After many months of negotiations, the Senate developed a compromise bill, called the Charity Aid, Relief and Empowerment (CARE) Act of 2002 (cosponsored by Senators Santorum and Lieberman). This focused primarily on encouraging greater private investment in FBOs. The CARE Act was eventually stripped to its barest essentials, and passed in spring 2003. In the midst of the seemingly endless legislative battle over CARE, the White House moved to push its agenda forward through some alternative avenues. It heightened its emphasis on national volunteer service, suggesting that this will serve FBOs since at least some new volunteers will contribute their labor to faith-based ministries. (The new Freedom Corps initiative was announced in the president's State of the Union address, January 29, 2002.) President Bush also issued new executive orders in December 2002 that direct various government agencies to review their administrative procedures and eligibility guidelines to ensure equal treatment of FBOs. (See Dana Milbank, "Bush Issues 'Faith-Based Initiative' Orders, Decrees Would Allow Religious Programs to Get Federal Money, Contracts," *Washington Post*, December 12, 2002.)

The tug-and-pull inside the Washington, D.C. beltway has led to only limited gains for the initiative. The CARE Act, by enabling citizens to gain a tax deduction for charitable contributions, could stimulate increased private giving to FBOs. Incorporating the use of vouchers for social programs, which the Administration is piloting in certain drug rehabilitation programs, will provide clients with more choice. The new Executive Orders have stimulated faith-friendly rule changes within the federal department of Health and Human Services and Housing and Urban Development. (See Alan Cooperman, "2 Faith-Based Proposals May Face Legal Challenge," *Washington Post*, January 30, 2003.) But the White House has had to limit its legislative goals, such as expanding the charitable choice guidelines to additional federal funding streams. Its Executive Orders have come under fire from church-state separationists, and there is still considerable media and political interest in the question of allowing FBOs that receive federal dollars to select staff based on their religion. Outside the beltway, however, there is ample evidence that the faith-based initiative is alive and well in communities across the nation, even if it is beleaguered in Washington, D.C.

A recent fifteen-state study on charitable choice implementation, for example, found that states and localities are interacting in creative, constructive ways with FBOs (Sherman et al. 2002). These new partnerships—worked out in the real world, in real communities, among real people—offer at least three lessons for policymakers interested in establishing a climate for a fruitful relationship between the faith community and government.

First, collaborations should capitalize on the faith community's unique strengths. The best rule of thumb for fruitful government-faith collaboration is simply this: Let the churches do what they do best, and let the government do what it does best. One of the faith community's greatest assets is its people—it can mobilize caring volunteers to be engaged in supportive relationships with struggling families. Many states and localities have recognized this. That is why there has been such an explosion of faith-based mentoring programs around the country. They exist now in approximately twenty-five states.

Some of these programs involve nonfinancial collaboration with government (e.g., the Texas Family Pathfinders program, which has engaged hundreds of congregations). Others involve dollars (such as several local contracts in various counties in Michigan that are underwriting mentoring initiatives). Through these initiatives, clients are receiving intensive emotional and practical support that caseworkers would never be able to offer, given their huge caseloads (Sherman 1998). The statistic noted earlier, regarding the National Jobs Partnership's impressive 83 percent job retention rate, has been achieved in large measure because of the program's strong mentoring component.

Another creative example of capitalizing on the faith community's strengths is the ACT Help Desks being used in several California cities. The Help Desks are staffed by trained volunteers drawn from local churches. The Desks are physically located in the lobby of the CalWORKS One Stop Career Centers. Volunteers are available to serve clients coming into the Centers for appointments. They can help manage the children while mom talks to the caseworkers, offer encouragement and comfort, and, if the client gets through the One Stop Center and still has unmet needs, the volunteer can refer her to a wide variety of resources in the private sector.

A third example is the way New York, Wisconsin, and Ohio have contracted with congregations to do outreach and recruitment work. In some cases, local welfare offices know that there are needy families in the community who could benefit tremendously from the various services they are eligible for—but these individuals have not formally applied for such services. Finding those "falling through the cracks" is difficult for government social workers. But congregations located in distressed communities often know who their needy neighbors are, speak their language, hold their trust, and can encourage them to get connected to services. In other cases, congregations are being asked to work with welfare clients sanctioned for noncompliance with mandatory work rules. New York City has engaged sixteen FBOs, many of them congregations, in a $6.4-million demonstration project focused on this. Faith partners are given lists of clients under sanctio. FBO staff then contact the individuals, assess why they are not working, refer them to training centers, and otherwise help them to lift the sanctions.

Second, policymakers should pursue "triple win" partnerships in which clients, churches, and local government benefit. One example would be Illinois's Front Door initiative. This program serves two types of clients: individuals who become employed while they are waiting for their TANF (welfare) applications to be processed, or people who need assistance with employment-related expenses in order to retain their jobs and avoid going back on welfare. The state Department of Human Services sends grant money to local faith partners according to a formula based on TANF applications in that church's neighborhood. Clients are referred from local DHS offices to the churches to get specific needs met—such as money for uniforms and transportation. The church contact meets with the client and processes the assistance for this need, and can offer the person additional aid available from the church's own benevolence programs.

The program is a win for clients because they get their pressing needs met quickly and because their contact with the church can connect them to additional resources the congregation may have to offer. It is also a win for the churches. Many want to do benevolence outreach, but are unaware of who is in need. Thus, the DHS's referral of specific clients is helpful. Other congregations are already operating benevolence programs, and the Front Door grants add to what they can make available to supplicants. The 8 percent administrative overhead fee faith partners retain under the Front Door program is also helpful in keeping their good work going. Finally, the program is a win for the local DHS office in at least two ways. Church volunteers conduct work with clients that otherwise overworked DHS social workers would have to do (thus leaving them free to concentrate energies on "harder" cases). Government also is interested in helping people to avoid reentry onto the welfare rolls, and the program advances this objective, too. Finally, program administrator Derrius Colvin reports that the Front Door initiative "has created a closer working relationship between the local office and faith-based organizations" and has built trust between the two parties. The partnership has given birth to additional collaboration, including new programs for senior citizens and a mentorship initiative (personal correspondence to the author, March 4, 2002).

Finally, to foster fruitful government-faith community collaboration, government can pursue contracting arrangements that make possible the involvement of small and mid-sized grassroots FBOs that often are highly effective, on a modest scale, among particularly hard-to-serve clients. Government can take several steps in this regard. First, indirect financial contracting via strategic intermediary organizations is a promising practice. Strategic intermediaries are organizations with credibility both in the eyes of the faith community (because they are known and their mission resonates with grassroots groups) and with the government (because they have the administrative capacity to account for and manage large contracts). Governments can contract with intermediaries, and intermediaries can then write subcontracts with smaller FBOs—often offering technical support in addition to the funds. Second, in the absence of intermediaries, government can offer contracts in smaller denominations, suiting the administrative capacity of grassroots FBOs. Third, public officials can work hard to inform FBOs of contracting opportunities and offer training workshops teaching FBOs about proposal writing and grant management. Indiana has done these things well through Indiana Faithworks, a technical assistance agency housed within the Family and Social Services Department. Faithworks operates a toll-free information number, hosts an up-to-date Web site with comprehensive information about contracting opportunities, and offers regional fundraising seminars. Through its efforts, FBOs have garnered over $3.5 million in state contracts. Ninety-five percent of the bidders for those contracts were FBOs that had never before received government funding.

Conclusion

Apart from the political battles on Capital Hill, the faith-based initiative is advancing throughout the country. The findings from the fifteen-state charitable choice tracking study reveal that most states examined truly are doing social welfare business in a new way. Often, government entities have contracted with new partners, FBOs that had not worked with them previously in formal contractual relationships. A survey of nearly four hundred leaders of the FBOs holding charitable choice contracts in these states found that 56 percent were new participants. They had no previous history of financial collaboration with government agencies prior to the passage of the charitable choice guidelines (Sherman and Green 2002). More often than not (66 percent of the time), government agencies are writing small and mid-sized contracts (under $100,000)—a scale that permits the involvement of smaller, grassroots FBOs. Far more often than just two years ago, governments are turning to FBOs as partners in efforts to fight poverty. My earlier study tracking charitable choice implementation had identified eighty-four examples of financial collaboration in nine states in 2000. The current survey uncovered 726 contracts in the fifteen states. Contracts are also being written for a wider diversity of social services, offered to a broader range of clients (children, youth, welfare recipients, the working poor, the low-income elderly, refugees and immigrants).

Compared with the total amount of federal dollars available for contracting under the four programs regulated by charitable choice, the $123 million of FBO collaborations uncovered in the fifteen-state study is modest. But it is an exponential increase over what was happening just two to three years ago. And it—combined with many other signs (special state or local "faith-based initiatives," new outreach endeavors, state-sponsored training conferences and regional seminars, appointments of faith liaisons)—is indicative of an attitude of eagerness by state and local officials to engage the faith community in a more extensive, creative, and systematic way than ever before.

In dialogue with local FBO leaders, these officials are leading the way in discovering—through creative experimentation that focuses on the practical result of serving low-income families better—how to partner constructively with faith-based charities. If Washington's decisions about how best to reinvigorate faith in communities are based more on this policymaking "from the ground up," and less on ideological debate, FBOs, low-income citizens, and American taxpayers will be the winners.

Bibliography

Abt Associates Inc. February 1999. *Evaluation of National and Community Service Programs First Annual Report—Program Profiles*. Cambridge, MA.

Abt Associates Inc and the Center for Human Resources, Brandeis University. February 1, 1994. *Evaluation of National and Community Service Programs: Briefing for the Corporation for National and Community Service on the Evaluation Information System*. Cambridge, MA.

Adams, James L. 1986. "The Voluntary Principle in the Forming of American Religion." In J. Ronald Engel, ed., *Voluntary Associations*. (pp. 171–200). Chicago, IL: Exploration Press.

_____. 1986a. "Voluntary Associations." In J. Ronald Engel, ed., *Voluntary Associations*. (pp. 250–53). Chicago, IL: Exploration Press.

Aguirre International. 1999. *Making a Difference: Impact of AmeriCorps*State/National Direct on Members and Communities 1994–1995 and 1995–1996*. San Mateo, CA.

Aguirre International. June 12, 1997. *AmeriCorps State/National Program Impact Evaluation: First Year Report*. San Mateo, CA.

Aguirre International. n.d. *AmeriCorps Members Life Skills Inventory*. San Mateo, CA.

America Gives: A Survey of Americans' Generosity After September 11. January 2002. The Center on Philanthropy at Indiana University and the Association of Fundraising Professions.

American Youth Policy Forum. June 1999. *More Things That Do Make A Difference for Youth: A Compendium of Evaluations of Youth Programs and Practices*. Washington, DC.

Ammerman, Nancy T. 1999. *Congregation and Community*. New Brunswick, NJ: Rutgers University Press.

Anderson, Beth B., J. Gregory Dees, and Jed Emerson. 2002. "Developing Viable Earned Income Strategies." In J. G. Dees, J. Emerson, and P. Economy, eds., *Strategic Tools for Social Entrepreneurs: Enhancing the Performance of Your Enterprising Nonprofit* (pp. 191–234). New York: John Wiley & Sons.

Andreasen, Alan R. 1996, November–December. "Profits for Nonprofits: Find a Corporate Partner." *Harvard Business Review*, 3–10.

Andrews, Catherine. 2002. "Shedding Some Light on Nonprofit Finances." *Foundation News and Commentary*, Sept/Oct, 12–14.

Astin, Alexander et al. 2001. *Executive Summary: How Service Learning Affects Students.* Los Angeles: University of California Los Angeles, Higher Education Research Institute.

Austin, James E. 2000. *The Collaboration Challenge: How Nonprofits and Businesses Succeed Through Strategic Alliances.* San Francisco, CA: Jossey-Bass.

Backman, Elaine V. and Steven R. Smith. Summer 2002. "Healthy Organizations, Unhealthy Communities?" *Nonprofit Management and Leadership,* 10, 4, 355–373.

Barber, Benjamin. 1998. *Strong Democracy: Participatory Politics for a New Age.* Berkeley: University of California Press.

Barstow, David and Diana B. Henriques. 2001. "Debate Over Rules for Victims Fund," *New York Times,* November 6.

Barstow, David and Diana B. Henriques. 2002. "Sorting Out Why U.S. Agency Spent So Little," *New York Times,* April 26.

Behn, Robert D. 2001. *Rethinking Democratic Accountability.* Washington, DC: Brookings.

Bellah, Robert, Richard Madsen, William Sullivan, Ann Swidler, and Steven Tipton. 1985. *Habits of the Heart: Individualism and Commitment in American Life.* New York: Harper and Row.

Berger, Peter and Richard J. Neuhaus. 1977. *To Empower People.* Washington, DC: American Enterprise Institute.

Bernstein, Susan. 1991. *Managing Contracted Services in the Nonprofit Agency: Administrative, Ethical and Political Issues.* Philadelphia, PA: Temple University Press.

Berresford, Susan V. 2002. "September 11th and Beyond." In *September 11 Perspectives from the Field of Philanthropy.* New York: The Foundation Center.

Berry, Jeffrey M. 1989. *The Interest Group Society.* 2nd ed. Glenview, IL: Scott, Foresman.

_____. 2003. *A Voice for Nonprofits.* Washington, DC: Brookings.

Billig, Shelley. 2000. "Research on K–12 Service Learning: The Evidence Builds." *Phi Delta Kappan,* 81: 9.

Billingsley, Andrew. 1999. *Mighty Like a River: The Black Church and Social Reform.* New York: Oxford University Press.

Bjorklund, Victoria B. 2002. "Reflections on September 11 Legal Developments." In *September 11 Perspectives from the Field of Philanthropy.* New York: The Foundation Center.

Bloomquist, John. December 15, 1992. *Measures of Attitudes and Personal Development Outcomes: An Annotated Summary.* Cambridge, MA: Abt Associates Inc.

Boris, Elizabeth T. and Jeff Krehely. 2002. "Advocacy and Civic Participation in the Nonprofit Sector." In Lester M. Salamon, ed., *The State of the Sector* (pp. 299–330). Washington, DC: Brookings.

Boris, Elizabeth T. and Eugene Steuerle, eds. 1999. *Nonprofits and Government: Collaboration and Conflict.* Washington, DC: Urban Institute Press.

Boschee, Jerr. 1995 March. "Social Entrepreneurship." *Across the Board*, 20–25.

Boyte, Harry. 1989. *CommonWealth: A Return to Citizen Politics*. New York: The Free Press.

Bremner, Robert H. 1988. *American Philanthropy*. 2nd ed. Chicago: University of Chicago Press.

Brody, Evelyn and Elizabeth J. Reid. Forthcoming. *Constitutional Perspectives and Democratic Governance*. Vol. 3, "Nonprofit Advocacy and The Policy Process." Washington, DC: Urban Institute Press.

Brostek, Michael. 2002. *Tax-Exempt Organizations: Improvements Possible in Public, IRS, and State Oversight of Charities*. Washington, DC: U.S. General Accounting Office.

Brown, Lawrence D. 1983. *New Policies, New Politics*. Washington, DC: Brookings.

Buckley, William. 1990. *Gratitude: Reflections on What We Owe To Our Country*. New York: Random House.

Buckmaster, Natalie, Mark Lyons, and Alan Bridges. 1994. "Financial Ratio Analysis and Nonprofit Organizations: A Review and an Exploratory Study of the Financial Risk and Vulnerability of Ninety Large Nonprofit Organisations in New South Wales." Working Paper #26, Center for Australian Community Organisations and Management, University of Technology Sydney, Australia.

Campaign Finance Institute. 2003. *Life After Reform: When the Bi-Partisan Campaign Finance Institute Meets Politics*. Lanham, MD: Rowman and Littlefield.

Carle, Robert D. and Louis A. DeCaro Jr. 1999. Revised. *Signs of Hope in the City: Ministries of Community Renewal*. Valley Forge, PA: Judson Press.

Center for Public Justice. 1997. *A Guide to Charitable Choice*. Washington, DC and Annandale, VA.

Center on Philanthropy at Indiana University and the Association of Fundraising Professions. January 2002. *America Gives: A Survey of Americans' Generosity After September 11*.

Chabotar, Kent J. 1989. "Financial Ratio Analysis Comes to Nonprofits." *Journal of Higher Education*, 60(2), 188–208.

Chambers, Simone and Jeffrey Kopstein. 2001. "Bad Civil Society." *Political Theory* 29 (December): 838–66.

Chapman, Bruce. 1990. "Politics and National Service: A Virus Attacks the Volunteer Sector." In *National Service Pro and Con*. Stanford, CA: Stanford University Press.

Chaves, Mark and William Tsitsos. 2001. "Congregations and Social Services: What They Do, How They Do It, and with Whom." *Nonprofit and Voluntary Sector Quarterly*, 30(4): 660–683.

Chrislip, Davis and Carl Larson. 1994. *Collaborative Leadership: How Citizens and Civic Leaders Can Make a Difference*. San Francisco, CA: Jossey-Bass.

Chronicle of Philanthropy. 2001. "The Nonprofit 400." November 1, p. 37.

Clemens, Elisabeth S. 1999. "Organizational Repertoires and Institutional Change: Women's Groups and the Transformation of American Politics, 1890–1920." In T. Skocpol and M. Fiorina, eds., *Civic Engagement in American Democracy* (pp. 81–110). Washington, DC: Brookings.

Cleverly, W. O. and K. Nilson. 1980. "Assessing Financial Position with 29 Key Ratios." *Hospital Financial Management*, 34, 30–36.

Cnaan, Ram. 1999. *The Newer Deal: Social Work and Religion in Partnership*. New York: Columbia University Press.

Cohen, Carolyn. 1997. *What Service Teaches About Citizenship and Work: The Case of AmeriCorps*. National Service-Learning Clearinghouse. <www.servicelearning.org>

Cohen, Diane and A. Robert Jaeger. 1998. *Sacred Places at Risk: New Evidence on How Endangered Older Churches and Synagogues Serve Communities*. Philadelphia, PA: Partners for Sacred Places.

Cohen, Jean and Andrew Arato. 1992. *Civil Society and Political Theory*. Cambridge, MA: MIT Press.

Cohen, Rick. 2002. "The US Non-Profit Sector in the Wake of September 11," *Alliance*, March.

Collins, Chuck, Pam Rogers, and Joan Garner. 2000. *Robin Hood Was Right: A Guide to Giving Your Money for Social Change*. New York: W.W. Norton.

Conservation Company and Public/Private Ventures. 1994. *Building from Strength: Replication as a Strategy for Expanding Social Programs That Work*. Public/Private Ventures. New York.

Constitutional Rights Foundation. n.d. *A Guide to Effective Citizenship Through National Service*.

Cordes, Joseph J. and Burton A. Weisbrod. 1998. "Differential Taxation of Nonprofits and the Commercialization of Nonprofit Revenues." In B. A. Weisbrod, ed., *To Profit or Not to Profit: The Commercial Transformation of the Nonprofit Sector* (pp. 83–104). Cambridge, UK: Cambridge University Press.

Corporation For National and Community Service. 1994. *Principles For High Quality National Service Programs*. Washington, DC.

Corporation For National and Community Service. 2000. *Transition Briefing Book November 2000*. Washington, DC.

Dahl, Robert. 1998. *On Democracy*. New Haven, CT: Yale University Press.

Dawkins, Andy, Bruce P. Corrie, and Dr. James Kielsmeier. *The Economics of the Forgotten Half: A Cost-Benefit Analysis of the Minnesota Youth Works Proposal (House File 2)*. Minnesota State House of Representatives.

Democratic Leadership Conference. 1988. *Citizenship and National Service: A Blueprint for Civic Enterprise*.

De Tocqueville, Alexis. 1956. *Democracy in America*. New York: New American Library.

DiIluio, John. 2001. "The State of Religion and Public Life." Speech presented at the Manhattan Institute, New York City, April 4.

DiMaggio, Paul and Walter W. Powell. 1983. "The Iron Cage Revisited: Institutional Isomorphism and Collective Rationality in Organizational Fields." *American Sociological Review*, 48 (April): 147–160.

Dionne, E. J. Jr., ed. 1998. *Community Works: The Revival of Civil Society in America.* Washington, DC: Brookings.

Doble, John. 1990. "Public Opinion about Charitable Solicitations and the Law." *Proceedings of New York University School of Law's Conference on Charitable Solicitations: Is There a Problem?* New York: New York School of Law.

Douglas, James. 1987. "Political Theories of Nonprofit Organization." In Walter W. Powell, ed., *The Nonprofit Sector: A Research Handbook* (pp. 43–54). New Haven, CT: Yale University Press.

Dowie, Mark. 2001. *American Foundations: An Investigative History.* Cambridge, MA: MIT Press.

Dudley, Carl S., and David Roozen. 2001. *Faith Communities Today.* Hartford, CT: Hartford Seminary. [Online.] Available from: <www.hartsem.edu>.

Eberly, Donald. 1968. *National Service and Manpower.* New York: Russell Sage Foundation.

Eberly, Donald. 1988. *National Service: A Promise to Keep.* Rochester, NY: John Alden Books.

Edington, Howard. 1996. *Downtown Church: The Heart of the City.* Nashville, TN: Abingdon Press.

Edsall, Tom. 2002. "New Ways to Harness Soft Money in Works." *Washington Post*, August 25, p.1.

Elliott, Barbara. 2000. "Teen Challenge's Remarkable Record." Houston: Center for Renewal.

Emerson, Jed. 2000. "The Nature of Returns: A Social Capital Markets Inquiry into Elements of Investment and the Blended Value Proposition." Harvard Business School Working Paper.

Erikson, Erik H. 1968. *Identity: Youth and Crises.* New York: Norton.

Esbeck, Carl. 1996. *The Regulation of Religious Organizations as Recipients of Government Funding.* Annapolis, MD: Center for Public Justice.

———. 2000. "Isn't Charitable Choice Government-Funded Discrimination?" [Online.] Available from: <www.cpjustice.org>.

Evans, Peter. 1996. "Government Action, Social Capital, and Development: Reviewing the Evidence of Synergy." *World Development*, 24, 6, 1119–32.

Evans, Peter, Dietrich Rueschemeyer, and Theda Skocpol. 1985. *Bringing the State Back In.* Cambridge, UK: Cambridge University Press.

Evers, William. 1990. *National Service: Pro and Con.* Stanford, CA: Stanford University Press.

Fazlollah, Mark and Peter Nicholas. 2002. "9/11 Tests Charities Sense of Fairness."*Philadelphia Inquirer,* April 29.

The Federal Domestic Volunteer Agency. September 1990. *Building Better Student Communities with Student Volunteers: An Evaluation Report on the Student Community Service Program.*

Finn, Chester E. and Kelly Amis. 2001. *Making It Count: A Guide to High-Impact Education Philanthropy.* New York: Thomas B. Fordham Foundation.

Fishman, James L. and Stephen Schwarz. 2000. *Nonprofit Organizations: Cases and Materials.* Westbury, NY: Foundation Press.

Foley, Michael and Bob Edwards. 1996. "The Paradox of Civil Society." *Journal of Democracy*, 7, 3 (September): 38–52.

Foundation Center. 2000. *The Foundation Directory.* New York: The Foundation Center.

Freedman, Samuel. 1993. *Upon This Rock: The Miracles of a Black Church.* New York: Harper Collins.

Friedman, Milton. 1989. "Service, Citizenship, and Democracy: Civic Duty as an Entailment of Civil Right." In *National Service Pro and Con.*

Frumkin, Peter. 2000. "After Partnership: Rethinking Public-Nonprofit Relations." In Mary Jo Bane, Brent Coffin, and Ronald Thiemann, eds., *Who Will Provide? The Changing Role of Religion in American Social Welfare.* Boulder, CO: Westview.

Fukuyama, Francis. 1995. *Trust: The Social Virtues and the Creation of Prosperity.* New York: Free Press.

Furco, Andrew, Parisa Muller, and Mary Sue Ammon. 1998. *Civic Responsibility Survey.* Service-Learning Research and Development Center. Graduate School of Education. University of California at Berkeley.

Gallagher, Janne. 2002. *Victims of Terrorism Tax Relief Act of 2001, H.R. 2884.* Council of Foundations, January 24.

Galston, William. 2001. "Political Knowledge, Political Engagement, and Civic Education," in *Annual Review of Political Science.*

Geary, Michael, Janet Greenlee, and John Trussel. 2000. "Risky Business? Nonprofits after Widespread Disclosure." Paper presented at the annual meeting of the Association for Research on Nonprofit Organizations and Voluntary Action, New Orleans, LA.

Glaser, John S. 1994. *The United Way Scandal: An Insider's Account of What Went Wrong and Why.* New York: John Wiley.

Glazer, Nathan. 1989. *The Self-Service Society.* Cambridge, MA: Harvard University Press.

Goddeeris, John H. and Burton A. Weisbrod. 1998. "Why Not For-Profit? Conversions and Public Policy." In E. Boris and E. Steuerle, eds., *Nonprofits and Government.* Washington, DC: Urban Institute Press.

Goddeeris, John and Burton A. Weisbrod. 1998. "Conversion from Nonprofit to For-Profit Legal Status: Why Does It Happen and Should Anyone Care?" In B. A. Weisbrod, ed., *To Profit or Not to Profit: The Commercial Transformation of the Nonprofit Sector* (pp. 129–148). Cambridge, UK: Cambridge University Press.

Government Printing Office. 1980. *Presidential Recommendations for Selective Service Reform: A Report to Congress Prepared Pursuant to P.L. 96–107.*

Grace, Kay Sprinkel and Alan L. Wendroff. 2001. *High Impact Philanthropy.* New York: Wiley and Sons.

Greene, Maria S., Yolanda Woodlee and Carol D. Leonnig. 2002. "Risky Ventures, Little Accountability." Washington, DC: *Washington Post*, Feb. 25, p. 1.

Greenlee, Janet S. 1993. "The Use of Information in Strategic Decisions: The Case of United Way." *Proceedings of American Accounting Association Annual Meeting.*

Greenlee, Janet S. and Karen Brown. 1999. "The Impact of Accounting Information on Contributions to Charitable Organizations." *Research in Accounting Regulation,* 13, 111–125.

Greenlee, J. S. and David Bukovinsky. 1998. "Financial Ratios for Use in the Analytical Review of Charitable Organizations." *Ohio CPA Journal.* January: 32–36.

Greenlee, J. S. and John Trussel. 2000 "Predicting the Financial Vulnerability of Charitable Organizations." *Nonprofit Management and Leadership,* 11, 199–210.

Gronbjerg, Kirsten A. 1993. *Understanding Nonprofit Funding: Managing Revenues in Social Service and Community Development Organizations.* San Francisco, CA: Jossey-Bass.

Gronbjerg, Kirsten A. and Steven R. Smith. 1999. "Nonprofit Organizations and Public Policies in the Delivery of Human Services." In C. T. Clotfelter and T. Ehrlich, eds., *Philanthropy and the Nonprofit Sector* (pp. 139–171). Indianapolis: Indiana University Press.

Gronbjerg, Kirsten A. and Steven R. Smith. Forthcoming. "The Government-Nonprofit Relationship." In Walter W. Powell and R. Steinberg, eds., *The Nonprofit Sector: A Research Handbook,* 2nd ed., New Haven, CT: Yale University Press.

Gumport, Patricia J. and Stuart K. Snydman. Forthcoming. "Higher Education: Fading Distinctions, Emerging Markets and Evolving Forms." In Walter W. Powell and R. Steinberg, eds., *The Nonprofit Sector: A Research Handbook,* 2nd ed., New Haven, CT: Yale University Press.

Gutch, Richard. 1993. *Contracting Lessons from the US.* London: National Council of Voluntary Organisations.

Gutmann, Amy, ed. 1998. *Freedom of Association.* Princeton: Princeton University Press.

Habermas, Jürgen. 1996. *Between Facts and Norms: Contributions to a Discourse Theory of Law and Democracy.* Translated by William Rehg. Cambridge, MA: MIT Press.

Hager, Mark. 2001. "Financial Vulnerability among Arts Organizations: A Test of the Tuckman-Chang Measures." *Nonprofit and Voluntary Sector Quarterly,* 30, 376–392.

Hall, Peter Dobkin. 1984. *The Organization of American Culture, 1700–1900.* New York: New York University Press.

_____. 1990. "The History of Religious Philanthropy in America." In Robert W. and V. Hodgkinson, eds., *Faith and Philanthropy in America* (pp. 38–62). Washington, DC: Independent Sector.

_____. 1992. *Inventing the Nonprofit Sector.* Baltimore, MD: Johns Hopkins University Press.

Hammack, David. 1998. *Making the Nonprofit Sector in the United States: A Reader.* Bloomington: Indiana University Press.

Hansmann, Henry. 1996. "The Changing Roles of Public, Private, and Non-profit Enterprise in Education, Health Care, and Other Human Services." In Victor R. Fuchs, ed., *Individual and Social Responsibility: Child Care, Education, Medical Care, and Long-Term Care in America* (pp. 245–75). Chicago: University of Chicago Press.

_____. 1980. "The Role of Nonprofit Enterprise." *Yale Law Journal*, 89: 835–901.

Harper, Nile. 1999. *Urban Churches, Vital Signs*. Grand Rapids, MI: Eerdmans.

Hasenfeld, Yeheskel and Benjamin Gidron. 2001. "Toward the Integration of Civil Society, Social Movement, and Third Sector Theories: Lessons from an International Study of Peace/Conflict Resolution Organizations." Paper presented at the annual meeting of the Association for Research on Nonprofit Organizations and Voluntary Action, Miami, FL.

Hatry, Harry P. 1999. *Performance Measurement: Getting Results*. Washington, DC: Urban Institute Press.

Heclo, Hugh. 1980. "Issue Networks and the Executive Establishment." In Anthony King, ed., *The New American Political System* (pp. 87–124). Washington, DC: AEI Press.

Held, David. 1996. *Models of Democracy*. 2nd ed. Stanford, CA: Stanford University Press.

Herrnson, Paul S. 2000. "Political Parties, Interest Groups, and Elections." In *Structuring the Inquiry into Advocacy* (pp. 9–22). Vol. 1 of "Nonprofit Advocacy and The Policy Process," edited by Elizabeth Reid. Washington, DC: Urban Institute Press.

Hill, Frances R. and Douglas M. Mancino. 2002. *Taxation of Exempt Organizations*. New York: Warren, Gorham, and Lamont.

Hirschman, Albert. O. 1984. *Getting Ahead Collectively: Grassroots Experiences in Latin America*. New York: Pergamon Press.

Hodgkinson, Virginia Ann and Murray S. Weitzman, eds. 1993. *From Belief to Commitment: The Community Service Activities and Finances of Religious Congregations in the United States*. Washington, DC: Independent Sector.

_____. 1996. *Giving and Volunteering in the United States*. Washington, DC: Independent Sector.

Hodgkinson, Virginia Ann, and Murray S. Weitzman, with John A. Abrahams, Eric A. Crutchfield, and David R. Stevenson. 1996. *Nonprofit Almanac: Dimensions of the Independent Sector: 1996–1997*. San Francisco, CA: Jossey-Bass.

Horowitz, Michael. 2000. "Subsidies May Cost Churches Their Souls," *Wall Street Journal*, December 16.

Howard, Alice and Joan Magretta. 1995, September–October. "Surviving Success: An Interview with The Nature Conservancy's John Sawhill." *Harvard Business Review*, 108–118.

Howard, Christopher. 1997. *The Hidden Welfare State: Tax Expenditures and Social Policy in the United States*. Princeton, NJ: Princeton University Press.

Independent Sector. 2002. *Obedience to the Unenforceable: Ethics and the Nation's Voluntary and Philanthropic Community.* Washington, DC: Independent Sector.

Independent Sector and the Urban Institute. 2002. *The New Nonprofit Almanac and Desk Reference.* New York: Jossey-Bass.

Internal Revenue Service (IRS). 1981. Chapter G "Social Welfare: What Does It Mean? How Much Private Benefit Is Permissible?" In *Continuing Professional Education Manual,* Professional Education Manual, Chapter G.

_____. 2002. "Tax Exempt Status for Your Organization." IRS Publication 557.

Internal Revenue Service Web Site. 2002. "Charities and Nonprofits." <http: www.irs.gov/ exempt/charitable/display/ 0,,i1%3D3%26i%3D18%26genericId%3D6874,00.html> (Accessed October 14, 2002.)

_____. 2002. "Social Welfare Organizations." <http://www.irs.gov/exempt/ welfare/display/0,,i1%3D3%26i2%3D29%26genericId%3D6898,00.html> (Accessed October 14, 2002.)

Intili, Jo Anne, Edward Kissam, and Heide Wrigley. September 1998. *AmeriCorps Impact on Members' Life Skills.* San Mateo, CA: Aguirre International.

Jahoda, Gustav. 1992. *Crossroads Between Culture and Mind: Continuities and Change in Theories of Human Nature.* Cambridge, MA: Harvard University Press.

James, Estelle. 1978. "Product Mix and Cost Disaggregation: A Reinterpretation of the Economics of Higher Education," *Journal of Human Resources,* Spring, pp. 157–186.

_____. 1983. "How Nonprofits Grow: A Model." *Journal of Policy Analysis and Management,* 2, 2, 350–365. Reprinted in *The Economics of Non-Profit Institutions: Studies in Structure and Policy,* ed. S. Rose-Ackerman. New York: Oxford University Press, 1986.

_____. 1984. "Benefits and Costs of Privatized Public Services: Lessons from the Dutch Educational System." *Comparative Education Review,* 28, No. 4, pp. 605–624. Expanded versions reprinted in *Private Education: Studies in Choice and Public Policy,* ed. D. Levy. New York: Oxford University Press, 1986, and *Private Schools in Ten Countries: Policy and Practice,* ed. G. Walford. New York: Routledge, 1988.

_____. 1986. "Cross Subsidization in Higher Education: Does It Pervert Private Choice and Public Policy?" In Daniel Levy, ed., *Private Education: Studies in Choice and Public Policy* (pp. 237–258). New York: Oxford University Press.

_____. 1987. "The Nonprofit Sector in Comparative Perspective." In Walter W. Powell, ed., *The Nonprofit Sector: A Research Handbook* (pp. 397–415). New Haven, CT: Yale University Press.

_____., ed. 1989. *The Nonprofit Sector in International Perspective: Studies in Comparative Culture and Policy.* New York: Oxford University Press.

_____. 1993. "Why Do Different Countries Choose A Different Public-Private Mix of Educational Services?" *Journal of Human Resources,* 28, pp. 571–592.

_____. 1998. "Commercialism among Nonprofits: Objectives, Opportunities, and Constraints. In B. A. Weisbrod, ed., *To Profit or Not to Profit: The Commercial Transformation of the Nonprofit Sector* (pp. 271–285). Cambridge, UK: Cambridge University Press.

James, Estelle and Egon Neuberger. 1981. "The Academic Department as a Non-Profit Labor Cooperative." *Public Choice*, pp. 585–612. Reprinted in *Collective Choice in Education*, ed. M. J. Bowman, Martinus Nijhoff, pp. 207–235.

James, Estelle and Susan Rose-Ackerman. 1986. *The Nonprofit Enterprise in Market Economies*, a monograph in *Fundamentals of Pure and Applied Economics and Encyclopedia of Economics*, ed. J. Lesourne and H. Sonnenschein. London: Harwood Academic Publishers.

Jeavons, Thomas H. 1993. "Identifying Characteristics of Religious Organizations: An Exploratory Proposal." A working paper of the Program on Nonprofits Organizations (#197). New Haven, CT: Yale University.

_____. 1994. *When the Bottom Line is Faithfulness: Management of Christian Service Organizations*. Bloomington: Indiana University Press.

Jeavons, Thomas H. and R. Cnaan. 1997. "Evolution of Small Religious Nonprofits." *Nonprofit and Voluntary Sector Quarterly*, 26 (S): S62–S84.

Jenkins, Craig and Abigail L. Halci. 1999. "Grassrooting the System? The Development and Impact of Social Movement Philanthropy, 1953–1990." In C. E. Langemann, ed., *Philanthropic Foundations: New Scholarship, New Possibilities* (pp. 229–56). Indianapolis: Indiana University Press.

Johnson, Byron R. 2000–2001. "A Better Kind of High: How Religious Commitment Reduces Drug Use Among Poor Urban Teens." Philadelphia, PA: Center for Research on Religion and Urban Civil Society.

_____. 2001–2002. "The Role of African-American Churches in Reducing Crime Among Black Youth." Philadelphia, PA: Center for Research on Religion and Urban Civil Society.

_____. 2002. "Objective Hope: Assessing the Effectiveness of Faith-Based Organizations." Philadelphia, PA: Center for Research on Religion and Urban Civil Society.

Johnson, Byron R., David Larson, and Timothy Pitts. 1997. "Religious Programs, Institutional Adjustment, and Recidivism among Former Inmates in Prison Fellowship Programs." *Justice Quarterly*. March.

Johnson, Byron R., Ralph Brett Tompkins, and Derek Webb. 2002. "Objective Hope: Assessing the Effectiveness of Faith-Based Organizations, A Review of the Literature." Philadelphia, PA: Center for Research on Religion and Urban Civil Society.

Johnston, David Cay. 1999. "Doing Good or Doing Well: It's Starting to Get Blurry." *New York Times* (Late Edition), November 17, H: 17, 1.

Kaplan, Ann E., ed. 2000. *Giving USA, 2000*. New York: AAFRC Trust for Philanthropy.

Kaplan, Robert S. and David P. Norton. 1992, January–February. "The Balanced Scorecard: Measures That Drive Performance. *Harvard Business Review*, 70, no. 1, 71–79.

_____. 1996, January–February. "Using the Balanced Scorecard as a Strategic Management System." *Harvard Business Review.*

Keating, Elizabeth K. and Peter Frumkin. 2003. "Reengineering Nonprofit Financial Accountability: Toward a More Reliable Foundation for Regulation." *Public Administration Review,* 63(1), 3–15.

Kemmis, Daniel. 1990. *Community and the Politics of Place.* Norman: University of Oklahoma Press.

Kent, Ros. 1993. "The Application of Financial Ratios in Analysing Nonprofit Organizations." Working Paper #20, QUT Program on Nonprofit Corporations, Brisbane, Australia.

Kirsch, Arthur D., Keith Hume, and Nadine Jalandoni, eds. 1999. *Giving and Volunteering in the United States.* Washington, DC: Independent Sector.

Kleiman, Neil and Sara Duitch. 2001. "Going on with the Show: Arts & Culture in New York City After Sept. 11." Center for an Urban Future. <www.nycfuture.org/content/reports/report_view.cfm?repkey=37&area=ecopol>

Kolbert, Elizabeth. 2002. "The Calculator: How Kenneth Feinberg Determines the Value of Three Thousand Lives." *New Yorker,* November 25.

Krasno, Johnathan S. and Daniel Seltz. 2001. "'Issue Advocacy' in the 1998 Elections." In Elizabeth J. Reid and Maria D. Montilla, eds. *Exploring Organizations and Advocacy, Strategies and Finances,* Issue 1 (pp.17–25). Washington, DC: The Urban Institute Press.

Krehely, Jeff and Kendall Golladay. 2002. "The Scope and Activities of 501(c)(4) Social Welfare Organizations." Paper presented at the Advisory Board Meeting of the Center on Nonprofits and Philanthropy, April 2002.

Lammers, Jennifer A. 2003. "Know Your Ratios? Everyone Else Does." *Nonprofit Quarterly,* Spring, 34–39.

Lampkin, Linda and Elizabeth Boris. 2002. "Nonprofit Organization Data: What We Have and What We Need." *American Behavioral Scientist,* 45(11), 1675–1715.

Landrum, Roger. 1992. *National Service: Roots and Flowers.* Youth Service America. Commission on Work, Family and Citizenship. Washington, DC.

Lappe, Francis M. and Paul M. Du Bois. 1994. *The Quickening of America: Rebuilding Our Nation, Remaking Our Lives.* San Francisco, CA: Jossey-Bass.

Laycock, Douglas. 1990. "Formal, Substantive, and Disaggregated Neutrality toward Religion." *DePaul Law Review,* 39, 993–1018.

Leonnig, Carol D. 2002. "HUD Loses Faith in Housing Program." *Washington Post,* February 19.

Lerner, Josh. 2000. *Venture Capital and Private Equity: A Casebook.* New York: Wiley and Sons.

Letts, Christine W., William P. Ryan, and Allen Grossman. 1997, March–April. "Virtuous Capital: What Foundations Can Learn from Venture Capitalists." *Harvard Business Review.*

Lindner, Eileen W., ed. 2000. *Yearbook of American and Canadian Churches, 2000.* Nashville, TN: Abingdon Press.

Lipman, Harvy. 2000. "Charities Zero-Sum Filing Game." *Chronicle of Philanthropy.* May 18.

Loconte, Joe. 1997. *Seducing the Samaritan.* Boston, MA: Pioneer.

Loprest, Pamela. 2001, April. "How Are Families That Leave Welfare Doing? A Comparison of Early and Recent Welfare Leavers." Washington, DC: The Urban Institute.

MacDonald, Heather. 2000. "The Billions of Dollars That Made Things Worse." In Myron Magnet, ed., *What Makes Charity Work* (pp. 145–171). New York: Ivan R. Dee.

Macro International. November 1997. *Study of Race, Class, and Ethnicity in AmeriCorps Programs.* Washington, DC.

Markus, Gregory, Jeffrey Howard, and David King. Winter 1993. *Integrating Community Service and Classroom Instruction Enhances Learning: Results from an Experiment: Educational Evaluation and Policy Analysis* 15(4): 410–419.

Marris, Peter and Martin Rein. 1982. *Dilemmas of Social Reform.* 2nd ed. Chicago: University of Chicago Press.

Masaoka, Jan. 2003. "The Effectiveness Trap." *Stanford Social Innovation Review,* 1(1), 82–83.

Mayer, Lloyd H. 2002. "Summary of Bipartisan Campaign Reform Act of 2002 Provisions Affecting Tax-Exempt Organizations." In *Independent Sector* web site. <http://www.independentsector.org/PDFs/campfin3.pdf> (Accessed October 14, 2002.)

McCaffrey, Arthur. 2002. "Los Angeles Urban Funders." Cambridge, MA: Kennedy School of Government Case Program.

McCarthy, John and Jim Castelli. 1998. "Religion-Sponsored Social Service Providers: The Not-So-Independent Sector." *Aspen Institute Nonprofit Sector Research Fund Working Paper.*

McConnell, Michael W. and Richard A. Posner. 1989. "An Economic Approach to Issues of Religious Freedom." *University of Chicago Law Review,* 56, 1–60.

McCurdy, Dave. 1990. "Citizenship and National Service." In *National Service Pro and Con.* Stanford, CA: Stanford University Press.

McIlnay, Dennis P. 1998. *How Foundations Work.* San Francisco, CA: Jossey-Bass.

McKnight, John. 1995. Section 1: "Professionalism." In *The Careless Society: Community and Its Counterfeits,* pp. 3–52. New York: Basic Books.

MDC, Inc. 1988. *America's Shame, America's Hope: Twelve Million Youth at Risk.* Chapel Hill, NC.

Mesch, Debra, Mary Tschirhart, James Perry, and Geunjoo Lee. Fall 1998. "Altruists or Egoists? Retention in Stipend Service." *Nonprofit Management & Leadership,* 9(1).

Meyer, Jack A., ed. 1982. *Meeting Human Needs.* Washington, DC: AEI Press.

Monsma, Stephen V. 1993. *Positive Neutrality.* Westport, CT: Greenwood.

_____. 1996. *When Sacred and Secular Mix: Religious Nonprofit Organizations and Public Money.* Lanham, MD: Rowman and Littlefield.

_____. 2000. "Deciding Whether and When to Seek Government Funds." In Edward L. Queen II, ed., *Serving Those in Need.* San Francisco, CA: Jossey-Bass.

_____. 2002a. "Nonprofit and Faith-Based Welfare to Work Programs: Government Partners or Government's Captives?" A paper presented to a conference on "How Independent Is the Independent Sector?" Washington, DC. March 7, 2002.

_____. 2002b. *Working Faith: How Religious Organizations Provide Welfare-to-Work Services.* Philadelphia, PA: Center for Research on Religion and Urban Civil Society.

Morgan, Gareth. 1986. *Images of Organizations.* Newbury Park, CA: Sage Publications.

Morino Institute. 2001. *Venture Philanthropy: The Changing Landscape.* Reston, VA: Morino Institute.

Morone, James. 1990. *The Democratic Wish.* New York: Basic Books.

Moskos, Charles. 1990. "National Service and Its Enemies." In *National Service: Pro and Con.* Stanford, CA: Stanford University Press.

Munter, Judith. June 1988. *Experiencing AmeriCorps: The Beginning of a Journey That Will Change Lives Forever.* Corporation for National and Community Service.

Nakatani, Laura. 1998. *Examining a Life of Service: A Study of AmeriCorps Leaders Program Alumni's Civic Involvement.* Corporation for National Service.

National Campaign for Jobs and Income Support. 2000. "Leaving Welfare, Left Behind: Employment Status, Income, and Well-Being of Former TANF Recipients." October 2.

National Center for Charitable Statistics (NCCS), Statistics of Income File (SOI). 1998.

_____. Core Files. 2001.

_____. Core Files. 2002.

National Commission on Civic Renewal. 1998. *A Nation of Spectators: How Civic Disengagement Weakens America and What We Can Do About It.*

Neumann, George R. et al. 1995. *The Benefits and Costs of National Service: Methods for Benefit Assessment with Application to Three AmeriCorps Programs.*

Newmann, Fred and Robert Rutter. 1983. *The Effects of High School Community Service Programs on Students' Social Development.* Center for Education Research. Madison, WI: University of Wisconsin.

Nisbet, Robert A. 1953. *The Quest for Community.* New York: Oxford University Press.

O'Connor, A. 1999. "The Ford Foundation and Philanthropic Activism in the 1960s." In Ellen Condliffe Langemann, ed., *Philanthropic Foundations.* Bloomington: Indiana University Press.

_____. 2001. *Poverty Knowledge: Social Science, Social Policy, and the Poor in the Twentieth Century U.S. History.* Princeton, NJ: Princeton University Press.

O'Connor, Thomas, Patricia Ryan, and Crystal Parikh. 1997. "The Impact of Prison Fellowship on Inmate Infractions at Lieber Prison in South Carolina." Center for Social Research, April.

Oi, Walter. 1990. "National Service: Who Bears the Costs and Who Reaps the Gains." In William Evers, ed., *National Service Pro and Con.* Stanford, CA: Stanford University Press.

O'Neill, Michael. 2002. *Nonprofit Nation: A New Look at the Third America.* San Francisco, CA: Jossey-Bass.

Orosz, Joel J. 2000. *The Insider's Guide to Grantmaking*. San Francisco, CA: Jossey-Bass.

O'Rourke, Dara. 2001. "Community-Driven Regulation: Towards an Improved Model of Environmental Regulation in Vietnam." In P. Evans, ed., *Livable Cities: The Politics of Urban Livelihood and Sustainability*. Berkeley: University of California Press.

Osborne, David and Ted Gaebler. 1991. *Reinventing Government*. New York: Plume.

Ostrander, Susan A. 1995. *Money for Change*. Philadelphia, PA: Temple University Press.

Ostrom, Elinor. 1996. "Crossing the Great Divide: Coproduction, Synergy, and Development." *World Development*, 24, 6:1073–1087.

Parsons, Talcott. 1971. *The System of Modern Societies*. Englewood Cliffs, NJ: Prentice-Hall.

Penn, William. 1971. *The Select Works of William Penn*. New York: Kraus Reprint.

Perrow, Charles. 1986. *Complex Organizations: A Critical Essay*, 3rd ed. New York: Random House.

Perry, James and Ann Thompson. 1997. *Building Communities Through AmeriCorps*. Bloomington, IN: Schools of Public and Environmental Affairs.

Peter D. Hart Research Associates. August 1998. *New Leadership for a New Century: Key Findings from a Study on Youth, Leadership, and Community Service*. Conducted for Public Allies. Funded by Surdna Foundation.

Peters, B. Guy. 2000. "Institutional Theory: Problems and Prospects." Institute of Advanced Studies, Vienna.

Pffefer, Jeffrey and Gerald D. Salancik. 1974. "Organizational Decision Making as a Political Process: The Case of a University Budget." *Administrative Science Quarterly*, 19 (June):135–151.

_____. 1978. *The External Control of Organizations: A Resource Dependency Perspective*. New York: Harper & Row.

Porter, Michael E. 1980. *Competitive Strategy*. New York: Free Press.

Portes, Alejandro. 1998. "Social Capital: Its Origins and Applications in Modern Sociology." *Annual Review of Sociology*, 24: 1–24.

Powell, Walter and P. DiMaggio, eds. 1991. *The New Institutionalism in Organizational Analysis*. Chicago: University of Chicago Press.

Powell, Walter and Jason Owen-Smith. 1998. "Universities as Creators and Retailers of Intellectual Property: Life-Sciences Research and Commercial Development." In B. A. Weisbrod, ed., *To Profit or Not to Profit: The Commercial Transformation of the Nonprofit Sector* (pp. 169–193). Cambridge, UK: Cambridge University Press.

Pressman, Jeffrey L. 1975. *Federal Programs and City Politics*. Berkeley: University of California Press.

Princeton Survey Research Associates. 2001. *BBB Wise Giving Alliance Donor Expectations Survey: Final Report*. Accessed from <www.give.org> March 2002.

Putnam, Robert D. 1993. *Making Democracy Work*. Princeton, NJ: Princeton University Press.

_____. 1995. "Bowling Alone: America's Declining Social Capital." *Journal of Democracy*, 6: 65–78.

_____. 1999. *Bowling Alone: The Collapse and Revival of American Community.* New York: Simon and Schuster.

Rangarajan, Anu and Tim Novak. 1999. "The Struggle to Sustain Employment: The Effectiveness of the Postemployment Services Demonstration." Princeton, NJ: Mathematica Policy Research, Inc.

Raynor, Gregory K. 1999. "The Ford Foundation's War on Poverty: Private Philanthropy and Race Relations in New York City, 1948–1968." In *Philanthropic Foundations*, pp. 195–228.

Regnerus, Mark D. 2001–2003. "Making the Grade: The Influence of Religion upon the Academic Performance of Youth in Disadvantaged Communities." Philadelphia, PA: Center for Research on Religion and Urban Civil Society.

Reid, Elizabeth J. "Nonprofit Membership Organizations: Regulation, Organizational Formation, and Political Practice." Presented at Annual Meeting of American Political Science Organization, August 31, 2003.

Reid, Elizabeth J. and Janelle Kerlin. 2003. "Complex Organizational Structures in the Nonprofit Sector: Structuring and Financing Political Advocacy." Revised paper presented at 2002 APPAM Annual Conference, Houston, TX, 2003.

Reid, Elizabeth J., and Jeff Krehely. 2001. "Idiosyncrasies of Nonprofit Membership in Regulation and Political Practice." Prepared for and presented at the National Council of Voluntary Organizations Conference, London, England, September 4–5, 2001; and ARNOVA 2001, Miami, FL,

Rein, Martin. 1986. "The Public/Private Mix." In M. Rein and L. Rainwater, eds., *The Public/Private Mix in Social Protection: A Comparative Study* (pp. 3-24). Armonk, NY: M. E. Sharpe.

Rein, Martin and Lee Rainwater, eds. 1986. *The Public/Private Mix in Social Protection: A Comparative Study.* Armonk, NY: M. E. Sharpe.

Reinhardt, Forest. 1992. "Environmental Defense Fund." Rev. 1994. Harvard Business School Case # 1-793-037. Boston: Harvard Business School Publishing.

Renz, Loren. 2002. *Giving in the Aftermath of 9/11: Foundations and Corporations Respond.* New York: The Foundation Center.

Rhoads, Robert A. 1997. *Community Service and Higher Learning.* New York: State University of New York Press.

Roberts Enterprise Development Fund. 1997a. "The Challenge of Change: Implementation of a Venture Philanthropy Strategy." San Francisco, CA: Roberts Enterprise Development Fund.

Roberts Enterprise Development Fund. 1997b. *SROI Reports.* San Francisco, CA: Roberts Enterprise Development Fund.

Roof, Wade C. 1994. *A Generation of Seekers.* San Francisco, CA: Harper San Francisco.

_____. 1999. *Spiritual Marketplace: Baby Boomers and the Remaking of American Religion.* Princeton, NJ: Princeton University Press.

Rose, Richard. 1998. "Getting Things Done in an Anti-Modern Society: Social Capital Networks in Russia." Center for the Study of Public Policy, University of Strathclyde, working paper.

Rosen, Jeffrey. 2000. "Is Nothing Sacred?" *New York Times Magazine.* January 30, pp. 40–45.

Rosenblum, Nancy L. 1998, *Membership and Morals: The Personal Uses of Pluralism in America*, Princeton, NJ: Princeton University Press.

Rothenberg, Randall. 1984. *The Neoliberals: Creating the New American Politics*. New York: Simon and Schuster.

Roundtable on Religion and Social Policy. 2002. Transcript of a panel on *The View from the States* held on October 23, 2002. Retrievable at <http://www.religionandsocialpolicy.org/docs/annualconference/10-23-2002>.

Ryan, William P. 1999, January–February. "The New Landscape for Nonprofits. *Harvard Business Review*, 127–136.

Sagawa, Shirley. 1998. "Ten Years of Youth Service in America." *American Youth Policy Forum*. Washington, DC.

Saidel, Judith R. 1991. "Resource Interdependence: The Relationship Between State Agencies and Nonprofit Organizations." *Public Administration Review*, 51 (6): 543–553.

Salamon, Lester M. 1995. *Partners in Public Service: Government-Nonprofit Relations in the Modern Welfare State*. Baltimore, MD: Johns Hopkins University Press.

_____. 1999. *The Nonprofit Sector: A Primer*. 2nd ed. New York: Foundation Center.

_____., ed. 2002. *Tools of Government Handbook*. New York: Oxford University Press.

Salisbury, Robert H. 1984. "Interest Representation: The Dominance of Institutions." *American Political Science Review*, 78: 64–76.

_____. 1990. "The Paradox of Interest Groups in America—More Groups, Less Clout." In A. King, ed., *The New American Political System* (pp. 203–230). 2nd ed. Washington, DC: AEI Press.

Schadler, B. Holly. 1998. "The Connection: Strategies for Creating and Operating 501(c)(3)s, 501(c)(4)s and PACs." Washington, DC: The Alliance for Justice.

Schambra, W. 2003. "The Evaluation Wars." *Philanthropy,* May/June. Accessed from <www.philanthropyroundtable.org>, June 2003.

Schmeigelow, Toni. 1993. *National Service: Not Just Another Job Training Program*. City Volunteer Corps. New York, NY.

Scott, W. Richard. 1987. *Organizations: Rational, Natural and Open Systems*. 2nd ed. Englewood, NJ: Prentice-Hall.

Segal, Lewis M. and Burton A. Weisbrod, 1998. "Interdependence of Commercial and Donative Revenues. In B.A. Weisbrod, ed., *To Profit or Not to Profit: The Commercial Transformation of the Nonprofit Sector* (pp. 105–127). Cambridge, UK: Cambridge University Press.

September 11th Fund. 2002. "The First Six Months." Publication of the September 11th Fund, New York.

September 11 Interim Report on the Response of Charities. 2002. Report to the Honorable Charles E. Grassley, Ranking Minority Member, Committee on Finance, U.S. Senate. Washington, DC: United States General Accounting Office, September.

September 11 Perspectives from the Field of Philanthropy. 2002. New York: The Foundation Center.

Shaiko, Ronald G. 1999. *Voices and Echoes for the Environment*. New York: Columbia University Press.

Sherman, Amy L. 1997. *Restorers of Hope: Reaching the Poor in Your Community with Church Based Ministries That Work*. Wheaton, IL: Crossway Books.

_____. 1998, January–February. "Little Miracles: How the Churches Are Responding to Welfare Reform." *American Enterprise*.

_____. 1999, September–October. "The Seven Habits of Highly Effective Charities." *Philanthropy*.

_____. 2001. *Collaborating for Employment Among the Poor: The Jobs Partnership Model*. Indianapolis, IN: Hudson Institute.

_____. 2002. *Reinvigorating Faith in Communities*. Indianapolis, IN: Hudson Institute.

_____. 2003. "The Community Serving Activities of Hispanic Protestant Congregations: A Report to The Center for the Study of Latino Religion at the University of Notre Dame" (unpublished paper).

Sherman, Amy L. and John C. Green. 2002. *Fruitful Collaborations: A Survey of Government-Funded Faith-Based Programs in 15 States*. Indianapolis, IN: Hudson Institute.

Sherman, Amy L. et al. 2002. *Collaborations Catalogue: A Report on Charitable Choice Implementation in 15 States*. Indianapolis, IN: Hudson Institute, March 2002.

Showalter, Susan, "Seizing Opportunity: Strategic Planning at the Northwest Area Foundation." Showalter & Company, June 1998.

Sider, Ronald J., Philip N. Olson, and Heidi Rolland Unruh. 2002. *Churches That Make a Difference: Reaching Your Community with Good News and Good Works*. Grand Rapids, MI: Baker Books.

Sider, Ronald J. and Heidi Rolland Unruh. Forthcoming. "Typology of Religious Characteristics of Social Service and Educational Organizations and Programs." *Nonprofit and Voluntary Sector Quarterly*.

Sievers, Bruce. 1997, November–December. "If Pigs Had Wings." *Foundation News and Commentary*.

Simon, Christopher A. 2002. "Testing for Bias in the Impact of AmeriCorps Service on Volunteer Participants: Evidence of Success in Achieving a Neutrality Program Objective." *Public Administration Review* 62(6).

Simon, Christopher A. and Changhua Wang. 1999. *Impact of AmeriCorps on Members' Political and Social Efficacy, Social Trust, Institutional Confidence and Values in Idaho, Montana, Oregon, and Washington*. Portland, OR: Northwest Regional Educational Laboratory.

Simon, Christopher A. and Changhua Wang. 2000. *First Follow-Up Study: Impact of AmeriCorps on Members' Political and Social Efficacy, Social Trust, Institutional Confidence and Values in Idaho, Montana, Oregon, and Washington*. Portland, OR: Northwest Regional Educational Laboratory.

Sirianni, Carmen and Lewis Friedland. 2001. *Civic Innovation in America*. Berkeley: University of California Press.

Skocpol, Theda. 1999. "Advocates Without Members: The Recent Transformation of American Civic Life." In Theda Skocpol and Morris P. Fiorina, eds., *Civic Engagement in American Democracy*, Washington, DC: Brookings.

Sloan, Frank A. 1998. "Commercialism in Nonprofit Hospitals." In B. A. Weisbrod, ed., *To Profit or Not to Profit: The Commercial Transformation of the Nonprofit Sector* (pp. 151–168). Cambridge, UK: Cambridge University Press.

Smith, David H. 1997. "The Rest of the Nonprofit Sector: Grassroots Associations as the Dark Matter Ignored in Prevailing 'Flat Earth' Maps of the Sector." *Nonprofit and Voluntary Sector Quarterly*, 26, 114–131.

Smith, Steven R. 1998. "Can Voluntary Agencies Build Community." Paper presented at the annual meeting of the American Political Science Association. Chicago.

Smith, Steven R. 2002. "Social Services." In Lester M. Salamon, ed., *The State of the Nonprofit Sector* (pp.149–86). Washington, DC: Brookings.

Smith, Steven R. and M. Kosin. 2001. "The Varieties of Faith-Related Agencies." *Public Administration Review*, 61, 6 (November/December): 651–670.

Smith, Steven Rathgeb and Michael Lipsky. 1993. *Nonprofits for Hire*. Cambridge, MA: Harvard University Press.

Stehle, Vince. 1998. "Study: Americans Confident in Charities' Integrity." *The Chronicle of Philanthropy*, September 10.

Steinberg, Richard. 1986. "The Revealed Objective Functions of Nonprofit Firms." *Rand Journal of Economics*, 17(4), 508–526.

Steinberg, Richard and B. A. Weisbrod. 1998. "Pricing and Rationing by Nonprofit Organizations with Distributional Objectives." In B. A. Weisbrod, ed., *To Profit or Not to Profit: The Commercial Transformation of the Nonprofit Sector*. Cambridge, UK: Cambridge University Press.

Steinmo, Sven, Kathleen Thelan, and Frank Longstreth eds. 1993. *Structuring Politics*. Cambridge, UK: Cambridge University Press.

Stewart, Richard B. 1975. "The Reformation of American Administrative Law." *Harvard Law Review*, 88, 8: 1669–1813.

Streeter, Ryan. 2001. *Transforming Charity: Toward a Results-Oriented Social Sector*. Indianapolis, IN: Hudson Institute.

Tabori, John, I. Rogard, Margarita Gordon, and Ron L. Martinez. August 1, 1997. *The Sustainability of AmeriCorps*Vista Programs and Activities*. PeopleWorks, Inc.

Tarrow, Sidney. 1994. *Power in Movement: Social Movements, Collective Action and Mass Politics in the Modern State*. New York: Cambridge University Press.

Tendler, Judith. 1997. *Good Government in the Tropics*. Baltimore, MD: Johns Hopkins University Press.

Tinkelman, Daniel. 1999. "Factors Affecting the Relation Between Donations to Not-for-Profit Organizations and an Efficiency Ratio." *Research in Government and Nonprofit Accounting*, 10, 135–161.

Tschirhart, Mary. December 1997. "Valuing Diversity in AmeriCorps: Does Service in Diverse Groups Change Diversity Attitudes?" *Annual Conference of the Association for Research on Nonprofit Organizations and Voluntary Action (ARNOVA)*. Indianapolis, IN.

Tuckman, Howard P. and Cyril F. Chang. 1991. "A Methodology for Measuring the Financial Vulnerability of Charitable Nonprofit Organizations." *Nonprofit and Voluntary Sector Quarterly*, 20, 445–460.

U.S. House of Representatives. 2001. Testimony of J. Brent Walker on behalf of the Baptist Joint Committee on Public Affairs before the Subcommittee on the Constitution of the Committee on the Judiciary, regarding "State and Local Implementation of Existing 'Charitable Choice' Programs," April 24.

U.S. House of Representatives. 2002. Ways and Means Oversite Committee. *Hearings on Response of Charities to Recent Terrorist Attacks.* November 8. <http://waysandmeans.house.gov/oversite/107cong/ov-7wit.htm>

Van den Haag, Ernest. 1979. "Should Government Subsidize the Arts?" *Policy Review,* 10 (Fall): 63–74.

Van Til, Jon. 2000. *Growing Civil Society: From Nonprofit Sector to Third Space.* Bloomington: Indiana University Press.

Wagner, Antonin. 2000. "Reframing Social Origins Theory: The Structural Transformation of the Public Sphere." *Nonprofit and Voluntary Sector Quarterly,* 29, 4: 541–553.

Waldman, Steven. 1995. *The Bill: How The Adventures of Clinton's National Service Bill Reveal What Is Corrupt, Comic, Cynical—and Noble—About Washington.* New York: Viking.

Walker, Jack L. 1988. "Interests, Political Parties, and Policy Formation in American Democracy." In Donald T. Critchlow and Ellis Hawley, eds., *Federal Social Policy: The Historical Dimension* (pp.141–70). University Park, PA: Pennsylvania State University Press.

Wallis, Jim. 2001. "Eyes on the Prize." *Sojourners Magazine,* Vol. 30, 3 (May/ June): 7–8.

Wang, Changhua and Kim Owens. 1995. "A Cost-and-Benefit Study of Two AmeriCorps Programs in the State of Washington."

Warren, Mark E. 2000. *Democracy and Association.* Princeton: Princeton University Press.

_____. 2001. *Dry Bones Rattling: Community Building to Revitalize American Democracy.* Princeton, NJ: Princeton University Press.

_____. 2003. "A Second Transformation of Democracy?" In Bruce Cain, Russell Dalton, and Susan Scarrow, eds., *Democracy Transformed.* Oxford: Oxford University Press.

Weisbrod, Burton A. 1998. *The Growing Commercialism of the Nonprofit Sector.* Cambridge, UK: Cambridge University Press.

_____. 1998a. *To Profit or Not to Profit: The Commercial Transformation of the Nonprofit Sector.* Cambridge, UK: Cambridge University Press.

_____. 1998b. "Modeling the Nonprofit Organization as a Multiproduct Firm: A Framework for Choice." In B. A. Weisbrod, ed., *To Profit or Not to Profit: The Commercial Transformation of the Nonprofit Sector* (pp. 47–64). Cambridge, UK: Cambridge University Press.

Welles, Edward O. 1998. "Ben's Big Flop." *Inc.,* 20, 12, 40-57.

The White House. 2001. *Unlevel Playing Field: Barriers to the Participation by Faith-Based and Community Organizations in Federal Social Service Programs.* Washington, DC, August.

Wind, J. P. and J. Lewis, eds. 1994. *American Congregations* (2 Vols). Chicago: University of Chicago Press.

Winston, Diane. 1999. *Red Hot and Righteous: The Urban Religion of the Salvation Army.* Cambridge, MA: Harvard University Press.

Woodson, Robert L. 1981. *A Summons to Life: Mediating Structures and Youth Crime.* Washington, DC: AEI Press.

_____. 1998. *The Triumphs of Joseph.* New York: Free Press.

Woolcock, Michael and Deepa Narayan. 2000. "Social Capital: Implications for Development Theory, Research and Policy." *World Bank Research Observer,* 15, 2 (August): 225–249.

Working Group on Human Needs and Faith-Based and Community Initiatives. 2002. *Finding Common Ground: 29 Recommendations of the Working Group on Human Needs and Faith-Based and Community Initiatives.* Washington, DC: Search for Common Ground.

Worth, David. 1996. Social Advocacy Organisations and Financial Ratio Analysis. Unpublished masters thesis. Sydney, Australia: University of Technology.

Wuthnow, Robert. 1988. *The Restructuring of American Religion.* Princeton, NJ: Princeton University Press.

_____. 1994. *Sharing the Journey: Support Groups and America's New Quest for Community.* New York: Free Press.

_____. 1998. *After Heaven: Spirituality in America Since the 1950's.* Berkeley: University of California Press.

Youniss, James and Martha Yates. 1997. *Community Service and Social Responsibility in Youth.* Chicago, IL: University of Chicago Press.

Young, Denise R. and Lester M. Salamon. 2002. "Commercialization, Social Ventures, and For-Profit Competition." In Lester M. Salamon, ed., *The State of Nonprofit America.* Washington, DC: Brookings.

Young, Iris Marion. 2000. *Inclusion and Democracy.* Oxford: Oxford University Press.

Young, Mark C., John Gartner, Thomas O'Connor, David Larson, and Kevin Wright. 1995. "Long-term Recidivism Among Federal Inmates Trained as Volunteer Prison Ministers." *Journal of Offender Rehabilitation,* 22 (1/2).

Zaff, Jonathan F. and Erik Michelsen. October 2002. "Encouraging Civic Engagement: How Teens Are (or Are Not) Becoming Responsible Citizens." *Child Trends Research Brief.*

Zald, Meyer N. and Patricia Denton. 1963. "From Evangelism to General Service: The Transformation of the YMCA." *Administrative Science Quarterly,* 8 (September): 214–234.

Contributors

Beth Battle Anderson is lecturer and managing director at the Center for the Advancement of Social Entrepreneurship (CASE) at Duke University's Fuqua School of Business. Previously, she served as a research associate and acting administrative director at Stanford Business School's Center for Social Innovation and as a summer associate at McKinsey & Company. With Professor J. Gregory Dees, she has co-authored papers on blurring sector boundaries, for-profit social enterprise, scaling social innovations, and the process of social entrepreneurship. While at Stanford, she researched, wrote, and helped edit several cases on social entrepreneurship and philanthropy and coauthored "Developing Viable Earned Income Strategies," a chapter in *Strategic Tools for Social Entrepreneurs* (Wiley, 2002). Additionally, she helped develop and served as a teaching assistant for a Stanford Public Policy course, "Business Skills for the Social Sector." She received her MBA from Stanford after working for five years in the nonprofit sector and graduating from Williams College.

J. Gregory Dees is adjunct professor of social entrepreneurship and nonprofit management at Duke University's Fuqua School of Business. He also serves as an entrepreneur-in-residence with the Kauffman Foundation's Center for Entrepreneurial Leadership. With Jed Emerson and Peter Economy, he recently produced two books on the topic of social entrepreneurship: *Enterprising Nonprofits* (Wiley, 2001) and *Strategic Tools for Social Entrepreneurs* (Wiley, 2002). Prior to coming to Duke, Greg served as the Miriam and Peter Haas Centennial Professor in Public Service at Stanford University's Graduate School of Business, where he was also the founding codirector of the Center for Social Innovation. Much of Greg's prior academic career was spent at Harvard Business School where he helped launch the Initiative on Social Enterprise. In 1995, Greg received HBS's Apgar Award for Innovation in Teaching, for his new course on "Entrepreneurship in the Social Sector." In 1996, he interrupted his academic career for two years to work on economic development in central Appalachia at the Mountain Association for Community Economic Development in Berea, Kentucky. He previously taught at the Yale School of Management and worked as a management consultant with McKinsey & Company. He holds a masters in public and private management from Yale and a Ph.D. in philosophy from Johns Hopkins.

Peter Frumkin is a senior fellow of the New America Foundation and an associate professor of public policy at Harvard University's John F. Kennedy School of Government, where he is affiliated with the Hauser Center for Nonprofit Organizations. At the Kennedy School, he teaches courses on philanthropy and nonprofit management. Frumkin is the author of numerous articles on all aspects of philanthropy, including the formulation of grantmaking strategy, the changing profile of major individual donors, theories of philanthropic leverage, the professionalization movement within foundations, and many other topics. His book, *On Being Nonprofit* (Harvard University Press, 2002), considers the changing roles and responsibilities of nonprofit organizations in American democracy and the evolution of public policies shaping the sector's growth. He is the author of numerous articles on topics related to nonprofit management, including nonprofit compensation policies, the impact of fundraising strategies on nonprofit revenue generation, and the effects of public funding on nonprofit mission definition. Before coming to Harvard, Frumkin worked as a foundation program officer, the manager of a nonprofit organization, and as a program evaluator in both nonprofit and public agencies. Frumkin received his Ph.D. in sociology from the University of Chicago in 1997.

Janet Greenlee is an associate professor of accounting at the University of Dayton, where she teaches both graduate and undergraduate courses. Her research focuses on the impact of decision making in the nonprofit sector. Greenlee, who is a CPA, received her Ph.D. in accounting from the University of Kentucky. She is active in both the Association for Research in Nonprofit Organizations and Voluntary Action (ARNOVA), an interdisciplinary scholarly organization devoted to research in the nonprofit arena, and the American Accounting Association. In addition, she regularly speaks to nonprofit organizations regarding nonprofit issues. Her work on nonprofit organizations have appeared in *Accounting Horizons, Nonprofit and Voluntary Sector Quarterly, Nonprofit Management and Leadership, The CPA Journal, Research in Accounting Regulation, The Journal of Public Budgeting, Accounting and Financial Management,* and *Research in Governmental and Nonprofit Accounting.* She is currently working on two projects: (1) an examination of alternative models of predicting financial vulnerability in the nonprofit sector, and (2) a study of the impact of A-133 (Single Audit Act) audit findings on auditor choice.

Mark Hager is a research associate in the Center on Nonprofits and Philanthropy at the Urban Institute, a policy research organization in Washington, D. C. Since 2000, he has worked with a small team of researchers to study fundraising and administrative expenditures by nonprofit organizations, which has led him toward critiques of financial reporting, resulting data quality, and accountability of nonprofit organizations. Hager earned his Ph.D. in organizational sociology at the University of Minnesota in 1999. His work on the behavior of nonprofit organizations has appeared in *Public Administration Review, Nonprofit and Voluntary Sector Quarterly*, the *American Behavioral Scientist, the International Journal of Nonprofit and Voluntary Sector Marketing*, and the *International Journal of Arts Management*. His current research efforts focus on data collection in the field of the performing arts, the financial stability of nonprofits, and volunteer management capacity of nonprofit organizations and religious congregations.

Jonathan B. Imber is Class of 1949 Professor in Ethics and professor of sociology at Wellesley College. He is editor-in-chief of *Society*. Formerly editor of *The American Sociologist*, he has been editor-in-chief of *Society* since 1997. He is a former fellow of the Woodrow Wilson International Center for Scholars in Washington, D.C. and a recipient of the National Endowment for the Humanities Fellowship for College Teachers. His books include: *Trusting Doctors: The Decline of Moral Authority in American Medicine* (forthcoming), *Searching for Science Policy* (2002), *The Feeling Intellect: Selected Writings of Philip Rieff* (1990), and *Abortion and the Private Practice of Medicine* (1986).

Estelle James has recently joined the Urban Institute as a visiting fellow, is a consultant at the World Bank and other organizations, and a member of the President's Commission to Strengthen Social Security in the United States. Previously she was director of the Pension Flagship Course at the World Bank Institute and lead economist in the Policy Research Department of the World Bank. She is the principal author of *Averting the Old Age Crisis: Policies to Protect the Old and Promote Growth*, a World Bank study that provided the first global analysis of economic problems associated with population aging. This study has become the basis for much of the World Bank's advice in this area and for reforms that are now taking place in many countries. Her recent research has focused on social security reform, including the political economy of the reform process, administrative costs of individual account systems, and how to handle the annuitization stage. Dr. James's previous work concentrated on the interaction between the public and private sectors in the provision of education and the role of the third sector—nonprofit, nongovernmental organizations. She has lectured extensively and advised governments in China, Costa Rica, India, and Thailand, among others. Before joining the Bank in 1991, she was professor of economics at the State University of New York, Stony Brook, where she also served as chair of the Economics Department and provost, Social and Behavioral Sciences. She received her B.S. from Cornell University and her Ph.D. from MIT.

Thomas H. Jeavons is the general secretary (chief executive) of the Philadelphia Yearly Meeting of the Religious Society of Friends, the largest Quaker judicatory in the United States, a position he has held since 1996. He is also a visiting fellow at the Yale University Program on Nonprofit Organizations, at the Yale Divinity School. He earned a B.A. in philosophy from the University of Colorado (1975), a M.A. in theology from the Earlham School of Religion (1978), and his Ph.D. in management and cultural studies from the Union Institute (1992). He also holds a graduate certificate in business administration from Georgetown University, and a certificate in fund raising management (CFRM) from Indiana University. His major publications include: *Growing Givers' Hearts: Fundraising as a Ministry* (Jossey-Bass, 2000), *When the Bottom Line Is Faithfulness: The Management of Christian Organizations* (1994), *Public Libraries and Private Fund Raising: Opportunities and Issues* (1994), and *Learning for the Common Good: Liberal Education, Civic Education and Teaching about Philanthropy* (1991). He is the author as well of numerous chapters and articles.

Stephen V. Monsma is professor of political science and chair of the Social Science Division at Pepperdine University, Malibu, California. He has served on the Pepperdine faculty since 1987. He has also taught at Calvin College, Grand Rapids, Michigan (1967–1972), and served in the Michigan House of Representatives (1972–1978) and Michigan Senate (1978–1982). He also was a member of the Michigan Natural Resources Commission (1983–1985) and part of the top management team in the Michigan Department of Social Services (1985–1987). He has his associate's degree from Calvin College, his M.A. from Georgetown University, and his Ph.D. from Michigan State University. He is the author of many books, including *The Challenge of Pluralism: Church and State in Five Democracies* (1997), *When Sacred and Secular Mix: Religious Nonprofit Organizations and Public Money* (1996), and *Positive Neutrality: Letting Religious Freedom Ring* (1993). In addition, he has contributed chapters to numerous books, and has authored articles in many journals, including *The Journal of Church and State*, *Policy Studies Review*, *Public Opinion Quarterly*, and *American Journal of Political Science*.

Note: I would like to thank the Smith Richardson Foundation for a grant that made this study possible. Also, I wish to express my appreciation to my associate researcher on this project, Carolyn Mounts, who was active at every stage of collecting the data. She also read and made helpful comments on an early draft of this essay. For more complete reports on the study, see Stephen V. Monsma, "Working Faith: How Religious Organizations Provide Welfare-to-Work Services" (Center for Research in Religion and Urban Civil Society, the University of Pennsylvania, 2002) and Stephen V. Monsma, *Serving Those in Need: Public-Private Welfare-to-Work Partnerships* (Ann Arbor: University of Michigan Press, forthcoming).

Elizabeth (Betsy) Reid is a research associate at the Urban Institute, Center on Nonprofits and Philanthropy where she directs research on nonprofit advocacy. She recently edited a four-volume series, "Nonprofit Advocacy and the Policy Process," drawn from ten seminars examining the impact of current law and regulation on nonprofit contributions to civic and political engagement. She is also the author of "Nonprofit Advocacy and Political Participation," in *Nonprofits and Government: Collaboration and Conflict* and "Building a Policy Voice for Children" in *Who Speaks for America's Children?* Ms. Reid has twenty-five years' experience in labor and community organizations. During the 1980s, she directed the national political committee for the American Federation of Government Employees union. During the 1990s, she served as adjunct faculty to the Corcoran School of Art where she taught courses in politics and international affairs. She holds an M.A. in comparative politics from the School of International Service, American University. The writer wishes to thank Kendall Golladay, Jeff Krehely, Janelle Kerlin, and Jennifer Auer at the Center on Nonprofits and Philanthropy, Urban Institute, for their contributions to this chapter.

Amy L. Sherman (Ph.D., University of Virginia) is a senior fellow at the Hudson Institute's Welfare Policy Center. She also serves as urban ministries advisor at Trinity Presbyterian Church in Charlottesville, VA. She is the author of four books and dozens of essays published in a variety of religious and secular periodicals. Sherman is the founder and former executive director of Charlottesville Abundant Life Ministries, a church-based outreach to a low-income urban neighborhood of approximately 380 families.

Steven Rathgeb Smith is associate professor of public affairs at the Daniel J. Evans School of Public Affairs, University of Washington. His current research interests focus on the relationship between government and nonprofit organizations. He is presently conducting research on the role of nonprofit organizations and community partnerships in building and rebuilding local communities, and the impact of welfare reform and devolution on faith-related service agencies. Professor Smith is the coauthor of *Nonprofits for Hire: The Welfare State in the Age of Contracting* and *Adjusting the Balance: Federal Policy and Victim Services.* He is also coeditor of *Public Policy for Democracy.* He is the editor of *Nonprofit and Voluntary Sector Quarterly* (NVSQ), the journal of the Association for Research on Nonprofit Organizations and Voluntary Action (ARNOVA).

Mark E. Warren is professor of government at Georgetown University, and specializes in democratic theory. He is the author of *Democracy and Association* (Princeton University Press, 2001) and editor of *Democracy and Trust* (Cambridge University Press, 1999).

Index

Abortion, 25
Accountability of nonprofits, 11. 13, 17-19, 33, 44-46, 58, 66, 77, 85, 90, 94, 104
Accounting practices, for nonprofits, 91-95
ACT Help Desks, 196
ACTION, 132
Advantage Schools, 106
Advocacy/action organizations, 20, 24-26, 30-31, 34, 62, 110
AIDS movement 7, 12-13, 39, 61
Alliance for Children and Families, 54
Alternative energy production, 55
America Works, 53
American Association of Retired People, 29, 53
American Bar Association, 44
American Cancer Society, 87
American Civil Liberties Union (ACLU), 19, 181, 186
American Institute of Certified Public Accountants, 92
American Institute of Philanthropy, 88
American Red Cross, 87, 102, 115, 117-120, 122-123, 127, 129
Americans United for Separation of Church and State, 186
AmeriCorps, 131-149
Anderson, Beth Battle, 51-71, 219
Animal welfare, 39
Anonymous giving, 108
Armed Forces Services, 123
Arts, the, 15, 90, 127
ASPCA Disaster Relief Fund, 119
Assessment of nonprofits, 11, 17, 109-111, 129, 139, 141, 146-148
Assisted living, 81
Association of State Democratic Chairs, 33
Associations, civic, 20, 40

Atlantic Philanthropies, 115
Audits, financial, 45, 95
Autonomy, nonprofit, 4, 11, 31, 33

Balanced Scorecard, 111
Beaver Creek Popcorn Festival Corp., 23
Benchmarks, nonprofit performance, 90, 92-95, 109
Berger, Peter, 5, 7
Big Brothers/Big Sisters, 135
Bipartisan Campaign Reform Act (BCRA), 27-28, 32-34
Blood donations, 117
Board, nonprofit, 13, 69, 83, 90, 186
Bonds, tax-exempt, 8
Boundaries, blurred (nonprofit/profit), 77, 83
Boy Scouts, The, 12
Boys and Girls Clubs of America, 135
Buckley v. Valeo, 34
Business tools for nonprofits, 57-58, 66, 85, 90-91, 101, 107-108, 110-111, 113

Campaign finance reform, 32-33, 45
Campaigning, political, 24, 45
Capital, 70, 79, 103
CARE (Charity, Aid, Recovery, and Empowerment) legislation, 59, 194-195
Carnegie, Andrew, 128
Carnegie Corporation of New York, 115
Cat Fanciers' Association, 23
Catholic Charities USA, 119-120, 164, 188
Change, 79
Charity/charities/charitable, 65, 68, 85-89, 94, 103, 108, 115, 117, 122, 125, 128-130, 162
Charity Navigator, 86, 88, 92, 95
Charitable choice, 168, 180, 184-186, 198
Charitable organizations, 22, 64, 75, 83, 118

Charities, rating/ranking of, 87-88
Charter schools, 55, 61
Checks and balances, 27
Chicago Public Education Fund (CPEF), 111
Children's Home & Aid Society of Illinois, 55
Children's services, 10, 76
Christian Community Development Association, 188
Christian Social Services Agencies, 188
Churches that Make a Difference, 193
Citizen Schools, 107
Citizens for Sensible Control of Acid Rain, 29
City Year, 54, 142
CitySkills, 55
Civil Rights Act, 186
Civil rights movement, 6, 25
Classification of nonprofits, 21
Coca-Cola Company, 116
Coercive utopianism, 134
Collaboration, nonprofit, 54
Collateral sources, 125
Collective action, 41-42
Combined Federal Campaign, 88
Commercialism, 103
Commission on National and Community Service, 137
Communitarians, political, 134
Community and Services Block Grant Program, 180
Community development, 13, 22, 55, 101, 162, 165
Community level, national service, 137-139, 143-144
Community Outreach, 123
Community Solutions Act, 194
Competition, nonprofit/for-profit, 53
Congregations, religious, 155-169, 187
Conservatives, political, 133-134, 143
Constituency, 28
Contractors, nonprofit, 54
Contracts, 8, 10
Conversion, 79, 84
Corporate giving, 116-117
Corporation for National and Community Service (CNCS), 132-149
Corporation of Presiding Bishop v. Amos, 183
Council on Foundations, 187
Cross-subsidization, 77-79, 83-84

Day care, 64, 76, 81, 187
Dees, J. Gregory, 51-71, 219
Definition of nonprofits, 22
Delta Dental of Pennsylvania, 23
Democracy and nonprofits, 35-38, 40-42, 44-47, 138, 143
Democratic National Committee, 33
Democratic State Party Organization, 33
Democrats, 100-101
Dependence model, 32
Deutsche Bank, 116
Developmental disabilities, 7
Devolution, 16
Disaster relief, 118-122, 126-127
Disclosure, 33-35
Doerr, John, 105
Domestic Volunteer Service Act (DVSA), 136
Domestic violence shelters, 7
Donors/donations, 28, 32. 56-58, 62, 65, 67-70, 73-75, 84-90, 93-96, 99, 101-106, 108, 110-112, 115, 117, 159
Drug rehabilitation, 180, 191
Due diligence, 100, 105
Dues, membership, 26

Economies of scale, 79
Ecotourism, 55
Edison Schools, 51, 80
Education, 53, 55, 76-78, 80, 101, 105
Edwards v. Aguillard, 180
Effectiveness of nonprofits, 120-122, 127, 131, 166
Efficiency of nonprofits, 120-122, 127, 142, 166
Election regulations, 26-27
Electioneering communication, 28
Emergency relief, 13
Engagement strategy, 103. 107-108, 113, 129
Entitlement programs, 101
Environment, 25, 101
Environmental Defense Fund, 62
Equity of nonprofit results, 120, 123-127
Ethics, 108
ExxonMobil, 116

Faith Communities Today, 157
Faith-Based & Community Initiatives, 3,185-186
Faith-based organizations (FBOs), 110, 135, 148, 153-169, 185-198

Faith-government collaboration, 194-195
Family Service America, 54
Fannie Mae Foundation, 116
Federal Election Commission (FEC), 27-31
Federal Emergency Management Agency (FEMA), 117
Fee schedule, nonprofit, 103
Financial reliance model, 32
Firefighter benefit associations, 23
First Amendment, 34, 181
501(c)(3) charitable designation, 8-10, 19-25, 30-31, 33-33. 39, 45, 168
501(c)(4) social welfare organizations, 8, 19-27, 30-31, 33, 39, 45
Form 990 (IRS), 89-90, 92, 94-96
Foundations, 67, 99, 101-102, 115-117, 128-129
Franchise model for nonprofits, 102-103
Freedom Corps, 195
From Belief to Commitment, 157
Front Door, 196-197
Frumkin, Peter, 99-113, 115-149, 220
Fund/funding/fundraising, 6, 8, 10, 12-13, 17, 25-27, 31, 56-57, 59, 65-66, 77, 79, 92, 103-106, 112-113, 165, 167-168

Georgia Amateur Wrestling Association, 23
Girl Scouts, 51, 64
Goodwill Industries, 51
Government/nonprofit divisions, 39
Government Performance Review Act (GPRA), 148
Grameen Bank, 57
Grants/grantmaking, 8-9, 14, 74, 82, 84-85, 99, 101, 103-104, 106-108, 112-113, 116, 128, 129, 142
Grassroots, 6, 17, 62, 167, 197
Greenlee, Janet, 85-96, 220
Group Health Cooperative of Puget Sound, 23
GuideStar, 86, 88, 95

Habitat for Humanity, 52-53, 57, 64, 135
Hager, Mark, 85-96, 220-221
Hartford Seminary Faith Communities Today Survey, 187
Harvard Business School Press, 53
Health Insurance Plan of Greater New York, 23

Health maintenance organizations (HMOs), 51
Health Plan of the Upper Ohio Valley, 23
Health services, 10-11, 15, 56, 101
Healy, Bernadine, 123
Heroes Fund, 125
Hospices, 68
Hospitals, nonprofit, 39l 42, 44, 51, 53, 56, 67, 74, 76-79
Housing & Urban Development, 44, 74, 177-178
Human rights, 25
Human services, 56
Hybrid nonprofit organizations, 54-55, 71

Ideologies, nonprofit, 75-76, 80
Imber, Jonathan B., 221
Immigrant services, 13
Income, earned, 65, 67
Income, fee-based, 64
Independent sector, 4, 7, 17, 20, 37, 39, 43, 45, 51, 161-162
Individual level, national service programs, 137-139
Infrastructure for nonprofits, 12
Institutional forms, 78, 82-84
Institutional functions, 38, 44
International Association of Fire Fighters (IAFF), 124
International Union of Gospel Missions, 188
Internet-based/online fund-raising, 119-120, 197
Iowa Health System, 23
Issue advertising, 27
Istook, Rep. Ernest (Okla.), 3, 7

James, Estelle, 221
Jeavons, Thomas H., 153-169, 222
Jewish Council for Public Affairs, 186
Jewish Federations, 188
Johnson Foundation, Robert Wood, 116
Jumpstart, 105
Junior League, 63

Kiwanis, 39

Learn and Serve America, 132, 136
Legitimacy of nonprofits, 19
Liberals, political, 133, 139, 143

Libertarians, political, 143
Liberty Disaster Relief Fund, 118, 123
Lilly Endowment, 115
Lions Clubs, 25
Literacy training, 171
Lobbying, 24, 31
Low-income housing, 13
Low Income Housing Tax Credit (LIHCT), 8
Lumberjack World Championships Foundation, 23
Lumina Foundation for Education, 116
Lutheran Social Services, 164

Making Democracy Work, 5
Management consulting for nonprofits, 103
Marketing, 67
Markets and nonprofits, 40-43, 45-47, 56, 58-59, 69, 80
Media of organizational operation, 39-40, 42-43, 45
Medicaid, 8
Medicare, 44
Medical societies, 23
Mellon Foundation, Andrew W., 115
Mentoring, 196
Mergers, 79-80
Membership, 12, 24-26, 28-30, 35-36, 43, 45, 157-158, 163, 165
Mentally ill, 7
Michigan Militia, 39
Ministry, 159
Mission, nonprofit, 9, 60, 62, 70, 73-74, 85, 87, 93, 103, 108, 122-123, 135, 144, 146, 164-165, 186, 190
Missouri Government PAC and Colorado Republican Party v. FEC, 34
Money and nonprofits, 40, 42, 44-45, 68
Monitor Group, 107
Monsma, Stephen V., 171-184, 222
Moose lodges, 19, 22

NAACP v. Alabama, 34
National and Community Service Trust Act, 132-133, 136-137
National Association for the Advancement of Colored People, 39
National Center for Charitable Statistics (NCCS), 21, 31, 33-34, 91
National Congress of Community Economic Development Corporations (NCCED), 188

National Disaster Fund, 119
National Geographic, 53-54
National Jobs Partnership, 189, 196
National Organization for Women, 19
National Rifle Association, 19, 25, 29, 39
National Right to Life Committee, 19
National service, 131-149
National Wetlands Committee, 29
Nature Conservancy, 54, 58
Neighborhood associations, 8
New Profit Inc., 105, 107
New Schools Venture Fund (NSVF), 105-107
New York Blood Center, 117
New York City Police Foundation, 125
New York Community Trust, 118
New York Fire Fighters 9-11 Disaster Relief Fund, 119, 124
New York Times 9-11 Neediest Fund, 119
Newhouse, Richard John, 5
NGOs (Brazil), 14-15
9/11 United Services Group, 122
Nisbet, Robert, 4-5
Nixon v. Shrink, 34
Nobel Learning Communities, 51
Norms and nonprofits, 40-46, 70
Nursing homes, 76

Objective Hope: Assessing the Effectiveness of Faith-Based Organizations, 189
O'Connor, Sandra Day, 43
Office of National Service in the White House, 132
Operation Compassion Under Fire, 119
Operation Noble Eagle, 119
Organizational level, national service programs, 137, 139-142
Organizational models for nonprofits, 31
Overhead, administrative, 121-122, 130
Over the Hill Soccer League, 23

Para-church organizations, 154
Partnerships, 79
Peace Corps, 117, 133, 149
Performance standards for nonprofits, 11, 13, 85, 110
Pfizer Foundation, 116
Philanthropic Giving Index, 126
Philanthropic Research Inc., 91

Philanthropy, 11-13, 56-57, 65, 68, 86, 99-103, 106, 108-113, 115-120, 127-130, 137, 162
Piaget, 138
Pioneer Human Services, 51, 57
Points of Light Foundation, 132
Police benefit associations, 23
Policy-making role, 19
Political Action groups (PACs), 5, 7, 9-10, 14-15, 22, 24, 30, 33-34, 37
Political role of nonprofits, 39, 68, 138
Power and nonprofits, 40-44, 68
Presidents' Summit for America's Future, 143, 147
Prison Fellowship, 190-191
Privacy, 33-34
Privatization, 16, 44
Profitability, potential, 69
Programs and projects, charitable/nonprofit, 31-32, 88, 102-105, 109-111, 129-131, 139, 143-144, 146-147, 149
Progress for America, 33
Progressives, 143
PTA, 3, 64
Public Broadcasting System, 54
Public opinion, 44
Public policies, toward nonprofits, 73
Public-private divide, 15-16
Public sphere, 38
Putnam, Robert, 5-7, 143

Quest for Community, 4-5

Racing Association of Central Iowa, 23
Rape crisis centers, 7
Religious organization, definition, 154
Religious service entities, definition, 161
Regulation and nonprofits, 30, 47
Rehabilitation services, 53
Reid, Elizabeth, 19-36, 223
Reinvigorating Faith in Communities, 189
Religious organizations, 37, 43, 76
Republicans, 3, 147-148, 194
Responsibility, 42, 79, 135, 138
Resources, nonprofit, 47, 56, 69, 70, 121, 160-161
Revenue stream, nonprofit, 103
Roberts v. Jaycees, 43
Roberts Enterprise Development Fund (REDF), 109-110
Roberts, George, 109

Robin Hood Foundation, 104, 119, 122
Rockefeller, John D., 128
Rotary Clubs, 25, 63

Salvation Army, 102, 119-120, 122, 164, 188
Save the Children, 58
Scientific philanthropy, 128-129
Section 537 organization, 30, 32, 34
Sector-bending, 51-52, 55-56, 59-60, 64-68, 71
Security Health Plan of Wisconsin, 23
Senior Service Corps, 117, 136
September 11, 2001, 94, 115-130, 148-149
September 11th Fund, 115, 118-120
September 11th victims' database, 122
September 11th Victims Compensation Fund, 125
Share Our Strength, 54
Sherman, Amy L., 185-198, 223
Sierra Club, 19, 23, 30, 39
Sierra Club Foundation, 30
Sierra Club Political Committee, 30
Silicon Valley, 100-101
Smith, Steven Rathgeb, 3-18, 223
Social capital, 41, 63
Social movements, 6
Social Venture Partners (SVP), 107
Social welfare groups, 19
Soup kitchens, 13
Special interest groups, 45
Special purpose social welfare organizations, 29
SROI Reports, 109-110
Staff development, nonprofit, 147
Starr Foundation, 115
State, the, and nonprofits, 40, 43. 46-47
Strategic Blood Reserve, 123
Strategic plans, nonprofit, 102
Structure/governance of nonprofits, 25-26, 31-32, 51-52, 68-71, 81
Subsidies, funding, 10
Substance abuse and Mental Health Service Administration, 180
Supreme Court, 34, 180-182

Tax credits, 8, 10, 186
Tax deductions, 75, 86
Tax designation, 39, 70
Tax-exempt bonds, 8
Tax exemption, 35-37, 75-76, 95, 179

Tax incentives, 35
Tax privileges, 82
Tax-Exempt Status for Your Organiza-tion, 20
Teen Challenge, 191
Terrorist Attack Relief Fund, 119
Texas Family Pathfinders, 196
Theory of change, nonprofits, 128, 144-146, 149
To Empower People, 5
Toqueville, Alexis de, 4, 6-7, 40, 134
Trustworthiness, nonprofits, 77, 79, 81
Twin Towers Fund, 118-119, 121-122, 129

Umbrella coalition, 9-11, 55
United Way, 11-12, 127
United Way of New York City, 118
Unrelated Business Income Tax (UBIT), 70
Urban Institute, 20
USA Freedom Corps, 117

Venture capital investing, 100, 104
Venture philanthropy, 99-113, 129
Veterans of Foreign Wars, 39
Verizon Foundation, 116

Volunteers in Service to America (VISTA), 132-133, 136
VITAS, 53
Volunteering, 18, 43, 70, 117, 131-149, 156
Vouchers, 8

War on Poverty, 133
Warren, Mark E., 37-47, 223
Welfare reform, 10
Welfare-to-work, 53, 55, 171-184
Welfare-to-Work Act, 180
White House Office of Faith-Based and Community Initiatives, 185, 194
Wise Giving Alliance (Better Business Bureau), 88
Wofford, Harris, 146
Women's health clinics, 7
Women's movement, 6-7
Worship, 158
Wuthnow, Robert, 154

Yearbook of American and Canadian Churches, 156-157, 160
YMCAs, 51, 135, 188